Praise for *Transition to Postsecondary Education for Students With Disabilities*

"Today, students with disabilities have more postsecondary options than ever before. They need to make knowledgeable decisions about their futures. This timely resource provides critical guidance educators and families need to transition into postsecondary education and careers with purposeful success. The authors offer a powerful storehouse of information and suggestions that fills a long-standing vacuum in our professional resources."

Patricia K. Ralabate
Senior Policy Analyst, National Education Association

"This book is a primer for teaching all students with special needs who are moving from the protective environment of our secondary schools to self-reliance, self-advocacy, and independence. The need for this resource is growing as the number of students with disabilities entering our postsecondary institutions continues to increase. Moreover, this resource is a lifeline for parents who are asking *what's next, where do we go from here, and who can we go to for services when needed?* This book fills a void in our profession's capacity to identify the key elements, strategies, and resources required for successful transition into postsecondary education."

Dr. Robert N. Ianacone
Associate Dean, Graduate School of
Education and Human Development
The George Washington University
(former President of the International Division on Career Development)

"IDEA 2004 recognized that a focus on postsecondary outcomes *must* drive transition planning for students with IEPs. For far too long, these outcomes have reflected high unemployment and underemployment rates, incomes below the poverty level, and participation in postsecondary education at rates not commensurate with their peers without disabilities. Secondary educators have more resources than ever before to teach the skills necessary for academic success and transition to the next setting. This has opened up a need for practitioner-friendly information on what persons with disabilities need to access postsecondary education and careers as well as how their participation in such training can improve their outcomes. Kochhar-Bryant, Bassett, & Webb do a fine job in responding to this need."

Michael J. Ward
Coordinator, Transition Special Education Distance
Education Certificate Program
The George Washington University Department of
Teacher Preparation and Special Education
(former Director, National Center on Self-Determination;
former Branch Chief, Office of Secondary Education and
Transition Services U.S. Office of Special Education)

"This book meets the need for a comprehensive set of strategies for assisting the transition of young adults into the postsecondary education and work environments. A wide variety of stakeholders, including general, special, and career and technical educators; counselors; disability advocates; representatives of community agencies; teacher educators; employers; and, of course, families will find this book useful. This resource is well written, easy to read, and addresses many facets and avenues for transitioning effectively. A must-have!"

Jane Williams
(former Professor and Chairperson,
Department of Special Education
Towson University, Towson, Maryland)

Transition to Postsecondary Education for Students with Disabilities

Carol Kochhar-Bryant

Diane S. Bassett • Kristine W. Webb

A Joint Publication

Division on Career
Development and Transition

For information:

Corwin Press
A SAGE Company
2455 Teller Road
Thousand Oaks, California 91320
www.corwinpress.com

SAGE Ltd.
1 Oliver's Yard
55 City Road
London EC1Y 1SP
United Kingdom

SAGE Pvt. Ltd.
B 1/I 1 Mohan Cooperative
  Industrial Area
Mathura Road, New Delhi 110 044
India

SAGE Asia-Pacific Pte. Ltd.
33 Pekin Street #02-01
Far East Square
Singapore 048763

Printed in the United States of America

Library of Congress Cataloging-in-Publication Data

Kochhar-Bryant, Carol A.
Transition to postsecondary education for students with disabilities/Carol Kochhar-Bryant, Diane S. Bassett, Kristine W. Webb.
    p. cm.
"A joint publication with Division on Career Development and Transition (DCDT)."
Includes bibliographical references and index.
ISBN 978-1-4129-5278-1 (cloth)
ISBN 978-1-4129-5279-8 (pbk.)
    1. Youth with disabilities—Education—United States—Decision making.
2. Postsecondary education—United States. 3. Youth with disabilities—Vocational education—United States. 4. School-to-work transition—United States. I. Bassett, Diane S. II. Webb, Kristine W. III. Title.

LC4031.K63 2009
371.9'0474—dc22   2008022894

This book is printed on acid-free paper.

08 09 10 11 12   10 9 8 7 6 5 4 3 2 1

Acquisitions Editor:	David Chao
Associate Editor:	Cassandra Harris
Production Editor:	Veronica Stapleton
Copy Editor:	Amy Rosenstein
Typesetter:	C&M Digitals (P) Ltd.
Proofreader:	Dennis W. Webb
Indexer:	Sheila Bodell
Graphic Designer:	Lisa Riley
Cover Designer:	Monique Hahn

Contents

About the Authors

Dr. Carol Kochhar-Bryant, Ph.D., is a Full Professor of Special Education at The George Washington University. For twenty-one years she has developed and directed advanced graduate and doctoral leadership preparation programs related to secondary and transition services for youth with disabilities. She teaches courses in special education, legal issues and public policy, systemic change and leadership, interdisciplinary planning, and development. She currently consults with public school districts, state departments of education, and federal agencies and has collaborated in international special education and transition policy research with the World Bank and the Office of Economic Cooperation and Development. She has conducted evaluations of state systemic reform initiatives, national technical assistance centers, transition services in correctional systems, and a variety of community-based agencies. Before her university career, Dr. Kochhar-Bryant was a former teacher of individuals with intellectual disabilities, a residential program director, case management program director, and evaluator. Dr. Kochhar-Bryant is widely published in areas of disability policy, leadership development, interagency service coordination, career-vocational programming, and secondary to postsecondary transition for special learners. She is a past president of the International Council for Exceptional Children's Division on Career Development and Transition (DCDT) and a parent of four young adults.

Diane S. Bassett, Ph.D., is a Professor in the School of Special Education at the University of Northern Colorado (UNC). She has taught general and special education in elementary, secondary, and postsecondary institutions in public and private schools. She currently coordinates the Generalist Masters Program and teaches coursework in secondary services, adolescent and adult development, transition from school to adulthood for students with exceptionalities, self-advocacy and self-determination, and transition services in a standards-based system. Dr. Bassett is the coauthor of two books, *Student-Focused Conferencing and Planning* and *Aligning Transition and Standards-Based Education: Issues and Strategies*. Other publications center on self-determination, effective services for students with mild/moderate disabilities, and efficacy-based transition practices. Dr. Bassett is a past president of the Council for Exceptional Children's DCDT and was also honored to receive the Oliver P. Kolstoe award from DCDT for her work in transition. At UNC, she has been awarded the Provost's Award for Excellence in Graduate Education, the College of Education Outstanding Scholar Award and Outstanding Service Award, the Mortar Board Award, and the Panhellenic Outstanding Professor Award.

 **K**ristine (Kris) W. Webb, Ph.D., is an Associate Professor in the Department of Exceptional Student and Deaf Education and Director of the Disability Resource Center at the University of North Florida (UNF). Dr. Webb is a past president of the International DCDT, an organization dedicated to improving life for adolescents and adults with disabilities. In 2007, she was awarded the Outstanding Faculty Service Award at the University of North Florida. In addition, Dr. Webb was the UNF 2003 CASE Undergraduate Teaching Award nominee and received the Outstanding Undergraduate Teaching Award for 2001–2002. In 2003, she was awarded the Transition Champion by the Division for Career Development and Transition. Before coming to UNF, Dr. Webb served as the Director of the Florida Network: Information and Services for Adults and Adolescents with Disabilities housed at the University of Florida. Prior to that position, she was the coordinator of a collaborative special education intern program at the University of New Mexico. Before her own transition to higher education, Dr. Webb was a high school teacher for seventeen years in Colorado and New Mexico. Along with her interest in teacher preparation, Dr. Webb has a long-standing passion for promoting successful postsecondary education experiences for individuals with disabilities, family involvement and collaboration, and transition to adult life for individuals with disabilities.

Introduction

Life transitions are about change, and about movement, and about becoming something other than what you are at this very moment.

—Kochhar-Bryant and Bassett, 2002

In the past two decades, students with disabilities have made greater progress than ever before in gaining access to postsecondary education. Individuals with disabilities, including those with significant disabilities, are successful in careers as teachers, doctors, lawyers, politicians, business leaders, computer specialists, and technical workers in a variety of industries. How has this happened? It is our belief that this trend has resulted from the combined efforts of (1) students who are setting higher goals for themselves and working to achieve them; (2) parents believing in and supporting those goals; (3) teachers, counselors, and related professionals who appreciate students' abilities and are willing to collaborate to assist them in the transition process; and (4) the advocacy of postsecondary support personnel and employers dedicated to opening doors for such students and providing supports. Shifts in attitudes and practices of secondary and postsecondary personnel are increasing the likelihood that competent and promising students are not denied an advanced education and the opportunity to pursue their career ambitions.

NATIONAL FOCUS ON POSTSECONDARY TRANSITION

Americans have recognized the power of education to transform the lives of all people and strengthen their ability to fully participate in their communities. Rapid changes in the employment market have made a postsecondary education essential for career advancement and success in many fields and industries. The past several decades have witnessed a growing national investment in youth development to help students access education and employment preparation programs and increase their social and economic independence. Interest in transition to postsecondary education is greater than it has ever been in the past, both in the United States and around the globe. For example, the U.S. Department of Education's Office of Vocational and Adult Education (OVAE) conducted a National Community College Symposium in June 2008 to examine research on promising practices and policy issues in several priority areas. These include research on (1) practices that facilitate student transitions across high schools, community colleges, and two- and four-year institutions, as well as linkages between community colleges and the workforce; (2) identification of innovative approaches to improving student access and persistence in postsecondary education; (3) nonacademic barriers to access of underrepresented groups as well as counseling and related support services; and (4) approaches that address students' remediation and developmental education needs (U.S. Department of Education, 2008).

Successful transition from secondary school is becoming recognized as a *chief indicator of the effectiveness* of our educational system for preparing youth and young adults for employment, postsecondary education, and adult independence (Baer, et al., 2003; Madaus & Shaw, 2004; Wagner, Newman, Cameto, & Levine, 2005).

POSTSECONDARY OPTIONS FOR YOUTH WITH DISABILITIES

The point of transition from high school to the postsecondary world is a challenging crossroads for all young people. They have to make choices about what college they will attend, what they will study, where they will live, whether they will work while they study, and how they will pay for their living expenses. If they choose to enter employment directly, they may be concerned about the kind of job for which they should interview, whether they have the skills and the stamina to work the long hours, how they will save and budget their earnings, and how they will juggle all of life's demands.

FACING MANY QUESTIONS ABOUT POSTSECONDARY CHOICES

During the time of transition to college life, individuals with disabilities have the same choices to make as their nondisabled peers but have on their plate many additional considerations that add uncertainty and stress. They may ask:

- What colleges have the support services, accommodations, and assistive technology I need, and will the Disability Support Services office need proof of my disability?
- Will I get into a dorm with my disability, and will I make friends in my classes?
- Will professors help accommodate me if I cannot finish the tests on time because of my reading disability, or will they be suspicious of my motives?
- Will there be counselors if I run into difficulty and need help?
- Will the campus be accessible for my wheelchair?
- Will people accept me as an equal in my new job?

Because these additional uncertainties place extraordinary demands on the young adult, supportive services are often (though not always) needed to help in the transition and adjustment to the college or work setting.

For most students, participation in postsecondary education is not limited to being physically present in a lecture hall. It is the possibility to ask questions, to discuss ideas with classmates, to have a critical conversation with professors about papers, to reflect upon readings, to explore the library, to have access to information in accessible formats at the same time as their nondisabled classmates, to work on a research project, to have coffee with friends, to participate at campus social and cultural events, and to really take part in the college experience (National Council on Disability, 2003a).

Many postsecondary options for youth with disabilities exist in the United States. *Four-year colleges and universities* offer Bachelor of Arts or Bachelor of Science degrees. Some also offer graduate and professional degrees. *Community colleges* are public, two-year colleges that typically serve people in the surrounding communities and offer academic, technical, and continuing-education courses. The programs often lead to a license, a certificate, or Associate of Arts or Science degrees. Community colleges often operate under an *open admissions* policy, and admissions requirements may vary. Some community colleges offer programs for individuals with cognitive disabilities, autism, and other disabilities and are focused on developing functional and employment skills.

Vocational and technical colleges offer a variety of options, including associate degrees, certificates, and work apprenticeships. Associate degree programs prepare students for technical occupations (e.g., accounting, dental hygienist, computer programmer). Technical diploma programs meet the needs of businesses and industry and provide employees with required certification for employment (e.g., automotive maintenance, accounting assistant, information technology, carpenter's assistant, pharmacy technician). *Apprenticeships* are typically geared toward those interested in working in industrial or service trades (e.g., carpentry, plumbing, machining). *Military service* can also help young people achieve their career goals; however, the military branches are not required to accommodate individuals on the basis of disability (Brown, 2000; HEATH Resource Center, 2005). Finally, *employment* in competitive jobs or supported work settings are common postsecondary goals for many youth, even if they plan eventually to enter into a two- or four-year college.

Employment After High School

Different types of employment opportunities are available for young men and women with significant disabilities, including competitive, supported, and sheltered employment.

Competitive employment. *Competitive employment* means a "mainstream" full-time or part-time job with competitive wages and responsibilities. Typically, competitive employment means that no long-term support is provided to the employee to help him or her learn the job or continue to perform the job. The absence of ongoing or long-term support distinguishes competitive employment from both *supported employment* and *segregated employment* (described below). All sorts of jobs are considered competitive employment—restaurant service worker, mechanic, teacher, secretary, factory worker, file clerk, or computer programmer. The amount of education or training a person needs will vary depending on the type of job.

Supported employment. Supported employment programs assist young people with the most significant disabilities to become and remain successfully and competitively employed in integrated workplace settings. Supported employment is designed for people who are not ready for competitive employment, or for whom competitive employment has been interrupted or is intermittent because of the disability. It is also designed for those who, because of the severity of their disability, need intensive or extended support services in order to work competitively (U.S. Department of Labor, 2005). Supported employment models include the following:

1. *Individual Placement.* Consumers/employees obtain employment independently and then contact the supported employment providers to get assistance or support, as needed.

2. *Agency Supported.* A rehabilitation or community services agency places the consumer in a job and provides or coordinates the ongoing support services needed to help assist him or her to retain the job.

3. *Entrepreneurial.* The consumer/employee is supported by the rehabilitation or community services agency to get the services and supports needed to successfully run his or her own business.

Supportive services in an employment setting may include job development and placement; intensive job-site training; facilitation of natural supports; special skills training; supplementary assessment; contact with employers, parents, family members and advocacy organizations; teaching compensatory workplace strategies. *Job development* means locating jobs for people with disabilities through networking with employers, businesses, and community leaders. The use of Business Advisory Councils is an excellent way to develop contacts that lead to employment for people with disabilities. An *Employment Specialist/Consultant (Job Coach)* is typically employed by a job training and placement organization serving people with disabilities who matches clients with jobs, provides necessary supports during the initial employment period, and then facilitates the transition to natural workplace supports while reducing his or her role.

Sheltered (Enclave) Employment. When employment is *sheltered*, individuals with disabilities work in a separate, self-contained center unit and are not integrated with nondisabled workers. This type of employment is generally supported by federal or state funds. The type of training that workers receive varies among programs, as does the type of work. Typical tasks include sewing, packing boxes, putting together packages or envelopes for mailing, or collating. In the past, segregated employment was thought to be the only option available for individuals with significant cognitive disabilities or autism. Today, many individuals with severe disabilities can work in community settings when provided with adequate support.

PURPOSE OF THE BOOK

This book is designed for secondary general and special education teachers, transition coordinators, counselors, postsecondary professionals, families, advocates, and anyone concerned with the successful transition of youth from high school into postsecondary education. It provides guidance to professionals who are preparing students for transition from high school to make informed choices and decisions regarding their future educational and career goals. The authors respond to the questions:

- Who is the student in transition to postsecondary settings?
- What changes for the student as he or she moves from the secondary to the postsecondary world?
- Why are self-determination and self-advocacy skills essential for successful transition to postsecondary?

- What should students know about documenting disability and seeking accommodations in the postsecondary setting?
- How can professionals help students plan for transition?
- How can families support students in transition?
- What is the role of community agencies in supporting transition to postsecondary?
- What can we learn from students about what helps them most as they navigate transition to postsecondary education?

Chapter 1, "Who Is the Student in Transition to Postsecondary?" introduces readers to the young people who are in the process of transition to postsecondary settings and the developmental tasks they face. It provides an overview of current national trends in the participation of youth with disabilities in postsecondary education and the elements of successful transition. The chapter discusses what we know about barriers to transition and the roles of students and families and professionals in supporting successful transition.

Chapter 2, "What Changes as the Student Moves from the Secondary to the Postsecondary World?" explores the laws affecting the education and support for students, how they change as students move beyond the secondary years, and how they protect and support the young adult in the postsecondary setting. The chapter presents the changes in programming and services for the student as he or she moves from the secondary to postsecondary world. We explore the questions that students need to ask about postsecondary institutions. Transition planning is presented as a unifying framework for coordinated services and support.

Chapter 3, "Self-Determination and Self-Advocacy Skills Essential for Successful Transition to Postsecondary," defines self-determination and self-advocacy skills and explains why they are essential for successful transition to postsecondary settings. Case illustrations—and the voices of students—are provided to illustrate who is the "self-determined youth," what do they know, and what can they do? The chapter explores how professionals can facilitate self-determination skills.

Chapter 4, "Guided Pathways: Colleges and Universities," presents the experiences of students in transition to postsecondary education through descriptions of 'guided pathways' in which we follow a student from the secondary world into a college setting. The description includes the stages of educational decision making and how students make postsecondary choices, how students plan in *high school* to achieve their postsecondary goals, how students prepare in their *final year* for transition to college, what professionals need to know to help students make *successful transition*, and the families' role in supporting transition for their child. Issues related to two- and four-year colleges include courses of study, integrating transition planning into the academic curriculum, transition assessment, and how high stakes testing affects career decision making. Case examples are presented to illustrate the concepts and strategies.

Chapter 5, "Guided Pathways: Career-Technical Education," presents the experiences of students in transition to career and technical education through descriptions of "guided pathways" in which we follow students from the secondary world into a career–technical school. The description includes the ranges of options for career-technical training; what professionals do and what students do; the stages of educational decision making and how students make postsecondary choices, how students plan in *high school* to achieve their postsecondary goals, how students prepare in their *final year* for transition to career-technical education, what professionals need to know to help students make *successful transition,* and the families' role in supporting transition of their child. Case examples are presented to illustrate the concepts and strategies.

Chapter 6, "Focus on the Year After High School" examines preparation of students for the postsecondary setting. It presents the Family Educational Rights and Privacy Act (FERPA) requirements and their importance in transition. Disability documentation requirements in two- and four-year colleges and in vocational rehabilitation agencies are discussed, as well as their importance for the student. The enrollment and admissions process for students with disabilities is presented along with services that enable students to remain successful in postsecondary education, including accommodations, use of technology, study skills and strategies for learning, and services of the campus disability support offices. Case examples are presented to illustrate the concepts and strategies.

Chapter 7, "Role of Community Agencies in Supporting the Transition to Postsecondary Education," discusses the central role of coordinated services in planning and transition to postsecondary education. It presents the variety of agencies required under law to collaborate, including vocational rehabilitation services. Financial supports for transition to employment for students who plan to work while they study are discussed, including the Ticket to Work and the Plan to Achieve Self-Support, or PASS, plan. Case examples illustrate how agencies can work together to support postsecondary planning and success.

Chapter 8, "Student Voices," presents the perspectives of students and explains why it is important for professionals to listen to them. Students speak about what was useful and helpful in the secondary planning processes, the final year transition stage, their first year after high school, and their first years in college. Nontraditional students speak about returning to high school to complete transition goals.

Chapter 9, "Considerations for Students with Specific Disabilities," uses a case approach to present transition considerations associated with different disabilities and support needs, including intellectual disabilities, learning disabilities, sensory disabilities, physical and chronic health disabilities, and culturally and linguistically diverse students. Such considerations include life demands of students, special accommodations, strategies for obtaining specialized supports, family issues, and cultural issues.

Box 0.1 — **Circle of Support at the University of Hawai'i**

Fasy ('Faz-ee') grew up in a small island country in the Pacific Ocean. He became paralyzed as a teenager when he fell from a cliff and suffered a serious spinal injury. Unable to walk, he learned to use a wheelchair. Neither the schools nor other government services provided much in special services for people like Fasy. However, with his determination and academic capabilities, he earned entry to the University of Hawai'i at Manoa. A number of support services were available to him there. Due to the seriousness of his disability, Fasy required assistance to get around campus and take care of his basic needs, but extensive aide services were not available. Fortunately, in keeping with the family orientation of his Pacific Island culture, some of his family members were able to come to Hawai'i specifically to support him to reach his postsecondary education goals. During much of his academic career, one or two of his brothers were always at his side, and when they were not available, other family members assisted him. With the support of his family, Fasy earned his bachelor's degree and then two master's degrees, one in history and the other in Pacific Islands Studies. The challenges presented by his disability as well as cultural and language differences resulted in his taking several extra years to complete his studies. However, his own efforts, the supports provided by his family, and supports provided by the university, were successful, and now, in his late 30s, he is the director of one of the four campuses of his country's national university.

This case study illustrates how a cultural strength (individuals giving priority to the success of the family as a whole) can be built upon to support a CLD student with disabilities to achieve postsecondary educational success. What is notable in this case is the ready and coordinated participation of the entire family. This 'collectivist' orientation contrasts with the 'individualistic' orientation of mainstream American society, and should be taken into account when addressing the support needs of persons with disabilities from collectivist cultural backgrounds (Leake & Cholymay, 2002, by permission).

1

Who Is the Student in Transition to Postsecondary?

INTRODUCTION

Although career development for children, youth, and adults of all exceptionalities has been evolving since the turn of the nineteenth nineteenth century, the concept of high school transition and preparation for careers has only emerged since the 1950s. More recently, educators and policy makers are recognizing how important it is to understand the role of career development and postsecondary planning within the overall framework of adolescent development. Researchers are interested in the range of interventions believed to be positively associated with improved graduation rates and transition of youth with disabilities from school to employment and adult life roles.

Societal interest in career awareness, career choice, graduation pathways, and adjustment to adult roles has emerged as a new subfield within education. Preparation for transition from high school to postsecondary education and adult life involves changes in the self-concept, motivation, and development of the individual and is a fragile passage for the adolescent seeking to make difficult life choices (German, Martin, Marshall, & Sale, 2000; Michaels, 1994). This passage is even more delicate for youth with disabilities who need additional support and preparation to make the journey. For professionals seeking to help students on this journey, the process involves forming linkages among education and other human service agencies, including employment and training, adult services, and rehabilitation.

This chapter introduces readers to the young people who are in the process of transition to postsecondary settings and the developmental tasks they face during that transition. It provides an overview of current national trends in the participation of graduates with disabilities in postsecondary education and the success of youth in the transition process. The chapter discusses what we know about barriers to transition and the roles of students, families, and professionals in supporting successful transition to postsecondary settings.

WHO PARTICIPATES IN POSTSECONDARY OPTIONS? PARTICIPATION IN AND OUTCOMES OF POSTSECONDARY EDUCATION

Although young adults with disabilities who complete a college degree are just as likely to become employed as their peers without disabilities, they are much less prepared to enter college, less likely to enroll, and much less likely to complete college (National Center on Secondary Education and Transition, 2004a; Wagner, Newman, Cameto, Garza, & Levine, 2005).

Preparation for postsecondary settings. Many youth with disabilities are not adequately prepared to meet the entrance requirements and academic rigor of postsecondary institutions. Students with disabilities are less likely than their peers without disabilities to complete a full secondary school academic curriculum, especially in the math and science curriculum areas. Furthermore, many are not encouraged in high school to extend their education beyond secondary school. It remains true today that secondary students with disabilities seldom attend or have minimal involvement in their Individualized Education Plan (IEP) meetings and therefore are unprepared with a postsecondary transition plan or to self-advocate for their needs (Miller, Lombard, & Corbey, 2006; Wagner, Newman, Cameto, & Levine, 2005). When ranked according to qualifications for college admission, students with disabilities remain less likely than their peers to be minimally qualified, based on an index score of grades, class rank, National Education Longitudinal Study (NELS) composite test scores, and SAT/ACT scores (National Center for Education Statistics [NCES], 2000a). However, attention to helping youth prepare for postsecondary education is strengthening access across the nation.

Increased number of students in college who report disabilities. The number of postsecondary students (all types of institutions) reporting a disability has increased dramatically, climbing from 2.6 percent in 1978 to 9.2 percent in 1994, 19 percent in 1996 (Blackorby & Wagner, 1996), and 20 percent in 2002 (Wagner et al., 2005). This increase is partly a result of changes in the Higher Education Act, Section 504 of the Rehabilitation Act, and Americans with Disabilities Act that require institutions of higher education (two- and four-year colleges and universities, and vocational and technical schools) to provide reasonable accommodations for students with disabilities. Since 1990, there has been a 90 percent increase in the number of colleges, universities, technical institutions, and career technical centers offering opportunities for persons with disabilities to continue education (National Center for the Study of Postsecondary Educational Supports, 2000; Pierangelo & Crane, 1997; Sharpe, Bruininks, Blacklock, Benson, & Johnson, 2004; Skinner, 2004).

Long-term outcomes of participation in college. While substantial federal and state investments in creating a "seamless" transition for students with disabilities have increased enrollment in postsecondary education programs, they have not had a significant impact on the completion of programs by students with disabilities (Blackorby & Wagner, 2002; Gilmore, Bose, & Hart, 2002). Large gaps remain in comparison to students without disabilities. Studies have found that only 27 percent of students with disabilities enroll in postsecondary education compared with 69 percent of students without disabilities (U.S. Department of Labor, 2005). More than 26 percent of freshmen with disabilities at four-year colleges *do not return* for their sophomore year (Izzo, Hertzfeld, Simmons-Reed, & Aaron, 2001) compared with 73 percent of students without disabilities (ACT, 2008). Students with disabilities who enroll in postsecondary institutions are less likely than their nondisabled counterparts to complete a bachelor's degree (16 percent and 52 percent, respectively) (U.S. Government Accountability Office, 2003a).

The good news is that students with disabilities who do earn a bachelor's degree do almost as well with employment as do those individuals without a disability (67 percent of youth with disabilities with a bachelor's degree were working full time compared with 73 percent for persons without disabilities holding the same degree) (National Center for Education Statistics, 2000; Office of Vocational and Adult Education (OVAE), 2008). Nonetheless, the enrollment of people with disabilities in postsecondary institutions is *still 50 percent lower than enrollment among the general population* (Getzel, Stodden, & Briel, 2001; Roessler & Rumrill, 1998; Sharpe & Johnson, 2001; Vreeburg-Izzo, Hertzfeld, Simmons-Reed, & Aaron, 2001). This gap in educational attainment effects long-term employment prospects.

What Are the Barriers to Participation in Postsecondary Education?

Many college students with and without disabilities are faced with challenging physical and social environments. These challenges are compounded for students with disabilities because they are faced with architectural barriers, attitudinal misperceptions about their skills and abilities by faculty, staff, and their nondisabled peers (Justesen & Justesen, 2000), as well as scarce support services. Youth face several barriers as they prepare for and participate in postsecondary schools education.

Lack of identification of the disability in early school years. Many students with disabilities are not appropriately identified and provided special education and related services during childhood and adolescent years. For example, 31 percent of national survey respondents with specific learning disabilities (SLD) indicated that their disability was first identified at the postsecondary level (University of Hawai'i at Manoa, 2000). When declaring a primary disability, 44 percent of participants with an attention deficit disorder (ADD) indicated that their disability was first identified at the postsecondary level (Izzo & Lamb, 2002). Delayed identification prevents students from benefiting from years of needed services and often requires that they seek support services on the college campus. Greater attention to early identification and intervention can prevent these difficulties.

Lack of access to guidance counseling. Dropout rates and receipt of alternative diplomas are much higher for youth with disabilities than for their nondisabled peers. Many youth with disabilities at the high school level are pulled out of content classes and placed into special education classes and as a result may not meet the entry requirements of many postsecondary schools. Others face barriers to tests and assessments, such as the SAT Reasoning Test, which may require testing accommodations. Finally, many academic and career counselors lack the necessary skills to provide guidance to students with disabilities. Secondary students are often left with inadequate guidance because of poor coordination among teachers and counseling staff (Stodden, Galloway, & Stodden, 2003; Stodden, Jones, & Chang, 2002). Strengthening counselor understanding of the needs of youth with disabilities can overcome these challenges.

Lack of financial support through college. Individuals with disabilities are more likely to face financial barriers during postsecondary education. Individuals with disabilities are more than twice as likely to live below the poverty line as individuals without disabilities (U.S. Department of Health and Human Services, 2003). At the same time, research has shown that few students with disabilities are accessing disability benefits that are available to them in postsecondary study. As one study shows, only 8.3 percent of postsecondary students with disabilities participate in supplemental security income (SSI) and social security disability insurance (SSDI) disability programs. In general, postsecondary students with disabilities, when compared with nondisabled peers, receive less financial aid and are unable to participate in assistance programs because of a lack of awareness about SSI or SSDI disability benefits or work incentive programs (Berry & Jones, 2000). Educating students about available benefits and resources while they are in high school can make the difference between independence and long-term dependence.

Attitudes and stigma. Many youth who attend college experience negative self-concept, poor socialization skills, stress and anxiety, and professors who are reluctant to help (Chadsey & Sheldon, 1998; Wolanin & Steele, 2004). Students with disabilities choose to remain invisible because they may be concerned about the *"stigma of accommodations,"* believing that "Teachers and other students think I'm getting away with something when I'm given accommodations" (National Center for the Study of Postsecondary Educational Supports [NCSPES], 2000, p. 11). Preparation for self-advocacy in high school and a welcoming attitude on the part of postsecondary institutions can reduce these stresses.

Barriers for culturally and linguistically diverse students. Entering postsecondary education from high school can be a stressful process for students with disabilities. These gaps are even greater for students with significant disabilities and who are culturally and linguistically diverse (CLD). Compared with their non-CLD peers, CLD students with disabilities are more likely to face language and social barriers and the negative effects of having grown up in poverty, and have difficulty processing "standard English" oral and written information, all of which may contribute to their risk of school failure (Kochhar-Bryant & Greene, 2008; Greene & Nefsky, 1999).

Furthermore, students with disabilities who are from diverse cultures are less likely to disclose their disability and receive support services in postsecondary schools (Flowers, Edwards, & Pusch, 1996; Hart, Zafft, & Zimbrich, 2001; Hasnain, 2001; Stodden et al., 2002). These conditions point to the need for greater assistance to culturally and linguistically diverse postsecondary students.

Gap in technology access. Lack of access to technology impedes students' ability to achieve their potential in high school and to use technology in the postsecondary environments. Only 28.4 percent of Americans with disabilities have access to the Internet at home or work, compared with 56.7 percent of those without disabilities. Almost 60 percent of Americans with disabilities have never used a personal computer, compared with less than 25 percent of Americans without disabilities (Kaye, 2000; National Organization on Disability, 2000). When students with disabilities do have access to technology in high school, it is more than likely that they *will not be able to take the technology with them after graduation* (Gaylord, Johnson, Lehr, Bremer, & Hasazi, 2004). Students must be prepared to advocate for their technological needs in the postsecondary setting.

Inadequate preparation of college faculty. A very important factor that affects students' persistence and retention is the lack of awareness of faculty members of the disability needs of students, available supports on campus, and their responsibility for making accommodations. Failure to make needed accommodations may lead to diminished student performance and invite misunderstanding or conflict that could lead to dropping out or to adversarial relationships with the institution (National Council on Disability, 2003b). Postsecondary institutions can promote student persistence and retention by educating faculty in accommodations for students with disabilities, and promoting understanding of students' educational challenges. **Box 1.1** describes the postsecondary experiences of a twenty-one-year-old student with learning disabilities in his first year.

Box 1.1 — **Reflection on My Cousin's Postsecondary Experience**

My cousin Brian is a 21-year-old student at Cypress College and he has a learning disability. He struggles with reading and writing, has difficulty understanding assignments, has very poor hand writing and has difficulty with written expressive language skills. As a result, he uses a computer for all his assignments and note taking. Brian worked very hard in high school and knew early on that he wanted to attend Cypress College. Although Brian did not believe that he faced special barriers to admission, once he enrolled in college he faced many obstacles. He found that it was too difficult for him to take the recommended full freshman course load and it took him longer to complete assignments and grasp academic concepts.

While Brian was in college, he struggled in English and Sociology classes, which were required, but he excelled in math and business courses. He had difficulty completing exams in the required time period so through student disability services he participated in special test taking facilities which allowed him extended time on tests. As a result, Brian saw a huge improvement in his grades and in his self-confidence. At Cypress College Brian has also had a lot of support from his professors. His supported him and made themselves available to assist with his academics outside of class. Some professors were willing to review lessons with him after class or during office hours. At first Brian was very hesitant to ask his professors for this extra help because he didn't want them to think that he was incapable of learning the material. However, later Brian realized that his teacher's time and patience with him was a key component to assisting him through the sometimes difficult course material.

Brian's support system of his family and teachers to encourage, assist and support him has played an important role in Brian's achievements. When I asked Brian where he sees himself in five years, he hesitated and said that was a very difficult question for him to answer. He is majoring in accounting and hopes to be as successful as he can in the field. Brian wants to use the skills he has learned in college to help him succeed in his career. He does not want his learning disability to interfere with his desire to succeed. He understands that he will have to continue to work hard, stay focused and set realistic and achievable goals for himself. Brian knows that just because he has been able to be successful in college doesn't mean that his challenges will end when he graduates. He knows he will have lifelong struggles in certain areas and he feels that college has prepared him for many challenges he may face once he graduates. In his final year of college, Brian was offered a job at a top level accounting firm for when he graduates.

Brian's recommendations to postsecondary students are that he feels it is important not to waste time trying to push yourself beyond what you can really handle. Seeking help and using the supports of the college will make the postsecondary experience much more pleasant if you are having difficulties. Brian believes that having open communication with professors is key so they can help assist. He also learned that having a positive mindset will keep you focused to achieve the goals you have set for yourself (S. Kauffman, Special Educator, 2007, reprinted with permission).

What Do We Know About Youth Employment After High School?

Large gaps continue to exist between young people with disabilities and the remainder of the population with regard to education, transition, economic, and independent living outcomes. Despite decades of federal and state initiatives to improve employment outcomes for youth with disabilities, employment outcomes continue to reflect the widest gulf between youth with disabilities and the general population (Blanck, 2000). According to the Census Bureau (McNeil, 2000), only three in ten working-aged people with disabilities are employed full time, compared with eight in ten people in the rest of the population. Two years after high school, only about 43 percent of young people with disabilities were employed, compared with 69 percent of their peers (Cameto, 2005; Fabian, Lent, and Willis, 1998). Currently, 20 percent of students in special education who complete high school are enrolled in postsecondary education compared with 68 percent of the general student population (Wagner, Newman, Cameto, & Levine, 2005; Wagner, Newman, Cameto, Garza, & Levine, 2005). And, three to five years after high school, only a little more than half become employed compared with 69 percent of their peers.

What Are the Barriers to Employment for Youth with Disabilities?

Lack of career-related course work. While more than half (56 percent) of students with disabilities had a goal of finding competitive employment after leaving high school, many who choose to enter directly into employment after completing high school are not adequately prepared to reach their goals (Wagner et al., 2005). Students with disabilities are less likely than students without disabilities to complete courses in high school that prepare them to succeed in skilled employment. Preparation must begin in the early school years to ensure that students participate in appropriate career development courses. *Schools can bridge the gap* by providing work experiences, career and academic counseling, job coaching, and mentoring opportunities while encouraging students to enroll in the kinds of academic courses that will prepare them to succeed in work and college.

Work-based learning experiences in school. Over the past 15 years, work-based learning experiences have become more available to youth with disabilities (Wagner et al., 2003). According to parents' reports, almost 60 percent of youth with disabilities were employed during a one-year period in high school, some at work-study jobs, but the vast majority at non–school-related jobs (Cameto, Marder, Wagner, & Cardoso, 2003). Approximately 15 percent of youth with disabilities held work-study jobs in a given year (6 percentage points more than in 1987); increases of 14 to 18 percentage points were significant for youth with cognitive disabilities, emotional disturbance, or multiple disabilities. The most common work-study placements are at food service (19 percent), maintenance (16 percent), and clerical (15 percent) jobs.

More than 90 percent of youth in work-study jobs receive school credit or pay for their work. Older youth are more likely than younger youth to have work-study jobs. Work-study employment rates are approximately 10 percent for youth fifteen years of age or younger, 15 percent for sixteen-year-olds, and 19 percent for seventeen-year-olds. The percentage of youth with work-study jobs varies for youth in different disability categories. Youth with speech impairments or learning disabilities are the least likely to have work-study jobs (7 percent and 10 percent, respectively). In contrast, approximately 30 percent of youth with mental retardation, autism, multiple disabilities, or deaf-blindness hold work-study jobs (Wagner & Cameto, 2004). Participation in work-based learning is associated with successful outcomes for youth with disabilities.

ADOLESCENT DEVELOPMENT, CAREER COUNSELING, AND POSTSECONDARY CHOICES

All adolescents face a range of developmental tasks as they make the transition from high school to adult roles and make difficult choices about relationships, careers, and postsecondary options. Exploring and forming a clear choice about a career path is a very important stage for older adolescents and young adults (Super, 1963). Transition from high school to postsecondary involves a series of complex decisions that begin with defining the end point (the postsecondary goal). Older adolescents enter the high school transition process with the goal of becoming independently functioning adults, as they strive to meet both personal and career-related needs.

Adolescent Development and the Brain

The adolescent brain. With the exception of infancy, early adolescence is the time when a child's body and brain grow and change faster than in any other phase of life. The student is in a process of change from child to adolescent, yet the change in environment from middle school to high school is a sudden *event*. Since most children are developing at different rates, some come into high school ready for the changes, others struggle to keep up, and still others fall behind. As with all school transitions, the transition to high school occurs as a "one-size-fits-all" event to which all youth are expected to adapt.

Recent brain research reveals that during the teen years up to age fifteen, the areas in the middle and back of the brain associated with associative thinking and language reach their peak growth rates (Wilson & Horch, 2004). The growth spurt is most predominant just before puberty in the prefrontal cortex, the part of the brain crucial to information synthesis. The prefrontal cortex is the area of the brain that controls planning, working memory, organization, insight, judgment, mood modulation, and inhibition of inappropriate behaviors (Arnsten & Shansky, 2004). This area of the brain is not mature until about eighteen years of age (Spinks, 2002). The prefrontal cortex appears to be the last region of the brain to mature (Casey, Giedd, & Thomas, 2000), undergoing major changes throughout puberty and continuing until age twenty-five. These recent findings about adolescent brain development have major implications for classroom practices, student supports, and transition. Only recently have educational researchers and practitioners begun to relate new brain research to learning, particularly for atypical learners.

Recent research also addresses new evidence that the nature of early adulthood is changing. The period before adulthood is lengthening, often spanning the twenties and even extending into the thirties. Pathways into and through adulthood have become less linear and predictable (Settersten, Furstenberg, & Rumbaut, 2004). These changes have significance for postsecondary institutions, employers, and policies that are aimed at supporting adolescents and young adults as they make the transition to adulthood.

Adolescent Development and Implications for Transition

The concept of transition was introduced as part of Ginsberg, Ginsberg, Axelrod, and Herman's (1951) developmental/self-concept theory. Ginsberg and colleagues' vocational choice theory described three stages—the Fantasy period, the Tentative period, and the Realistic period. The Fantasy period reflects the young child's arbitrary and unrealistic preferences about occupations and choices (Osipow, 1983; Osipow & Fitzgerald, 1996).

In the Tentative period, children consider what they are interested in and like to do, their abilities, and the value of different vocations. Ginsberg and colleagues define the Transition stage as the closing of the Tentative period, which occurs at about age seventeen or eighteen. In this stage, individuals begin to make immediate, concrete, and realistic decisions about their career future. The Realistic period involves the actual entry into work or college and the development of a career pattern and ultimately a career focus or specialization. As Ginsberg and colleagues' theory demonstrates, the logic of transition planning is rooted in several assumptions about the tasks of adolescent development, one of which is career decision making and vocational awareness. Understanding the characteristics of the stages of adolescence helps educators design the types of education and transition services most appropriate for middle and high school age youth. Adolescence is recognized as a stage, or "passage," in which the adolescent undergoes substantial transformations, physically, psychologically, emotionally, and socially (Adams, Gullotta, & Montemayor, 1992; Blos, 1962, 1979; Erikson, 1968). Krup (1987) synthesized literature to yield the following definitions of transition

> A transition is a natural process of disorientation and reorientation, caused by an event or non-event, that alters the individual's perception of self and the world, demands a change in assumptions or behavior, and may lead either to growth or deterioration; the choice rests with the individual. (p. 4)

Smith, Price, and Marsh (1986) describe adolescence as (1) a transitional period between childhood and adulthood, (2) the period during which an emotionally mature person reaches the final stages of physical and mental development, and (3) the period of attainment of maturity (p. 212). Michaels (1994) asserted that the period of adolescence may be better conceptualized as one of floundering and experimentation, during which many different roles, identities, and experiences will be "tried on" (p. 12).

Phelan, Davidson, and Yu (1998) eloquently describe adolescence as a "critical period fraught with promise and peril—a time of passage in which biological, emotional, and social factors converge to forecast the future of youth adults" (p. 2).

The processes of adjusting and adapting to the various "worlds" of adolescents—home, family, teachers, peer groups—requires competencies and skills for transitions to be successful, particularly for students with disabilities. Phelan, Davidson, and Yu point out that students' ability to move between these settings and adapt to different settings has great implications for the quality of their lives and their chances of using the educational system as a stepping stone to further education, productive work experiences, and a meaningful adult life. Transition planning needs to address these multiple borders and the complexity of youths' efforts to negotiate them.

Among the various developmental frameworks, there are some common "tasks" or developmental transitions that the adolescent must accomplish. They must do the following:

- Look toward their future for the first time in their lives, as well as deal with the present (Bee & Mitchell, 1980).
- Confront the development of an identity or concept of self (Erikson, 1968).
- Pursue an occupation.
- Enter into intimate relationships and consider marriage and family.
- Live apart from the family.
- Exercise citizenship and participate in the community.

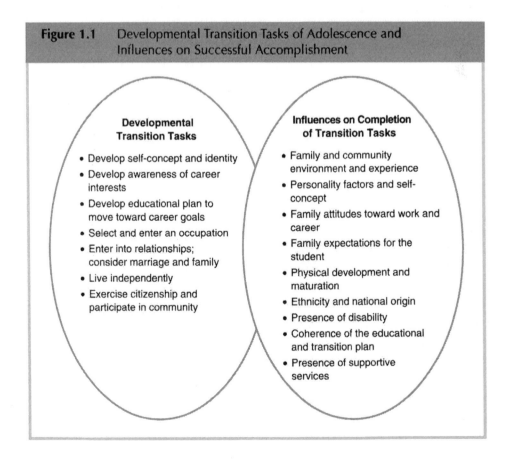

Figure 1.1 Developmental Transition Tasks of Adolescence and Influences on Successful Accomplishment

Developmental Transition Tasks

- Develop self-concept and identity
- Develop awareness of career interests
- Develop educational plan to move toward career goals
- Select and enter an occupation
- Enter into relationships; consider marriage and family
- Live independently
- Exercise citizenship and participate in community

Influences on Completion of Transition Tasks

- Family and community environment and experience
- Personality factors and self-concept
- Family attitudes toward work and career
- Family expectations for the student
- Physical development and maturation
- Ethnicity and national origin
- Presence of disability
- Coherence of the educational and transition plan
- Presence of supportive services

All adolescents vary in their rate of development and maturation and ability to negotiate the various tasks of childhood. The physical and social effects of disabilities, however, can provide special challenges and can interfere with the successful passage through each of the transitional areas outlined above. Transition service planning must be designed to respond to a wide range of disabling conditions, stages of adolescent adjustment, and family and environmental circumstances.

Career Counseling Needs

A longitudinal study by Amundson, Borgen, and Tench (1996) found that young people left high school unprepared for current career realities and that both the career and personal areas of their lives were in a state of change and uncertainty. At the end of their final year of high school, young people in the study expressed optimism about entering the career area of their choice and they expected to be successful workers in challenging jobs that offered personal satisfaction. About half of the respondents indicated some concern about meeting postsecondary entrance standards. Approximately nine and eighteen months following graduation, depression, self-esteem, and anxiety were correlated with a range of perceived problems, including money, lack of support from family and friends, internal attribution of general transition problems, external attribution of career/employment difficulties, and lack of job satisfaction.

At the end of the study, some of the young people were interviewed. They were asked about factors that helped or hindered the post–high school transition. Positive factors included supportive family and friends, making money, satisfying leisure activities, personal achievements, and educational success. Negative factors included relationship problems, career confusion, financial difficulties, unemployment, lack of satisfying work, lack of postsecondary educational opportunities, and difficulty in adjusting to postsecondary educational demands.

Developmentally, the young people were trying to meet personal and career-related needs, which were in a state of flux and uncertainty. It was apparent that a lack of progress in one area could have a negative influence on the other (e.g., an inability to gain postsecondary educational admission or paid work could drastically alter one's ability to move from being a dependent adolescent to an independent adult).

The above study, corroborated by additional recent studies (Amundson, Harris-Bowlsbey, & Niles, 2005; Borgen, Amundson, & Reuter, 2004), suggests a need for a broader view of career guidance and counseling— counseling that recognizes the developmental needs of young people, the influence of social and economic changes, and the importance of basing intervention strategies on personal and career competence, all within a context of diminished and changing opportunities for choice. To address this broader range of issues, Amundson and colleagues employed a competence model with eight main areas: *purpose, problem solving, communication skills, theoretical knowledge, applied knowledge, organizational adaptability, human-relations skills,* and *self-confidence.* Counseling strategies that facilitate a smoother transition include developing flexibility in career planning and multiple plans for transition; self-advocacy and marketing; managing change; meeting basic needs for meaning, physical, and emotional security; coping with stress; coping with loss; bridging programs that link education and work experience; and information and information access on careers and skill requirements. **Box 1.2** illustrates an innovative program that links postsecondary education and independent living experiences for young adults with intellectual disabilities.

Box 1.2 — **Learning into Future Environment (LIFE) Program Provides Postsecondary Education for Young Adults with Severe Challenges**

Over the past few years, some two- and four-year colleges and universities are providing innovative independent living programs and courses to students with disabilities. For example, the Kellar Institute for Human DisAbilities at the George Mason University in Virginia, has launched a new program to prepare students with disabilities for careers and independent living. The program blends functional instruction with academics to prepare young adults with significant disabilities for employment and independent living in their communities. The Learning into Future Environments (LIFE) Program, the first of its kind at a public four-year university, allows these students to obtain a postsecondary education in a supportive, inclusive environment. At the same time, the program provides Mason students majoring in disciplines such as education, psychology, assistive technology, and social work with practical experience in working with individuals with disabilities (George Mason University, Kellar Institute for Human Disabilities, 2002, reprinted with permission).

Personal and career issues are inextricably intertwined for young people. The ways in which young people make some of their transition experiences greatly influence their psychological well-being. Families and friends form a strong base for support during transition.

2 What Changes as the Student Moves From the Secondary to the Postsecondary World?

INTRODUCTION

Transition has been referred to as the "transition cliff" for young people with disabilities. Students age out of the special education system and into the adult service world at either age eighteen or twenty-two, depending on the program they are in or the state in which they reside. As they leave the "safety" of services and an individualized education plan, they face many barriers to transition into postsecondary settings and to adult adjustment. Many lose the health insurance coverage they had with their families. Many youth with mental health needs are diagnosed when they are in school and may be receiving a variety of services. However, the Individualized Education Plans (IEPs) do not follow them beyond high school, and mental health services usually end at age eighteen or twenty-two, depending on the state or program (National Collaborative on Workforce and Disability for Youth, 2007). As graduates enter the adult system of education, mental health services, vocational rehabilitation, social security or workforce development, eligibility requirements vary greatly among the systems of services. Eligibility is often restricted to those who have the greatest need for services, there are long waiting lists, and services may be very limited in rural areas. For example, in states operating under an "order of selection" system for vocational rehabilitation services, the majority of transition age students (sixteen to twenty-one) will not meet the definition of most significant disability and will be placed on a waiting list for services (Council of State Administrators of Vocational Rehabilitation [CSAVR], 2006; Lamb, 2007). Transportation to and from services also becomes the responsibility of the youth.

This chapter examines changes in programming and services for the student as he or she moves from the secondary to postsecondary world. It explores the ways that educational laws affecting the education and support for students change as they move out of the secondary years and how they protect and support the young adult in the postsecondary setting.

WHAT IS DIFFERENT FOR THE STUDENT IN THE POSTSECONDARY WORLD?

From the IDEA Entitlement to the Adult Service World

Secondary school students are entitled to receive the transition services they need as a part of their IEP and to expect school staff to coordinate with students, parents, and community agencies. Such service entitlements are designed to ensure that students receive appropriate services for which they are eligible while they are in K–12 education. When students with disabilities exit secondary education, they must rely on adult service agencies to continue providing supportive services that may be needed in employment or postsecondary education. *Services provided through adult agencies are not entitlements.* These agencies have various eligibility requirements and, because of limited funding, cannot always immediately offer services to eligible citizens. Applicants for services are often placed on a waiting list. Planning for ongoing support before a student exits school is key to accessing services in the postsecondary environment. Students can prepare by becoming aware of agency eligibility criteria, meeting agency staff, gathering information from state and federal agencies about adult service programs and postsecondary services, and learning about community resources. Such exploration provides valuable information for students, families, and teachers to guide transition planning.

According to the National Council on Disability (2003a), students with disabilities and their parents are not well informed about the differences in the rights and responsibilities of schools and students as they move from high school to higher education. The result is that students are often harshly surprised rather than prepared for the disparity between the two

---

Box 2.1 **Let's See It in Action! Teaching Case Example**

Question: I am a high school senior with a learning disability and I have just been admitted to the college of my choice. Will the accommodations that were provided to me in high school under my IEP automatically be provided to me in college?

Answer: First of all, NO accommodations will be provided to you unless and until you identify yourself to be a student with a disability, and provide documentation of your disability. Once the proper administrator has been notified, under Section 504 of the Rehabilitation Act, and under the Americans with Disabilities Act, the college must provide reasonable and appropriate accommodations and academic adjustments that specifically address your known disability. By providing such accommodations, they afford you an equal opportunity to participate in the institution's programs, courses, and activities. However, the college is *not* required to provide accommodations just because they appear in your IEP, though that information can certainly be very helpful to Disability Support Service (DSS) coordinators as they develop your personal accommodations plan. In fact, DSS personnel may determine that some accommodations you received in high school substantially alter aspects of the curriculum, and are therefore not reasonable. They were actually 'modifications' to the curriculum. In short, it will be useful to refer to your IEP when discussing possible accommodations for college-level work, yet be prepared to consider alternative accommodations or adjustments in the event that some in the IEP are no longer available to you (HEATH Resource Center, 2005).

---

levels of education (National Council on Disability, p. 8). In secondary school the teachers and other school professionals share the responsibility for the educational success with the student, but *in higher education it is up to the individual.* Student must have the skills to advocate for their needs in college or on the job, skills they may not have learned in high school. **Box 2.1** illustrates the importance of self-determination in advocating for services in the postsecondary world.

Self-advocacy skills needed for postsecondary participation: It's up to the student. Every state is now emphasizing the importance of transition services and working to ensure that students with disabilities who need such services are provided with adequate planning and support. However, only one half of secondary schools have specific curriculum to teach secondary students *self-advocacy and self-determination skills* (U.S. Government Accountability Office, 2003b; Study of State and Local Implementation and Impact of the Individuals with Disabilities Education Act [SLIIDEA], 2003). Postsecondary education is different from secondary school in many ways. Class schedules are more flexible, class offerings are more varied, and class periods are shorter. Students are expected to take full responsibility for their progress and to spend much more time and effort on independent study. **Box 2.2** presents the story of an extraordinary

Box 2.2   **A Professor's Story**

Katie was a graduate student who had survived a life-threatening brain injury in high school. She was told that she would never talk, walk, feed herself or ever complete high school. Defying all her doctors' predictions, she fought hard to achieve a remarkable recovery. She finished high school and went on to complete an undergraduate degree with distinction.

She made it clear to her advisor from the beginning that she was a survivor. She spoke openly and honestly about her past and her struggles. She met frequently with her advisor for counsel when she needed it. She spoke about her academic work, her struggles with relationships with peers, and about her long-range goals. Sometimes these meetings involved Kleenex, but that was a small price to pay if the time helped contribute to Kate's persistence in her classes and to her success. Mostly, Kate was very positive and dedicated to overcoming all of her struggles.

The professor became 'invested' in this student's success, understanding her disability along the way and gaining a great appreciation for her strength and her struggle. The professor became her strongest advocate.

college student for whom self-advocacy became a way of life. For students living on campus, there is a wide variety of social opportunities and often a great sense of freedom from parental supervision. However, postsecondary school is not free, and books can be very costly. Financial planning is very important for students who need additional resources to attend postsecondary education.

Laws governing secondary and postsecondary settings are different. For students with disabilities, the laws governing special assistance in the postsecondary setting are different from those in secondary education and change students' experiences in several ways:

1. While high school decision making is heavily parent and professional driven, in the postsecondary setting students are responsible for self-identifying their disabilities, providing documentation for the disability, and informing the institution of their need for accommodations (student driven).

2. Students make decisions about the services available; there is no professional team to decide for them.

3. Disability services personnel make decisions about services based on the "reasonable accommodations" requirements of the Americans with Disabilities Act (ADA) and Section 504 of the Rehabilitation Act, and not on services prescribed by the Individuals with Disabilities Education Act (IDEA).

4. Students with disabilities often have to repeat the process of requesting accommodations each new semester and often on a course-by-course basis, since different classes may require different accommodations (NCSET, 2004b).

Postsecondary education services under Section 504 of the Rehabilitation Act are not mandated for each individual by law as they are for students with IEPs in the secondary setting. Rather, they are based on (1) determination of eligibility for the services and (2) the requirement that the accommodation does not result in a change in content or standards expected for all students. In the postsecondary setting, supports are based on what is "reasonable," rather than what is "appropriate" and "least restrictive," as mandated by IDEA. Therefore, support services and accommodations are aimed at providing *access to content and reduction of barriers to learning,* rather than on promoting achievement. For example, a postsecondary school is more likely to provide a note taker than a tutor.

WHAT STRATEGIES ASSIST YOUTH WITH TRANSITION TO POSTSECONDARY EDUCATION?

Despite the challenges of entering a "different world" of postsecondary education, recent laws have greatly improved access and support for youth with disabilities. Most postsecondary institutions are responding to the mandates and developing greater capacity to recruit, retain, and support students with disabilities to help them complete a postsecondary degree.

Postsecondary Planning in the Last Year of High School

The IDEA legislation requires transition planning for youth preparing for graduation. An important part of transition planning is determining the student's postsecondary goal (e.g., enrolling in college or entering employment) and gathering information about the requirements for achieving it. Then, through "backward planning," the student's transition plan incorporates the secondary course of study, support services, needed assessments, and appropriate community-based experiences. The classes that secondary students take in their final years—both academic and career-technical—should not only meet requirements for graduating from secondary school, but also for entering postsecondary education or employment. The IEP team identifies and explores supports and accommodations that the student will need in postsecondary environments and plans for ways to prepare the student to transition to these supports (Baer & Kochhar-Bryant, 2008; NCSET, 2004a).

In the final year of high school, the student, in consultation with parents and guidance counselors, should identify potential colleges that (1) they can qualify for, (2) have programs that match their interests and abilities, (3) have student support services available, and (4) have a strong record of welcoming and supporting students with disabilities. If the student is planning to enroll in a two- or four-year college or technical school, he or she can ask their guidance counselor to help them (a) select colleges, (b) apply and negotiate for support services, (c) obtain appropriate documentation of their disability required by those colleges, (d) find information on how to access campus resources, (e) discuss interview techniques, (f) discuss self-advocacy techniques and ways to promote one's strengths, and the advantages and disadvantages of self-disclosure of the disability. There are several important questions that youth with disabilities should ask when preparing to apply for Disability Support Services.

- Who is responsible for coordinating services for students with disabilities?
- What documentation of my disability will the college need? What should I make sure I take with me from high school?
- Is there anyone to help me coordinate academic and other support services? Will I have an advocate or mentor?
- How many students does the disability services office serve and what is the ratio of support professionals to students?
- Is a program representative available to answer all my questions clearly and thoroughly?
- What do students pay for support services? Are these charges considered in the school's financial aid packet?

In the last year of high school, with the support and involvement of the family and transition team, each student should make sure the IEP includes transition plans and a *summary of academic and functional performance*, now required under IDEA 2004 (see a sample of the Summary of Performance in the Resources section). Finally, students should learn to discuss their disability and to describe accommodations that are necessary or helpful. If appropriate, they should contact the Vocational Rehabilitation (VR) agency or the Social Security Administration at age eighteen or earlier if there is a partnership between the school and VR to provide early eligibility determination.

Coordination with Community Service Agencies in the Last Year of High School

Adult service agencies provide a comprehensive system of services responsive to the needs of individuals with disabilities. These services typically include public health services, mental health counseling, vocational rehabilitation, assistive technology, developmental disabilities, employment, and independent living services. Examples of adult and independent living services include service coordination to access and obtain local services; therapeutic recreation; day activities; respite care; and residential services (group homes and supervised apartments).

The IDEA 2004 requires school-linked human service agencies to support students' transition from school to postsecondary education and employment. While the school system is required by law to provide the services that are written into the IEP/ITP, organizations that provide supportive services are expected to share the responsibility for transition support services. For example, if the student needs medical services, they can be sought and provided from Medicaid, public health agencies, private insurance, early periodic screening, diagnosis, and treatment programs. If transition support services are needed, they may be sought and provided from vocational rehabilitation agencies, employment services, adult service agencies, job training programs, Workforce Investment Act programs, or supported employment projects.

The student's IEP should contain a *statement of interagency responsibilities* or any linkages required to ensure that the student has the transition services needed from outside agencies and that representatives from those agencies are invited to attend IEP meetings. This requirement for interagency services means that there must be formal interagency agreements between schools and cooperating agencies.

CONCEPT OF "SUPPORTED EDUCATION"

Early efforts to address the needs of individuals with psychiatric disabilities in postsecondary settings are known as "supported education," a term that is based on the definition of supported employment in the Rehabilitation Act (Unger, 1998). According to Unger (1998), supported-education programs involve three prototypes: (1) a self-contained setting, where students are reintegrated into the postsecondary setting; (2) on-site support, where ongoing support is provided by the institution's disabilities support staff or a mental health professional; and (3) mobile support, where support is largely provided by community mental health service providers. Generally accommodations and strategies that appear to be the most common and effective include the following:

- Extra time and/or a private environment for exams
- Priority registration
- Audio recording of lectures

- Note takers for lectures
- Modified deadlines for assignments
- Reduced course load
- Preferential classroom seating
- Early availability of syllabus or textbooks (Sharpe, Johnson, Izzo, & Murray, 2003; Sharpe, Bruininks, Blacklock, Benson, & Johnson, 2004). There is much more that needs to be learned about the growing population of students with psychiatric disabilities and their needs within the postsecondary setting. For example, much more needs to known about how many students exhibit severe and persistent mental illness in relation to those whose illness is considered "mild."

HOW DOES IDEA 2004 PROMOTE POSTSECONDARY PARTICIPATION?

Collaboration and the Summary of Performance

The IDEA 2004 included a new requirement to assist students to make the transition from high school to postsecondary education or employment. Under IDEA 2004, local educational agencies must provide students with a summary of the student's academic achievement and functional performance (Summary of Performance [SOP]), which includes recommendations on how to assist the student in meeting their postsecondary goals (IDEA, 2004). The SOP also provides documentation of the disability, which is necessary under Section 504 of the Rehabilitation Act and the Americans with Disabilities Act to help establish a student's eligibility for reasonable accommodations and supports in *postsecondary* settings. It is also helpful in the Vocational Rehabilitation Comprehensive Assessment process to determine eligibility for VR services. Developing the SOP may be the responsibility of the special educator or school psychologist, but coordination and participation of teachers, counselors, and related services professionals are essential to gathering all relevant information on the student.

Postsecondary educational institutions do not typically accept an IEP from a high school as documentation of a disability for an academic accommodation (HEATH, 2005). However, colleges may use high school testing results, documented in the SOP if the information is current and disability-specific. For example, after consultation with the college, a student with a learning disability might submit the psycho-educational evaluation from eleventh grade as *documentation of the learning disability*. It is very important that students collect and maintain their high school records and summary of performance for the purposes of disability documentation (Hart, Zafft, & Zimbrich, 2001; Shaw, 2006; Shaw & Dukes, 2001).

Collaboration at the age of majority. Age of majority refers to the age at which a young person acquires all the rights and responsibilities of being an adult. In most states the age is eighteen. The IDEA outlined a procedure for the transfer of parental rights to the student when he or she reaches the age of majority. Collaboration and communication among school professionals and parents are essential. Schools must now notify the student and both parents about the student's rights when he or she reaches the age of majority. One year before the student reaches the age of majority under state law, the IEP must include a statement that he or she has been informed of the rights that transfer to the students once she reaches the age of majority. This transfer of rights is an enormous step toward the student's independence and participation in the decision making for further education and future planning (Bremer, Kachgal, & Schoeller, 2003; Eisenman & Chamberlin, 2001; Kupper, 1997).

Collaboration and Section 504 of the Rehabilitation Act

The 1998 Rehabilitation Amendments (P.L. 102–569) strengthened the collaboration and coordination among secondary schools, postsecondary schools, and rehabilitation agencies to support transition to employment or postsecondary settings. Interagency agreements were required in every state that transferred responsibility for transitioning students from the State Education Agency to the State Unit providing vocational rehabilitation services. This provision *links the IEP and the Individual Written Rehabilitation Plan (IWRP) in accomplishing rehabilitation goals prior to high school graduation.*

Vocational rehabilitation provides funds for eligible students with disabilities to attend postsecondary education or technical education programs. Vocational rehabilitation assists persons with cognitive, sensory, physical, or emotional disabilities to attain employment, postsecondary education, and increased independence. Students with disabilities are entitled to accommodations to help them succeed in the postsecondary program, but students are responsible for disclosing their disabilities and asking for the accommodations they need. Vocational rehabilitation services typically last for a limited period of time and are based on an individual's rehabilitation plan.

The 1998 Amendments to the Rehabilitation Act also required rehabilitation agencies to make information about services and providers available to students in their final two years of high school. Rehabilitation services such as early assessment for eligibility for services, vocational assessments, and counseling in work behaviors are now available to students in their final years of high school and after graduation. Close collaboration between secondary personnel and rehabilitation counselors after the student reaches age sixteen is vital to linking the student with VR services and engaging parents in planning. Many states are now specifically hiring VR specialists who visit schools and begin direct collaboration and planning with students, families, and professionals before high school graduation.

WHAT STRATEGIES ASSIST YOUTH WITH TRANSITION TO EMPLOYMENT?

Mull, Sitlington, and Alper (2001) conducted a synthesis of research on postsecondary education programs for students with learning disabilities between 1985 and 2000. Students with learning disabilities constitute the largest disability group participating in college, showing a tenfold increase since 1976. Eleven program factors that were examined included definition of learning disability, characteristics of adult learners, type of institution, special admission procedures, assessment services, program accommodations, support services, instructional adjustments, instructional staff training, direct staff training, and program evaluation.

The authors looked extensively at Section 504 of the Rehabilitation Act of 1973, which has been the defining legislation for the determination of accommodations at postsecondary institutions, as well as the ADA, which expanded coverage to all programs and services regardless of whether or not they received federal financial assistance. Several recommendations for practice were identified.

1. Students need to be prepared to determine which of the accommodations and supports used at the secondary level will also be needed at the postsecondary level.

2. Students need to be prepared to use the increasing number of assistive technology devices.

3. Secondary teachers need to be aware of the demands and expectations of postsecondary education environments in order to help students to acquire skills, supports, and accommodations.

4. More emphasis should be placed on the training of postsecondary admission staff, faculty, residence staff, and others to support students with disabilities.

The authors indicate while it has been twenty-eight years since the passage of the Rehabilitation Act of 1973, many of the recommendations and requirements of Section 504 are still not addressed in the literature. The transition to postsecondary is a key indicator of success of special education and of the transition process for all youth with disabilities. It is key to access, persistence, and retention that students be prepared to identify and request the accommodations and supportive services that they require to be successful in the postsecondary setting.

Collaboration and the Higher Education Act

The Higher Education Act of 1998 (HEA, P.L. 105–244) is designed to assist individuals to participate in postsecondary education, including students with disabilities. The HEA encourages collaborative partnerships between institutions of higher education (IHEs) and secondary schools, particularly those that serve low-income and disadvantaged students. The HEA encourages collaboration among IHEs, businesses, labor organizations, community-based organizations, and private and civic organizations to improve accessibility and support in higher education. It also promotes collaboration between IHEs, schools, and other community agencies for outreach to students with disabilities and aims to reduce attitudinal barriers that prevent participation of individuals with disabilities within their community. The HEA aims to improve college retention and graduation rates for low-income and first-generation college students with disabilities and to encourage programs that counsel students about financial aid and support services.

Coordination and the Americans with Disabilities Act in Postsecondary Institutions and Employment

The Americans with Disabilities Act (ADA) of 1990 promotes collaboration to provide accommodations in both public and private organizations, including public and private schools, colleges and universities, postsecondary vocational-technical schools, employer-based training programs, and other private training programs. Under ADA, transition activities can include preparation for college interviews, knowledge about reasonable accommodations provided in the programs, assistance with applications, and supporting documentation. The ADA prohibits discrimination against individuals with disabilities in postsecondary applications, postsecondary education, job training, job application procedures, hiring, advancement, and employee compensation. According to ADA regulations, *reasonable accommodations* at the postsecondary level include modifications to postsecondary education admission procedures to enable individuals to be considered for admission, modifications in classrooms, test taking, and instructional modifications that would help the student participate in and learn in the college setting. Through antidiscrimination provisions, the ADA encourages postsecondary institutions to consider applicants with disabilities in their recruitment of teachers, professors, and support personnel.

In most colleges and universities, students can expect to apply for and receive services from an office with a title such as "student support services" or "office of disability services. " While a student may not have an IEP or 504 plan in college, postsecondary institutions are required under ADA and the HEA of to provide reasonable accommodations to students with documented disabilities who require them (Shaw, 2006; McGuire & Shaw, 2002; Ekpone & Bogucki, 2002; HEATH Resource Center, 2006). Often students have support service plans that are similar to 504 plans because they specify the kinds of accommodations that the student is to receive in classrooms and in nonacademic activities. Accommodations that can be requested in postsecondary education include testing accommodations, physical accommodations, adaptations of technology, special software for large print, note takers, supplemental online tutorials, time extensions for papers and homework, tutors, and groups support sessions. If students plan to use telecommunications equipment as part of the educational program or in their work on campus, then accommodations for sensory deficits may also be requested.

The Vocational Rehabilitation Role

As the primary federal vehicle for assisting individuals with disabilities to obtain employment, the VR program is a critical link in assisting youths with disabilities to prepare for education, training, and employment opportunities beyond high school (U.S. Department of Education, 2007). Vocational rehabilitation professionals bring to the table valuable knowledge and expertise about the world of work and disability, including career planning, occupational trends and local employment opportunities, job-related education, training and skills, job seeking and retention skills, and accommodations. They also are knowledgeable about adult service systems and the range of benefits and resources available to assist individuals with disabilities. However, research shows that there is an ongoing gap between transition service needs and VR professional involvement in assisting students with disabilities during the transition years (National Longitudinal Transition Study-2 [NLTS-2], 2005).

Several provisions of the Rehabilitation Act address coordination with high schools to improve transition services for students who will be eligible for VR services after leaving school. Recognizing that some youth with disabilities leaving school will require assistance, state VR agencies are encouraged to participate in the cost of transition services for any student determined eligible to receive VR services (Horne, 2001). The State Educational Agency (SEA) is required to create plans that transfer the responsibility for transitioning students from the school to the vocational rehabilitation agency. This provision links the IEP and the Individual Written Rehabilitation Plan (IWRP) under the Rehabilitation Act to accomplish rehabilitation goals before high school graduation.

The Americans with Disabilities Act in Employment

The ADA prohibits discrimination by employers against "qualified individuals with disabilities (visible or hidden)"—those who possess the skills, experience, education, and other job-related requirements of a position and who, with or without reasonable accommodations, can perform the essential functions of the job. This antidiscrimination provision covers all aspects of employment, including application, testing and medical examinations, promotion, hiring and layoffs, assignments and termination, evaluation and compensation, disciplinary actions and leave, and training and benefit. Examples of reasonable accommodations include job restructuring, modified work schedules, reassignments of position, modifications to equipment, modifications of examinations, training materials or policies, and provision of readers or interpreters (Dixon, Kruse, & Van Horn, 2003). Employers are not required to lower their standards to make such accommodations, nor are they required to provide accommodations if they impose "undue hardships" on the business through actions that are very costly or disruptive of the work environment (National Information Center for Children and Youth with Disabilities, 1999). However, most accommodations cost less than $500. **Box 2.3** provides examples of accommodations worked out through discussions between employees and employers, in consultation with the Office of Disability Employment Policy's Job Accommodation Network (Job Accommodation Network [JAN], 2008).

Box 2.3 — **Simple Accommodations for Workers with Disabilities**

Situation: A bowling alley worker with a cognitive disability and limited finger dexterity in both hands was having difficulty wiping the bowling shoes that had been returned by customers. **Solution:** A local job coach service provider fabricated a device that allowed the individual to roll the shoes in front of a brush rather than run a brush over the shoes. **Cost:** no cost as scraps of wood that were left over from other projects were used to make the device.

Situation: A high school guidance counselor with attention deficit disorder was having difficulty concentrating due to the school noise. Solution: The school replaced the bell on his phone with an electric light bulb device that lights up when the phone rings, soundproofed his office and provided a floor fan for white noise. **Cost:** under $600.

Situation: A machine operator who developed arthritis had difficulty turning the machinery control switches. **Solution:** The employer replaced the small machine tabs with larger cushioned knobs and provided the employee with non-slip dot gripping gloves that enabled him to grasp and turn the knobs more effectively and with less force. **Cost:** approximately $130.

(Continued)

(Continued)

Situation: A 25-year veteran warehouse supervisor whose job involved managing and delivering company supplies was having difficulty with the physical demands of his job due to fatigue from cancer treatment. **Solution:** The employer provided the employee with a three-wheeled scooter to reduce walking but enable him to manage the warehouse. The employer also rearranged the layout of supplies in the warehouse to reduce climbing and reaching. **Cost:** $3,000.

Situation: A part-time college instructor had a learning disability, specifically auditory discrimination difficulties. This was causing problems for her during meetings and in class and prevented her from meeting time lines for projects. **Solution:** The employee was permitted to take notes during staff meetings and to provide written responses to all attendees on the questions raised during the meeting within a time frame agreed upon by the meeting participants. The employee also received a copy of meeting agendas and project expectations in advance of the face-to-face meetings and was thereby able to ask questions or provide follow-up responses in writing. **Cost:** $0.

Social Security Administration

The Social Security Administration operates the federally funded program that provides benefits for people of any age who are unable to do substantial work and have a severe mental or physical disability. Several programs are offered for people with disabilities, including Social Security Disability Insurance (SSDI), Supplemental Security Income (SSI), Plan to Achieve Self-Support (PASS), Medicaid, and Medicare. Examples of employment services include cash benefits while working (e.g., student-earned income), Medicare or Medicaid while working, help with extra work expenses the individual has as a result of the disability, and assistance to start a new line of work. Postsecondary services generally include financial incentives for further education and training.

Plan to Achieve Self-Support plan. To provide incentives for young people to enter the workforce, the Social Security Administration developed the PASS plan to help individuals make the transition without losing disability benefits (U.S. Department of Labor, 2004). A PASS plan lets the young worker use his or her income or other assets to reach work goals. For example, a young graduate could set aside money to go to school to get specialized training for a job or to start a business. The job that the individual wants should allow him or her to earn enough to reduce or eliminate the need for benefits provided under both the Social Security and Supplemental Security Income (SSI) programs. A plan is designed to help the individual to obtain services, items, or skills that are needed to reach their employment goals.

Three requirements are needed to qualify for a PASS plan: (1) desire to work; (2) currently receiving SSI (or can qualify for SSI by having this plan) because the person is disabled or blind; and (3) has other income or resources to get a job or start a business (U.S. Department of Labor, 2004). Under SSI rules, any income that the individual has reduces the SSI payment for disability. But, with an approved PASS plan, the individual can use that income to pay for the items needed to reach their work goal. Money set aside toward work-related goals is not counted under this plan when the SSI payment amount is determined. Money set aside can be used for transportation to and from work; tuition, books, fees, and supplies needed for school or training; child care; attendant care; employment services, such as job coaching and resume writing; supplies to start a business; equipment and tools to do the job; or uniforms, special clothing, and safety equipment. If the plan is approved, the coordinator/specialist will stay in contact make sure that the plan is followed and the goals are being met. **Box 2.4** illustrates how the PASS plan can open doors for individuals with disabilities transitioning to employment.

Box 2.4 — **Go for It!: The PASS Plan for Self-Support**

Dana Simpkins likes spending time in front of the computer. As an e-mail specialist for the Gap, Inc. in Columbus, Ohio, that's his job. But Dana has spinal muscular atrophy and relies on a wheelchair. There was a time when he didn't know the joy of job satisfaction. Supplemental Security Income (SSI) helped make ends meet, but he wanted to work. "My PASS (Plan for Achieving Self-Support) was what allowed me to work," Dana remembers. The PASS let him keep his SSI while he went to work. He used his SSI to meet his basic needs, and his wages were saved in a special PASS account to help meet his goal of getting a van modified for wheelchair transportation. Now, with his modified van, Dana no longer needs the help of SSI. "My advice to those who are considering work is to simply go for it. Don't be afraid to try and fail. The feeling I got cashing that first paycheck was sweeter having overcome greater challenges than most." (*Working While Disabled, a Guide to Plans for Achieving Self-Support,* Social Security Administration, 2004.)

Ticket to Work and Work Incentive Improvement Act. In late 1999, the Congress enacted the Ticket to Work and Work Incentive Improvement Act (TWWIIA, P.L. 106–170). The SSA administers the Act, and the Department of Health and Human Services administers the health care component. Under the voluntary Ticket to Work Program, individuals with disabilities can obtain job-related training and placement assistance from an approved provider of their choice. For example, youth in transition to work can receive employment services, vocational services, or other services to help them enter employment. *Employment Networks* are private organizations or government agencies that have agreed to work with the SSA to provide employment services to persons with disabilities at no cost. The second measure expands health care coverage so that individuals with disabilities will be able to become employed without fear of losing their health insurance (Imel, 2001; U.S. Department of Education, 2001). The Ticket to Work program has helped many young people make the transition into employment.

3 Self-Determination and Self-Advocacy Skills Essential for Successful Transition to Postsecondary Settings

INTRODUCTION

This scenario occurred three years ago. Adam decided to attend college and is currently a successful and happy sophomore. He receives services to help him with reading, math, note taking, and test taking. He speaks honestly about his need for accommodations to his professors and is linked to an advisor who understands the demands he faces with workload and studying. All of this might not have occurred had it not been for Adam's strong sense of self-determination and the ability to advocate for himself. These skills were not something he possessed naturally but were taught to him explicitly by his teachers and reinforced at both home and school.

Self-determination skills are considered some of the most important skills young adults can bring with them to colleges and universities (Durlak, Rose, & Bursuck, 1994; Hitchings, Retish, & Horvath, 2005; Sands & Wehmeyer, 1996; Sitlington, 2003; Thoma & Wehmeyer, 2005;

Webster, 2004; Wehmeyer, Agran, & Hughes, 1998). Although we acknowledge that academic skills are critical to future success in college, students may ultimately fail if they are not able to advocate for themselves. More than ever, young adults need to possess those attributes necessary to make clear choices and decisions, to state their needs, and to plan their futures. Most students with disabilities may have difficulties practicing self-determination and self-advocacy skills without explicit instruction and strategies. It is up to us as educators to not assume that self-determination and self-advocacy skills will magically appear upon a student's graduation. Rather, it is our responsibility to *explicitly teach* these skills and to provide opportunities for students to practice them. This chapter will provide guidelines to foster self-determination with eventual postsecondary education in mind.

WHAT IS SELF-DETERMINATION?

Many of us consider ourselves to be self-determined. We know how to ask for help, how to state our needs, how to make decisions, and how to assume responsibility for our actions. These skills typify successful adult behaviors and actions. In working with students, it is important we teach them to become aware of these behaviors and that they have ample opportunities to practice self-determination actions. Field, Martin, Miller, Ward, and Wehmeyer (1998) offer a list of attributes that are typically associated with self-determined behaviors. Some of these attributes are:

- Awareness of personal preferences, interests, needs
- Ability to set goals
- Ability to advocate for oneself
- Ability to be persistent
- Ability to be self-confident
- Ability to evaluate decisions

Other factors may include choice making, decision making, goal setting, independence, and assertiveness. In general, a student who can assume control and advocate for his or her needs, and then can take action on those needs, is considered to be self-determined. Self-determination theory includes the study of motivation, personality, and social development (Ryan & Deci, 2000; Wehmeyer & Schalock, 2001). Wehmeyer (1992) defined self-determination as "acting as the primary causal agent in one's life free to make choices and decisions about one's quality of life, free from undue influence or interference" (p. 302). Wehmeyer and Schwartz (1997) extended this definition to include four essential characteristics of a self-determined individual. They assert that self-determined individuals are:

Autonomous—acting according to their own preferences

Self-regulated—purposefully making decisions about which skills to use in a certain situation, act upon them, and evaluate their effectiveness

Psychologically empowered—acting based on the beliefs that they have the capacity to perform behaviors that will influence outcomes

Self-realized—having and using knowledge of themselves, including strengths and limitations

Individuals who demonstrate these abilities are found to have more successful academic, behavioral, and social outcomes, all of which lead to greater success as adults. These skills guide individuals to plan, initiate actions, follow-through on those actions, and evaluate the effectiveness of those actions, in turn leading to the next point of decision or action. Hoffman and Field (2005) have provided a framework regarding self-determination. Using this framework, students begin the path to self-determination by learning to know and value themselves so that they can then create quality goals and actions. Their five-step guide includes knowing yourself, valuing yourself, planning to reach goals, acting upon those plans, and learning from the experience. Hoffman and Field argue that youth must be allowed to practice these skills. Until youth are given both the **opportunity** to practice self-determined behaviors and the **support** from which to reflect and learn from the consequences of their actions, they will not develop the ultimate capacity to become responsible adults (Mithaug, 1996). To do so, these youth will need **explicit instruction** in learning how to be self-determined. They will need specific examples and scenarios in which to **practice** these skills, and they will need the *support* of caring and competent adults to guide them to self-determined actions.

Self-Determination and Changing Perspectives

Our world is undergoing remarkable and palpable changes. With the advent of technology and an emerging global economy as a foundation for nearly all we do, adolescents have had to adapt to changes in the workforce, more specialized careers, further and longer educational opportunities, and increased options for schooling, work, relationships, and living opportunities. Mortimer and Larson (2002) contend that a new phase of "postadolescence" or "emerging adulthood" (p. 11) has defined the time period when young adults leave high school to explore different jobs, lifestyles, relationships, and educational experiences. This developmental period of time extends through the early twenties and allows young adults to take much longer to transition to true adulthood with its concomitant responsibilities. However, this lengthening of adolescence does not exclude individuals from the societal pressures. As Mortimer and Larson state,

> Adolescents are not passive recipients of macrosocietal change, they are actors within it. In some cases they create it. Adolescence is above all a period in which youth are required to be agents, to find their own paths, and within the set of constraints and opportunities available to them, to model themselves in ways that enable them to obtain the adulthoods they desire. (p. 15)

Given this scenario, the need for self-determination is evident. Youth with disabilities must be able to make choices for themselves, to be adaptable to the changes occurring both within and around them, and to evaluate the consequences of their decisions. In a now classic study of successful adults with learning disabilities, Gerber, Ginsberg, and Reiff (1992) found that success for these adults resulted directly from behaviors we would consider to be self-determined. These included gaining control of their lives, having the desire to succeed, positively reframing their disability, garnering a strong circle of support, and being adaptable and persistent.

Conversely, poor self-determined actions can lead to poor outcomes. In a study conducted by Trainor (2007), adolescent girls from low socioeconomic backgrounds made many decisions that on face value reflected tenets of self-determination. However, because these girls lacked opportunities to practice positive and constructive aspects of self-determination, their decisions often result in deleterious consequences such as truancy, abuse, fighting, low self-esteem, and limited expectations for further postsecondary education. Trainor states that it is imperative that the sociocultural aspects of self-determination be critically analyzed and applied in systematic and respectful ways. Yuen and Shaughnessy (2001) speak of the need to equalize diverse students' "cultural capital" (p. 202) so that their desires and values are equally considered and respected along with those of the dominant culture. Given the scenario of a changing societal view of adolescence, and the need to be culturally responsive, the tenets of self-determination can assist teachers to respond more sensitively to the individual needs of our diverse population.

What We Know About Adult Outcomes and Self-Determination

There are numerous ways to teach self-determination, including curricula, strategies, and opportunities for school reform. We will investigate these options later in the chapter. However, just because we believe in teaching self-determination skills, *does it really make a difference?* This question is beginning to be answered as researchers can now see the longitudinal efforts of their teaching. Durlak, Rose, and Bursuck (1994) were among the first to investigate the value and potential for generalization to other settings. In their study, eight students with identified learning disabilities were taught a series of seven skills related to self-determination. These included the ability to (1) ask for clarification of course materials, (2) disclose to a teacher that one has a learning disability, (3) make an appointment with a teacher to discuss needs and accommodations, (4) ask to use a tape recorder in class, (5) ask for approval for a note taker, (6) ask library staff for assistance, and (7) make an appointment with other professional personnel for assistance. On average, results indicated that students improved their skill rate from 42 percent to 82 percent; further, these skills were generalized 100 percent to other settings on a subsequent maintenance check.

Wehmeyer and Schwartz (1997) measured the self-determination of eighty students with learning disabilities or cognitive disabilities when they were first in secondary school, and then one year after they exited school. Students in the high self-determination group were more than twice as likely to be employed (80 percent of the sample) and earn more per hour ($2.00). Wehmeyer and Palmer (2003) conducted a follow-up study of ninety-four postschool young adults with cognitive disabilities, half of whom had been taught self-determination skills. In assessing their progress one to three years out of school, more of the high self-determination group were found to be living independently, and employed with benefits, vacations, and sick leave.

Unfortunately, lack of explicit self-determination instruction has resulted in negative effects for youth with disabilities (Carter, Lane, Pierson, & Glaeser, 2006; Hitchings, Retish, & Horvath, 2005; Trainor, 2005, 2007). Carter et al. (2006) assessed the self-determination characteristics of students with identified learning disabilities and emotional disturbance. Their findings revealed that students with emotional disturbance were found to have lower ratings of self-determination; further, these students had fewer opportunities to practice self-determination skills, and educators and parents differed on their perceptions of available opportunities for youth with emotional and behavioral disabilities. Researchers suggest infusing self-determination instruction throughout the general education curriculum, beginning such instruction in earlier grades and with a strong commitment for implementation. Hitchings et al. (2005) queried tenth graders with disabilities regarding their desire to attend postsecondary education. The students were again queried as seniors. Students' desire to continue postsecondary education declined from 77 percent to 47 percent over the two-year period. Researchers speculate that few opportunities were provided to students to become involved in transition planning, with little opportunity to advocate for their needs in general education settings (which could ultimately provide the impetus to consider further education).

Trainor's work with culturally diverse students in the transition planning process (2005) has highlighted a significant lack of self-determination instruction and opportunities, resulting in lowered expectations and outcomes. Christle, Jolivette, and Nelson (2007) studied school characteristics related to dropout rates; they highlight the need for "student-centered environments" (p. 334) to promote school engagement and successful transition to adult life.

These studies illustrate the need for explicit instruction and opportunities for generalization. They also illustrate that self-determination strategies are not being systematically taught to students with disabilities, putting them at tremendous disadvantage if they choose to attend postsecondary schools (Durlak et al., 1994; Eisenman, 2007; Thoma, Williams, & Davis, 2005; Trainor, 2005). At this point, we again emphasize the need for strong advocacy and self-knowledge skills as critical to postsecondary success.

HOW CAN STUDENTS LEARN SELF-DETERMINATION SKILLS FOR POSTSECONDARY EDUCATION?

Increasingly, students with disabilities are entering colleges and universities. Wagner, Newman, Cameto, and Levine (2005) report a 17 percent increase between 1987 and 2003 in young adults with disabilities continuing to postsecondary education (contrasted to a 5 percent enrollment increase in postsecondary education for young adults without disabilities). However, it is unclear how many of these students actually finish college with degree in hand. To maximize the opportunities for young adults with disabilities to attain a degree, it is crucial that a variety of components be present in secondary schools. These include comprehensive transition planning, systematic use of self-determination curricula, resources and materials specific to transitioning to postsecondary opportunities, and opportunities to practice self-advocacy and self-determined actions. School personnel, including teachers, counselors, and administrators must also understand the unique learning and coping needs of students with disabilities as they assist with the transition to postsecondary education. Finally, school systems must realign their efforts to ensure that all willing students are encouraged to follow postsecondary educational opportunities if they desire.

Transition Planning

The most important element in ensuring successful transition to postsecondary education is effective and comprehensive transition planning. If developed in alignment with student interests, preferences, and needs, and with an eye always toward future goals, transition planning can guide a young adult to optimal postsecondary opportunities. Inherent in this planning are the self-determination skills used by young adults throughout the process and into the postsecondary community. It is crucial that students have the opportunity to engage in self-determined behaviors beginning in elementary school that continue through high school and beyond. Several effective strategies exist to facilitate the nascent acquisition of self-determination competencies. Children in elementary and middle school can lead their own parent-teacher-student conferences where they demonstrate a body of work to their families; they may present a portfolio of their best work, or they may guide family members to topically based centers around the room that showcase the work they have produced. Regardless of the means of demonstration, student-led conferences provide a powerful initiation to the self-knowledge and self-advocacy skills needed throughout life (Bassett & Lehmann, 2002; Picciotto, 1996).

Student-centered planning can also act as a precursor to transition planning. By convening a MAP session (i.e., McGill Action Plans; Forest & Pearpoint, 1992) or a similar person-focused meeting, a student and his or her invited guests are asked to share their perspectives on the student's dream, nightmares, strengths and needs, and desired action for the future. The student has the opportunity not only to hear others' *positive* perspectives, but she can begin to advocate for goals that will ultimately be translated onto the Individualized Education Plan (IEP) document. The PATH process (Planning Alternative Tomorrows with Hope) also helps young adults to articulate their goals from the perspective that the goals have already been achieved and through a series of targeted steps created by "backward planning" (Pearpoint, Forest, & O'Brien, 1998).

Transition planning is anchored by the development of an effective transition-focused IEP. The fundamental elements of this plan are girded in tenets of self-determination. Implicit in IDEA (2004) are mandates that reinforce self-determination principles. These include:

- *Student involvement in IEP meetings*—IEP teams are required to invite transition-aged students to IEP meetings. Students are not mandated to attend the meeting, but their input regarding their goals must be considered and documented. Research has found that the more students can be involved in the development of their IEPs, the more likely *their* goals are included in transition planning (Martin et al., 2006; Van Reusen, Bos, Schumaker, & Deshler, 1994).
- *Student interests and preferences*—Educators are expected to work with students to help them articulate their interests and preferences that will be shared at the IEP meeting. Students can use self-determination skills to ensure that their interests and preferences are heard, documented, and considered during IEP development.

- *Postsecondary goal statements*—Postsecondary goals are predicated on student interests and preferences, and may be related to information gleaned from assessment data as well as from student interests and preferences. Postsecondary goals provide the foundation for the development of annual goals and objectives. The postsecondary goals should link directly to the aspirations of each student.
- *Formal and informal transition assessment*—Some assessments require student input and self-report (i.e., Transition Planning Inventory, Clark & Patton, 2006). Students are asked to self-report on their strengths and needs, interests, and preferences. The results of these assessments are used to develop postsecondary goals and annual goals and drive the transition services to assist in reaching those goals. Student input and advocacy throughout the assessment process is critical to a holistic perspective.
- *Course of study*—Although students must take certain courses required for graduation, there is also flexibility in the type of courses students can take to complete their education. As educators work with students to plan their course of study, students can advocate for those courses that reflect their interests and future goals for careers. Guidance counselors can help students to understand which courses could best align with postsecondary goals.

Strategies That Can Foster Student Involvement and Self-Determination in the IEP Planning Process

Structured, guided approaches to student self-determination in the IEP process offer critical means by which a student's voice is heard in the planning and implementation of postsecondary goals. Student-directed IEP meetings offer students a conduit by which to authentically participate in transition-focused IEP meetings. Allowing a student to lead or help to facilitate her IEP meeting results in a larger percentage of student-initiated goals on the document. In studies conducted for the *Self-Advocacy Strategy*, Van Reusen et al. (1994) found an increase from 13 percent to 86 percent of student-initiated goals written into the IEP. If students are not authentically included in IEP development, their IEPs may not reflect their goals and preferences. In a study by Martin, Van Dycke, D'Ottavio, & Nickerson (2007), one hundred and nine students attended their IEP meetings, ostensibly to provide input into their goals. Although the students were present, they did not direct or facilitate the meetings; as a result, students talked only 3 percent of the total meeting time, as compared with education professionals, who spoke 66 percent of the time. Clearly, the need for systematic ways to involve students in IEP planning is warranted.

Teaching students to become more involved in the IEP planning process typically follows three phases: a *beginning* phase, a *during* phase, and an *after* phase. Students in the *beginning* phase learn the steps or process of student involvement which they will use to participate in the IEP meeting. Martin, Marshall, Maxon, and Jerman (1996) developed the *Self-Directed IEP* to teach students how to direct or facilitate IEP meetings. The curriculum includes videos and student workbooks that guide students to learn the eleven steps that they will use as they participate in the meetings. The steps are

1. Begin meeting by stating the purpose

2. Introduce everyone

3. Review past goals and performance

4. Ask for others' feedback

5. State your school and transition goals

6. Ask questions if you don't understand

7. Deal with difference in opinion

8. State what support you will need

9. Summarize your goals

10. Close the meeting by thanking everyone

11. Work on IEP goals all year

(Martin et al., 1996).

Using the support materials, teachers review the eleven steps with students. Often, students already experienced in using the self-directed IEP help to teach the strategy to the uninitiated. Students compose their strengths, needs, and goals and then role-play scenarios prior to the IEP meeting.

In the *during* phase, students attend the IEP meeting in one of four capacities: (1) student directs the entire meeting, (2) student and educator codirect the meeting, (3) educator facilitates the meeting and guides the student to direct certain pieces, and (4) educator directs the meeting and includes the students to provide information in certain areas. Regardless of the degree of participation, what is important is that the student has assumed a much more active role and is more likely to advocate for his or her needs. The *after* component of the strategy includes working on IEP goals during the year, as well as assisting students new to this level of involvement. Students are motivated to work on goals they have created and to follow through on their responsibilities for meeting these goals.

Van Reusen et al. (1994) developed the *Self-Advocacy Strategy* to prepare students to become stronger and more effective self-advocates during educational planning meetings, including transition-focused IEP meetings. The *beginning* phase for the strategy includes learning the SHARE behaviors to be able to demonstrate appropriate, adult behaviors during the meeting. These behaviors include:

S	Sit up straight
H	Have a pleasant tone of voice
A	Activate your thinking
R	Relax
E	Engage in eye communication

Following mastery of the SHARE behaviors, the gist of the self-advocacy strategy is taught. The strategy first begins by having students develop a document of their strengths, areas to improve, goals, and choices for learning that they can take to the IEP meeting with them to share with the IEP team. The students are then taught how to present their "inventory," how to listen, how to respond, and how to articulate their goals. Thus the strategy, I PLAN, is organized in the following manner:

- Step 1: **I**nventory your strengths, areas to improve, goals, and choices for learning or accommodations
- Step 2: **P**resent your interest inventory
- Step 3: **L**isten and respond
- Step 4: **A**sk questions
- Step 5: **N**ame your goals

(Van Reusen et al., 1994).

The *during* phase involves using the self-advocacy strategy (including the SHARE behaviors) to participate in the meeting. Students are asked not to direct the meetings, but to begin the meeting by reviewing their inventory, and then to actively participate throughout the meetings, listening to comments, asking questions, and stating their needs. The *after* phase replicates that of the self-directed IEP: to work on goals all year and to work with other students to learn the strategy.

These are just two of the many ways that students can be taught to use self-determination strategies in transition planning. Explicit instruction can benefit students as they work with disability support staff and instructors through their college careers.

Summary of Performance

The use of self-determination competencies during IEP development is equally important when developing the student's exit Summary of Performance (SOP). Mandated through IDEA 2004, the SOP document is intended to travel with a student as he exits school to the next educational or vocational environment. It is a summary of the students' academic and social strengths and needs, and also includes student preferences for learning as well as an explanation of accommodations and modifications needed to enhance success. Although each state (and often, each school district) can develop its own SOP document, typical areas of information include: (1) background information on the student, including demographic data, (2) student's postsecondary goals, (3) present levels of performance, (4) recommendations to assist the student in meeting postsecondary goals, and (5) student input (Kochhar-Bryant, Shaw, & Izzo, 2007). Because students will be the ones sharing the document with postsecondary professionals, they should play an integral role in SOP development. They must be able to explain the nature of their disability, their learning strengths, their postsecondary goals, and the need for specific accommodations and modifications. They need to understand and clarify the assessment data derived from previous educational plans. Finally, they need to advocate for the services they will require as college students. With the use of the SOP document, students can now employ the advocacy strategies they learned in school to fully communicate their needs.

Strategies That Enhance Self-Determination and Self-Advocacy Skills

Now that we have reviewed the importance of self-determination and self-advocacy skills for IEP planning, there are also resources that explicitly teach principles and strategies of self-determination skills. Students transitioning to postsecondary educational settings will use self-determination strategies consistently throughout their school careers to ensure that their needs are met. According to Izzo and Lamb (2002), American culture is strongly based on individuals' abilities to exercise power and control over influences in their lives. However, for individuals with disabilities, these foundations of self-determination may be limited because of a lack of opportunities to practice them. The explicit instruction of self-determination strategies provides a link to the metacognitive processes that allow students to think consciously about what strategies to employ, how to use them, and how to evaluate their effectiveness.

The *Steps to Self-Determination* program created by Field and Hoffman (1996) provides an explicit template for students to learn and practice self-determination skills. Students begin with learning about themselves and valuing the many strengths they possess. Students then learn how to plan for their goals, how to take action on their goals, and how to evaluate the outcomes of their actions. They are offered many options to practice these skills in a controlled way using a mentor (e.g., a parent, a teacher, an adult friend) who helps to guide them. Figure 3.1 presents the Model of Self-Determination that frames this process (Field and Hoffman, 1996).

Many fine resources exist that assist students in the transition from secondary schools to postsecondary educational settings (see Field, Hoffman, & Spezia, 1998; Halpern, Herr, Doren, & Wolf, 2000; Martin, Hughes, Marshall, Jerman, & Maxon, 2000; McGahee-Kovac, 2002; Powers, Ellison, Matuszewski, & Turner, 1999). All of these resources share a common thread—they address the need for students to acquire self-determination skills as they prepare to transition to college.

Getting Down to the Business: Using Self-Determination to Plan for Postsecondary Transition

As students become self-determined, they are ready to tackle the business of considering their postsecondary educational options. While the many details of how to choose an educational or training opportunity, how to apply, how to provide documentation, and how to stay organized for the transition will be covered in Chapters 4, 6, and 7, there are a number of excellent resources and guidelines that can assist students in their decision-making process. Students with strong self-determination skills still need assistance to make the myriad decisions that come with this important transition. Webb (2000) provides a cogent, user-friendly guide to students that outlines a process for considering postsecondary opportunities. Using self-guided student resources, she takes students through the decision to attend a postsecondary institution, preparing for the transition, exploring choices and selecting a postsecondary institution, and applying to the institution(s) of choice. Students learn the differences between a high school educational setting and a postsecondary one. She also speaks to the smaller details, such as parking and living situations, which surely confound many students. Arnold (1994) offers a similar format for youth who wish to attend college by relying heavily on building self-advocacy skills that lead to decision-making, applying, interviewing and writing skills, and knowing legal rights and responsibilities. Resource guides for parents are also available that parallel the content learned by students, helping them to acquire the knowledge and the appropriate advocacy skills to support their child. Taymans, West, and Sullivan (2000) offer a comprehensive collection of resources for students with learning disabilities and attention deficit hyperactivity disorder, including resources for those individuals who are nontraditional students and are newly identified with an invisible disability. All of these resources engage the student throughout and put self-determination skills to action.

Figure 3.1

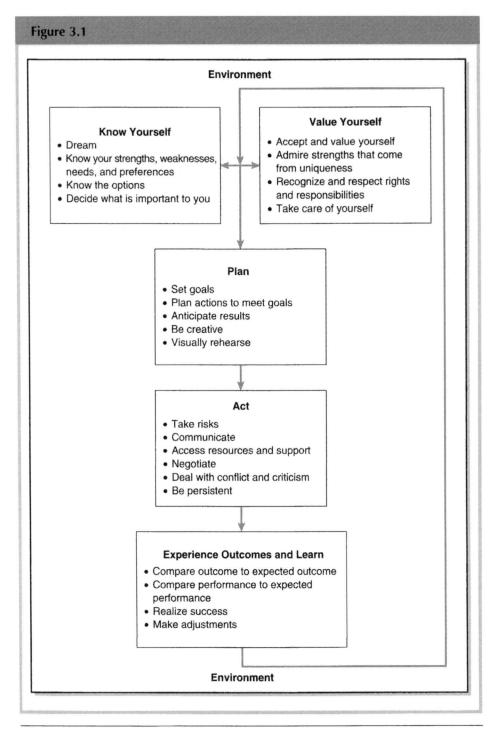

Source: Figure by Alan Hoffman and Sharon Field. Reprinted with permission from Pro-Ed: Austin, TX.

To truly understand the realities of postsecondary education for youth with disabilities, personal perspectives of those who have "been there" can motivate students and underscore the importance of self-determination skills. Mooney and Cole (2000) and Cobb (2003) provide engaging, humorous, and detailed explanations of how to transition to postsecondary settings as well as how to be successful learners. Their work relies heavily on personal experiences in using self-advocacy skills and teaching readers the "tricks" to success.

Having a strong sense of self-determination is a cornerstone for success for young adults as they transition to postsecondary opportunities. By providing explicit instruction from early grades through high school, in student involvement in the IEP process, to acquisition of explicit self-determination skills, to readiness to explore postsecondary options, to learning from others with disabilities who have survived the challenge, young adults can and will succeed and thrive.

WHAT CAN SCHOOLS AND PROFESSIONALS DO TO ASSIST STUDENTS?

Although the tenets of self-determination are grounded in intrinsic self-realization, motivation, and action, school systems and school personnel must acknowledge a huge responsibility to providing the opportunities for students to practice these skills. Because support services for transition to postsecondary settings continue to be inconsistent (Hong, Ivy, Gonzalez, & Ehrensberger, 2007), it is critical for schools to develop comprehensive programs that support this transition (Brinckerhoff, McGuire, & Shaw, 2002). Mellard (2005) offers the following guidelines that schools can implement to smooth the transition from high school to postsecondary settings:

- Develop effective study skills curriculum for students.
- Teach learning strategies.
- Arrange job tryouts to give all students opportunities to evaluate different career and vocational options.
- Arrange needed accommodations for college entrance exams and matriculation testing.
- Identify colleges that provide educational programs relevant to career interests.
- Identify the types of accommodations and support services that the student needs based on a student's disability.
- Assist in the application process.
- Assist in preparing the documentation that the student can carry to the college (Mellard, 2005, p. 10).

The use of the ACT and SAT exams with secondary students has highlighted the need for school systems to provide appropriate guidance to school personnel regarding the nature of testing accommodations and the way in which they are requested and implemented. Fuchs, Fuchs, and Capizzi (2005) discuss the ramifications of test accommodations for students with learning disabilities and conclude that although the use of such accommodations still vary widely and are used inconsistently (both on state tests and college entrance exams), teachers need to be supported in their decision making and provide objective means for identifying such accommodations in a way that is valid and appropriate. Brinckerhoff and Banerjee (2007) provide recommendations for ensuring that students are able to receive accommodations appropriate to their needs, based on a body of evidence from multiple sources that have demonstrated effectiveness.

Some schools have offered creative means by which to educate students and educational professionals regarding postsecondary education. Postsecondary academies offer a way to provide information to improve the recruitment and eventual success rates of students with disabilities (Kato, Nulty, Olszewski, Doolittle, & Flannery, 2006). The academies offer a one-day conference located at a college or university for high school juniors and seniors to explore the many facets of postsecondary education. Parents and high school teachers and staff are also welcome to attend. The academy is structured with break-out sessions designed to look like college classes. Students can tour the college campus, visit the disability support services office, and learn about counseling, tutoring, and advisement services. Suggestions for organizing and coordinating a postsecondary academy include four steps: (1) establishing a planning committee, (2) identifying funding, content, and format, (3) marketing and implementing, and (4) evaluating the results (Kato et al., 2006). Positive results from the academies are evident by the increasing numbers of participants each year as well as the systematic structural and curricular changes that high school transition programs have made in response. Clearly, the academies have provided a useful model to aid in the transition process.

HOW CAN SCHOOL PROFESSIONALS ASSIST IN STUDENTS' TRANSITION TO POSTSECONDARY EDUCATION?

Just as students with disabilities need to learn and practice self-determination and self-advocacy skills, so too do teachers, counselors, and other school personnel need to support their efforts. First and most importantly, professionals need to *believe* that students have the ability to exercise self-determination, that they have a right to choose a quality of life (Wehmeyer & Schalock, 2001) that meets their needs. This is not to say that professionals should condone risky or spurious behavior, but rather that students should be encouraged to take risks, and that professionals should be there to support their decisions and to help students to evaluate the consequences of their actions. Researchers believe that if secondary schools are to provide programmatic supports that enhance opportunities for students with disabilities to attend postsecondary settings, opportunities to practice self-determined choice and decision making must be available (Johnson, Stodden, Emanuel, Luecking, & Mack, 2002; Stodden, Galloway, & Stodden, 2003). Other researchers emphasize the need for schools to have resources to meet students' needs as they learn self-determination skills. These include access to technology (Burgstahler, 2002; Mull & Sitlington, 2003), authentic learning practices that blend standards and transition-focused competencies (Bassett & Kochhar-Bryant, 2006), career and technical education (Benz, Lindstrom, & Yovanoff, 2000), and social competence (Lane, Pierson, & Givner, 2004). Teachers themselves need to model the ways in which self-determined actions can be used. In reviewing elements of successful high schools, George, McEwin, and Jenkins (2000) note that effective teachers must create a climate of support and caring, encourage student self-knowledge and self-determination for learning, and serve as personal advocates for students.

The role of school counselors is essential in developing self-determination skills for young adults with disabilities as they transition to postsecondary education. Counselors can help provide students with information regarding essential elements to transitioning including knowledge of colleges and universities, knowledge of postsecondary support services at each college or university, knowledge of laws regarding disability supports, knowledge of documentation needed for postsecondary supports, knowledge of self-advocacy strategies needed in postsecondary settings, and knowledge of funding resources (Baumberger & Harper, 1999; Milsom & Hartley, 2005). Counselors can offer advisory programs that emphasize decision-making, problem-solving, and listening and verbal skills (George et al., 2000). Counselors are a necessary part of any team planning for a student's transition to postsecondary education.

4 Guided Pathways: Colleges and Universities

INTRODUCTION

There are many students for whom the idea of attending a college or university is akin to flying to the moon. Especially for some students with disabilities, postsecondary education is seen as a distant dream to be accomplished by others, but not by them. They may receive little encouragement from parents or teachers; if they would be the first in their family to attend college, the odds of their going sharply decrease yet again. Today, we have seen a 17 percent increase in the number of students with disabilities attending college from 1987 to 2003. Researchers from the National Longitudinal Transition Study Two (NLTS-2) reported postsecondary enrollment went from 15 percent in 1987 to 32 percent in 2003 (Wagner, Newman, Cameto, & Levine, 2005), indicating more than a doubling of students with disabilities enrolling in postsecondary education. The number of college freshmen with disabilities has increased tenfold since 1976 (Fuller & Wehman, 2003). These increases tell us that more youth than ever see postsecondary education as a viable option to shape their futures. An educated population of adults with disabilities provides our society with intelligent, creative, and self-sufficient individuals who can actively contribute to their communities.

Just as typical students need supports to attend a college or university, so do students with disabilities. These individuals will require the broad support of a number of significant people, structures to help them both transition from a secondary setting to a postsecondary setting, and the internal motivation and confidence to know that they can succeed through their efforts and the ongoing support of others. Gerber and Reiff (1994) identified adults with learning disabilities who had been nominated by others as "successful." Results of their ethnographic study indicated that these successful adults understood the nature of their disability and came to an acceptance of both the gifts and the challenges it brought to them. They demonstrated a "goodness of fit" between their educational and career expectations and their abilities and talents. Most importantly, they surrounded themselves with supportive friends, family, and professionals who believed in their dreams and encouraged them to take action. As educators, it is our obligation, our pledge, to support those students who wish to attend postsecondary institutions. We can help them to create and achieve their dreams. This chapter will outline the ways in which students, parents, educators, and educational systems can assist in this process.

WHAT FACTORS ARE ESSENTIAL TO HELP STUDENTS AS THEY CONSIDER ATTENDING COLLEGE?

More than anything, it is imperative that students have the intrinsic motivation and the extrinsic support to succeed in postsecondary settings. Mithaug (1996) speaks to the need for building the *capacity* and the *opportunity* for students to acquire self-determination and other skills they will need to master the myriad demands of college settings. Students must possess those intrinsic qualities of motivation, persistence, organization, goal setting, and decision making to allow them to envision a future framed through a college experience (Field, Martin, Miller, Ward, & Wehmeyer, 1998). Additionally, parents, educators, and other professionals must provide opportunities for these youth to practice the skills they will need to attend postsecondary institutions, including a strong academic background, appropriate social skills, strategies for studying, time management and organization, and confidence bred from past successes. At a minimum, there are five major elements that educators can include to assist the transition from secondary to postsecondary experiences. These include person-focused planning, appropriate Individualized Education Plan (IEP) development, strong Summary of Performance (SOP) documentation, partnerships with families, and opportunities for exploration.

Use Person-Focused Planning to Begin the Journey to Postsecondary Education

Person-focused planning has been used for a variety of purposes over the years. It was originally conceived to be used with adults with significant disabilities living and working in communities to help them to articulate their dreams, strengths, and challenges (O'Brien & Lovett, 1993). Today, variations of person-focused planning have been used to encourage inclusive practices (Forest & Pearpoint, 1992). Person-focused planning has also been used extensively as a component of transition planning (Bassett & Lehmann, 2002; Morningstar, Kleinhammer-Trammill, & Lattin, 1999; Pearpoint, Forest, & O'Brien, 1998). As students articulate an interest in pursuing postsecondary educational options, person-focused planning can assist them and their supporters to recognize the strengths, talents, interests, and challenges to these goals, and to plan for them accordingly through the IEP process. Person-centered planning acts as the catalyst for IEP development focused on postsecondary educational goals. As we have seen in Chapter 3, educators can employ a number of approaches to begin a person-centered process.

Teach and Provide Opportunities for Students to Practice Self-Advocacy Skills

Chapter 3 outlined the need for strong self-determination and self-advocacy skills and direct involvement in IEP development. For students who aspire to attend colleges or universities, there is probably no more important skill than that of self-advocacy. Without a clear knowledge of oneself, one's strengths, needs, preferences, and interests, and the ability to advocate for one's needs, students may not have access to the supports accorded to them by law. They may receive support in academic courses (e.g., note takers, extended time on tests, copies of lectures), support for their living situations (e.g., first-floor dorm room for a student with a physical disability, flashing lights for a student who is hard of hearing), support for learning executive functioning skills (e.g., study skills, time management skills), and emotional support (e.g., counseling). If students are to become strong self-advocates, they will need explicit instruction in high school coupled with opportunities to practice self-advocacy in authentic ways. This could include selecting one's course of study, advocating for an extended curfew or time with friends, choosing a part-time job, and even selecting clothes. One thing is clear, however; student self-advocacy is absolutely necessary for participation in higher education (Durlak, Rose, & Bursuck, 1994; Mellard, 2005; Webster, 2004).

Develop Transition-Focused, Standards-Based Individualized Education Plans to Guide the Transition to Postsecondary Education

Developing appropriate comprehensive transition-focused, standards-based IEPs offers the cornerstone for effective planning for postsecondary education. It is imperative that transition planning occur no later than age sixteen; indeed, the earlier the better. Because a student desires to attend a two-year or four-year institution of higher education, mastery of academic content standards is crucial. In the past, for many students, participation in special education services was relegated to "study hall"–type courses in resource settings. Students exited high schools not knowing how to read or compute at the high school level, nor did they possess a cogent grasp of the high school content expectations for history, science, foreign language, English, or math. Today, with more students accessing general education curricula in general education classrooms, students with disabilities must successfully complete the general curriculum so necessary to transition to college settings. Mastering this curriculum and its concomitant skills (e.g., reading, math, writing) depends in large part on the coordinated set of activities developed in a comprehensive IEP guided by the principles of transition and attention to postsecondary goals (Bassett & Kochhar-Bryant, 2006). Students who desire to attend colleges or universities and *want to succeed* must have a good grasp of high school content before they graduate. They must be able to succeed in general education classrooms and master general education curricula (Hitchings, Retish, & Horvath, 2005). Aligning a transition-focused approach to developing IEPs in a standards-based educational system can ensure student readiness for college settings (Kochhar-Bryant & Bassett, 2002).

Provide Strong Summary of Performance Documentation

In acknowledging the importance of transitioning youth with disabilities to the next environment with supports and documentation, the Individuals with Disabilities Education Act (IDEA) (2004) mandates an SOP for all students with disabilities formally exiting the school system (Kochhar-Bryant, Shaw, & Izzo, 2007). The language as stated in IDEA 2004 regarding the SOP is as follows:

> For a child whose eligibility under special education terminates due to graduation with a regular diploma, or due to exceeding the age of eligibility, the local education agency "shall provide the child with a summary of the child's academic achievement and functional performance, which shall include recommendations on how to assist the child in meeting the child's postsecondary goals." (§Sec. 300.305(e)(3))

The SOP is particularly important for students transitioning to college settings because it supplies the information needed by Disability Support

Service offices to appropriately identify students with disabilities who can receive accommodations and modifications as required by law. The SOP also provides a synopsis of a student's strengths, needs, preferences, learning styles, and suggested accommodations. We will explore the SOP in more depth later in this chapter.

Develop Authentic Partnerships with Parents and Families to Guide the Transition from Secondary to Postsecondary Opportunities

Developing strong and ongoing collaborative partnerships with parents and family members can assist the team in determining optimal strategies for a young adult's transition to postsecondary education. Studies have demonstrated that parent involvement is a predictor of school success; for students with disabilities, parent interest and involvement is critical (Eckes & Ochoa, 2005). Further, Madaus (2005) found that parents of students with disabilities in higher education tend to be more involved in their child's education than parents of typical youth. Although some parents can become overzealous or overprotective in their desires to find an optimal situation for their child (Eckes & Ochoa, 2005), strong support can help to provide students with the emotional anchor they need, as well as to offer ongoing monitoring and support. A strong team can help to empower students by emphasizing self-advocacy skills. Secondary school experiences can be seen as "dress rehearsal" for college life and beyond. It is important for educators and parents to find the balance between appropriate support and overprotection, to allow young adults to make mistakes and learn from them as they assume greater control of their decision-making responsibilities.

Provide Opportunities for Students to Explore Postsecondary Options

It is typical for many typical high school students to be unaware of the myriad possibilities for attending a postsecondary institution. This may be even more pronounced for students with disabilities, who may have not considered any options for attending a college setting. In our experience, many students opt for the closest and most familiar setting, because they have seen it and heard about it from other friends or family. However, these settings may not provide the quality of individual accommodations and support needed to succeed. It is important that students explore a wealth of opportunities, including community colleges and other two-year institutions, four-year public colleges and universities, and four-year private universities. Students can begin their search via the Internet or college guides found in most high school and public libraries. Internet searches can be followed up with phone interviews to college personnel. Ideally, students and their families can visit the campuses themselves, take informational tours, and meet with the disability support staff (Kato, Nulty, Olszewski, Doolittle, & Flannery, 2006). These opportunities allow students to find that "goodness of fit" so crucial to future success. The greater the opportunities to investigate different options, the more likely students can succeed in their future educational careers.

HOW DO STUDENTS MAKE POSTSECONDARY CHOICES?

As students consider options for postsecondary education, many variables come into play. Students must honestly assess their interests and capabilities and think strongly about the career options they may entertain. They will need to learn about the admissions requirements of various colleges. They need to consider the time they want to invest in a certificate program or a two- or four-year degree. For students residing in some states, they must decide with what type of diploma they wish to graduate, as that may determine the type of postsecondary institution they can attend. Also, they must consider the logistics of selecting a college or university. For example, will a student need to live at home to attend college? Will the college or university offer financial aid or might the student need to work? Is the university in an urban, suburban, or rural setting? What are the attitudes regarding students with disabilities on a campus?

Webb (2000) presents a college exploration worksheet that can be used by students to determine the best fit for the college or universities they prefer. The worksheet asks students to investigate a variety of areas that comprise the college experience (see Resource A).

HOW CAN STUDENTS PREPARE FOR POSTSECONDARY COURSEWORK IN THEIR HIGH SCHOOL YEARS?

The Need for Academic Coursework

As students begin to think about their options for postsecondary education, it is essential that they continue to succeed in high school courses that may be required for college admission (Hitchings et al., 2005). Students with disabilities have a twofold responsibility in preparing for college. First, they must possess a foundation of reading, writing, and mathematical skills so that they are able to pass any entrance exams that colleges may require (Getzel & Wehman, 2005). This foundation does not necessarily mean that they must be reading at grade level, or performing upper-level math. However, the ability to decode, comprehend, write cogently, and perform high school mathematical functions are necessary for taking college entrance exams and for working toward acceptable grades on high school courses. Many community colleges and universities offer developmental or remedial courses in these areas, and students may have to take and pass one or more of them to advance to freshman level coursework. However, students should know that although schools charge standard tuition rates for these courses, they may not count for credit or toward a degree. It is much more advantageous to leave high school with a credible skill base in these areas.

Second, students must successfully complete courses in general education curricula. While some students with disabilities may access academic content in special education resource settings, it is far more advantageous to learn the content from general educators who specialize in each area. Each state's college requirements differ somewhat, but most postsecondary institutions will require at least four years of English and two to three years of mathematics, social sciences, and science. Additionally, some universities require some foreign language, which may be particularly difficult for students with learning disabilities; these requirements must be scrutinized carefully. The point, however, is that students who wish to attend college should be taking courses in inclusive environments to the greatest extent possible. Because students with disabilities were identified in the first place as having special educational and behavioral needs, collaborative support between general and special educators is all the more essential given the high stakes of preparing students with disabilities for college settings. Strong, consistent student support must be evidenced in all general education courses.

The Need for Transition-Focused Individualized Education Plans and Guiding Postsecondary Goals

By the time high school students with disabilities begin to seriously consider postsecondary opportunities, transition planning is mandated. It becomes the foundation of the special education services they will receive. Transition planning includes consideration of student strengths, needs, interests, and preferences through goal setting and strong IEP development coupled with agency and community linkages (Kochhar-Bryant et al., 2007). Transition-focused IEPs can provide the roadmap into a student's future, through the use of postsecondary goals and a coordinated set of activities.

The postsecondary goals written into a student's IEP tells us what the student will do after graduation from high school. They state in specific terms what the student will accomplish in broad terms that are also measurable, tangible, and achievable. Teachers may confuse postsecondary goals with annual goals, but the two are very different; *postsecondary goals measure what the student will do after graduation, and annual goals measure what the student will do before graduation.* Postsecondary goals are written first, and annual goals are written to compliment the postsecondary goals. They are time limited to a year, whereas postsecondary goals are intended to start several years in the future. The National Secondary Transition Technical Assistance Center (NSTTAC) (2007) has developed examples of both appropriate and inappropriate postsecondary goals that set the foundation for IEP development at the secondary level. Notice the specific language and action that the student will be required to take to complete each goal. Notice also the "nonexamples" and how they do not provide information that is measurable.

Box 4.1 — **Examples and Nonexamples of Postsecondary Goals on the Individualized Education Plans**

1. This is an example of a measurable postsecondary goal in the domain of education/training.

Example:
- Upon completion of high school, John will enroll in courses at Ocean County Community College.
  a. Participation in postsecondary education is the focus of this goal.
  b. Enrollment at a community college can be observed, as in John enrolls in courses or he does not.
  c. The expectation, or behavior, is explicit, as John enrolls at the community college or he does not.
  d. Enrollment at a community college occurs after graduation, and it is stated that this goal will occur after graduation.

Nonexample:
- Upon graduation, John will continue to learn about life skills and reading.
  a. Participation in learning is the focus of this goal, but no specific place or program is specified.
  b. The expectation for learning, or behavior, is not explicitly stated.

2. This is an example of a **measurable postsecondary goal** for I-13 item #1 on the NSTTAC Indicator 13 Checklist in the domain of **education/training**.
- Allison will obtain a four-year degree from a liberal arts college with major in Child Development.
  a. Participation in postsecondary education is the focus of this goal.

b. Obtaining a degree at a college can be observed, as Allison gets a degree or does not.

c. Obtaining a college degree occurs after graduation from high school.

Nonexample:

- The fall after graduation from high school, Allison plans to enroll in a four-year university in the Southeast.

  a. "Plans" does not indicate something that must occur after high school and can be ongoing after exit: "Will enroll" would make this a measurable postsecondary goal.

Adapted from *Web-based Examples and Nonexamples for SPP/APR Indicator 13 Checklist* (NSTTAC, 2007).

Some teachers are hesitant to write postsecondary goals using a "will" statement (e.g., Allison **will** obtain a four-year degree). They mistakenly believe that there is a potential liability in writing such a strong statement. What if Allison decides that college is not for her? All of us change our minds; adolescents do this regularly. Postsecondary goals are written to underscore a positive, proactive approach to future goals, and if the goals need to be changed, new postsecondary goals can be created. There is no liability or danger in changing one's mind.

Postsecondary goals provide the framework from which to develop strong academic, behavioral, and transition annual goals. From the development of a student's future goals, the annual goals can reflect, from year to year, the strategies and supports needed to help students to progress, so that their postschool goals can ultimately succeed.

The Need for Aligning Content Standards and Transition-Focused Goals

It is easy to say that all students must adequately pass their general education coursework in preparation for college. However, for many students with disabilities, participation in general education courses continues to present major challenges. Students may find themselves falling farther behind with the demands of reading, writing, organization, and time management. And yet, general education courses offer the best preparation for postsecondary educational opportunities. Given that all students must now demonstrate competence in a standards-based world through rigorous content demands (and participate in high stakes assessment as well), we must learn to align a standards-based system grounded in transition-focused competencies to provide critical linkages to relevant knowledge and understanding (Bassett & Kochhar-Bryant, 2006; Kochhar-Bryant & Bassett, 2002: Stodden, Galloway, & Stodden, 2003). Although these two concepts appear at odds with each other, blending standards and transition can yield powerful results for students with disabilities in general education classrooms.

Developing standards-based, transition-focused curriculum and instruction relies on authentic practice and evaluation, process over product, and student empowerment and self-management (Kochhar-Bryant & Bassett, 2002). By using the principles of universal design and the use of applied academics to make instruction and content accessible to all learners, students learn to think more critically, solve problems, and evaluate their efforts in a way that lends relevance and meaning to their work (Hong, Ivy, Gonzalez, & Ehrensberger, 2007). We believe that a unique collaborative process occurs between the general education teacher, the repository of the content, and the special educator, the supplier of strategies and differentiated instructional design to enhance a relevant curriculum (Bassett & Kochhar-Bryant, 2006). This team can work together to build skills, reinforce standards-based content, and allow students to demonstrate mastery of their subject matter. Bassett and Kochhar-Bryant (2006) provide templates of how to align transition-focused competencies and standards-based curriculum into comprehensive lesson planning. Given this integrated approach, students are able to acquire more content, thus preparing them for postsecondary environments.

The Need for Effective Transition Assessments

Assessment for the purposes of transition is now mandated as a component of the IEP assessment process. Ideally, these assessments should be multidisciplinary and assess a variety of skills related to transitioning to adult life (e.g., academic, behavioral, interests and preferences, aptitude, self-management and self-advocacy). They should also be utilized over time, not just to capture a discrete moment of a student's processing or ability. Statewide assessments measuring academic growth can offer one snapshot of student achievement, but often this represents only a small fraction of student talents and abilities. For students with disabilities, there are other measures to assist them in their journey to postsecondary options.

Students may initially take a career inventory to ascertain their interests. Career surveys such as the Career Orientation and Placement Survey (COPS) (Educational and Industrial Testing Service [EdITS], 1995) and the informal assessments collected by Clark, Patton, and Moulton (2000) can also provide information for the student in a variety of areas, including personal interests, leisure activities, self-advocacy skills, healthy living, and more. The Transition Planning Inventory (TPI) (Clark and Patton, 2006) offers a comprehensive perspective of the transition-focused competencies needed by emerging adults. The TPI is administered to students, their parents, and the educators who work directly with the students. From comparing responses from the three perspectives, a clearer picture emerges of the transition-related strengths and needs of the student, which can then be translated to IEP goals and activities. Results from the TPI can be used to pinpoint those areas, at school, at home, and in the community upon which students can focus before leaving for college (e.g., money management, daily living skills such as cooking, health care, legal issues).

HOW DO STUDENTS PREPARE TO ATTEND POSTSECONDARY INSTITUTIONS?

Students with disabilities who desire to attend a college or university must begin to prepare for this transition throughout their high school careers. We already know the importance of taking academic courses, preferably in general education settings. Learning to use strong self-advocacy skills is also a prerequisite for considering college. However, students and their families must undertake a number of other responsibilities to ensure a smooth transition to postsecondary opportunities. Students must be aware of the college exams necessary for admission. They should be full partners in preparing the documentation for the SOP, through their involvement in IEP development. They should be aware of agencies such as Vocational Rehabilitation that may assist them with their educational goals. They should also become aware of the various adaptive technology and software options available in both high school and college that can assist their learning. Appropriate social skills, organizational skills, and time-management skills will help ameliorate problems during the college experience. The Wisconsin Department of Public Instruction has developed a concise yet comprehensive four-year plan to use when planning the transition to colleges or universities. We have adapted this timeline for use with students and their families.

Need to Consider Accommodations on the ACT and SAT Entrance Exams

The ACT and SAT are the two most widely used college entrance exams in the country. For students who wish to attend four-year colleges or

Table 4.1   Timeline for Preparing for Postsecondary Education

Ninth Grade	Tenth Grade	Eleventh Grade	Twelfth Grade
Design class schedule	Continue academic preparation	Continue academic preparation	Strengthen self-advocacy skills
Learn to understand nature of disability and how it affects learning and test-taking	Identify interests, aptitudes, accommodation needs	Focus on matching interests and skills with postsecondary education choice	Prepare SOP documentation
Learn about time-management, study skills, stress management, exam preparation	Develop self-advocacy skills	Take ACT or SAT	Role-play interviews
Explore career options	Meet with guidance counselor to discuss colleges and college requirements	Establish a tentative career goal	Talk with students who are receiving services at colleges
Participate in extracurricular activities	Make arrangements to take ACT or SAT; request accommodations if appropriate	Invite Vocational Rehabilitation (VR) counselor to IEP meeting	Prepare applications; meet with college personnel if appropriate
Continue to remediate or compensate for basic skill deficits	Gather information about colleges and services offered for students with disabilities	Tour postsecondary campuses; investigate services offered for disabilities	Jointly develop Individual Plan for Employment with VR counselor if eligible
Investigate assistive technology	Identify application deadlines	Learn to use public transportation options	Work on adult living skills such as cooking, finances
Learn to use as many kinds of software as possible	Investigate eligibility requirements for VR	Obtain current documentation of disability	Investigate financial aid options
	Participate in volunteer and paid work experiences		

Source: Adapted from *Opening Doors to Postsecondary Education and Training* (Wisconsin Department of Public Instruction, 2007).

universities, the ACT or SAT is required for consideration of admission. Both the Americans with Disabilities Act and Section 504 of the Rehabilitation Act acknowledge the legal rights accorded to students with disabilities to receive appropriate accommodations; these rights have been upheld through the courts as well (Fuller & Wehman, 2003). Many students desire accommodations before taking either of these exams; it is important to realize that unless adequate documentation is provided in a timely fashion, requests for accommodations may be denied. There are four classes of accommodations offered by both testing companies: (1) extended time, (2) alternative format, (3) alternative location, and (4) adaptive equipment. Extended time may be used as a result of using a tape-recorded format, sign language, Braille, or for students with reading deficits. It is the most commonly used accommodation; 90 percent of accommodation requests come from students with learning disabilities and of those, two thirds simply ask for extended time (Fuller & Wehman, 2003). Alternative format exams may utilize Braille, photo-enlarged test questions, or large type. Alternative locations may include small groups or spaces. Adaptive equipment is widely accepted as a reasonable accommodation for both the ACT and SAT. Accommodations can range from preferential seating for a person using a wheelchair, to directions read orally to a student, to snack breaks for students who have diabetes, to extended time for students with learning disabilities. The accommodations depend on the nature of the disability. Through her personal experience, Cobb (2003) outlines useful suggestions for requesting accommodations on the ACT and SAT. These include:

- Start the application process early
- Request a "common eligibility form" from either the ACT or SAT Web sites, or from the College Board Services for Students with Disabilities (SSD)
- Complete your section of the form; the school personnel also completes part of the form
- A letter of eligibility will be sent to the student and the school
- Accommodations may include extended time, a reader, specific color backgrounds, computer and technology accommodations
- Alternate testing formats are available
- Documentation must be current (not older than three years), conducted by qualified personnel, and include a specific diagnosis
- Qualified personnel must make recommendations for the accommodations requested and supply a rationale to support the recommendations. The disability must *substantially limit the major life function of learning*

Source: Adapted from Learning How to Learn: Getting into and Surviving College When You Have a Learning Disability by J. Cobb, 2003, Washington, DC: Child and Family Press.

Fuller and Wehman (2003) report that many students with disabilities perform much better on these exams when they are coached by professionals to gain knowledge of how their disability impacts test taking, to learn test-taking strategies, and to practice relaxation techniques. They also provide a brief comparison of the ACT and SAT so that students choose (if possible) the exam that fits their test-taking style.

The SAT	The ACT
One half of questions address vocabulary; so, work on improving vocabulary	Easy and difficult questions are worth the same. Do easy questions first, go back to harder ones later
One half of SAT is math skills, from arithmetic to algebra II. Be sure to have good working knowledge of what is already known	Not considered to have as many "tricks and traps" as SAT
SAT subtracts a quarter point for wrong answers, making guessing less attractive	No penalty for guessing on the ACT. Never leave an answer blank

Need to Develop Comprehensive Summary of Performance

In IDEA 2004, a new mandate was to develop a document that represents a compendium of information that students with disabilities can carry with them to their next adult environment. Known as the SOP, it specifies that "a local educational agency shall provide the child with a summary of the child's academic achievement and functional performance, which shall include recommendations on how to assist the child in meeting the child's postsecondary goals" (IDEA, 2004). According to Kochhar-Bryant and colleagues (2007), the goal of an SOP is to "describe students' current performance and functional limitations based on an historical review of assessments" (p. 77). It also identifies students' interests and preferences and describes accommodations and supports that were effective in high school. Current, valid assessment results may accompany the SOP.

When the mandate for an SOP was included into IDEA 2004, no specifics were added as to how to develop this documentation. Each state (indeed each district) is free to design its own SOP document. We believe each SOP should contain the following elements:

- Background information—including most recent formal and informal assessment information
- Student's postsecondary goals—goals should also indicate the postsecondary environment(s) to which the student wishes to transition
- Summary of performance—includes sections for academic, cognitive, and functional levels of performance; each includes accommodations and needed assistive technology

- Recommendations to assist the student in meeting postsecondary goals—includes suggestions for accommodations, strategies, adaptive devices, other supports in postschool environments (based on previous history and experience)
- Student input—helps professionals to complete the SOP, gain knowledge and advocacy for one's disability, and assist postsecondary personnel to more clearly understand this perspective

Student participation in crafting the SOP is vital. Not only can students share their interests and preferences, and strengths and needs from an historical perspective, they can blend these attributes into a body of evidence that is relevant to the next educational environment. Further, students should be able to orally describe the contents of the SOP; they can explain its contents to disability support service staff. Kochhar-Bryant and Izzo (2006) argue that the introduction of the SOP will encourage postsecondary institutions to be clearer in their documentation expectations, improve access to technology, assist faculty members to understand individual learning needs of their students, and address variations among postsecondary institution regarding the quality of their services. Martin, Van Dycke, D'Ottavio, and Nickerson (2007) argue that the SOP can be a more effective document if its development is directed by the student; the student can practice the valuable skills of self-advocacy through the SOP process.

Resource A contains a Summary of Functional Performance Model Template, which was developed by the National Transition Document Summit and adopted by the Council for Exceptional Children (CEC), the Division on Career Development and Transition (DCDT), and other professional associations (Kochhar-Bryant & Izzo, 2006). It provides a comprehensive yet user-friendly model for educators.

5 Guided Pathways: Career-Technical Education

INTRODUCTION

Career and technical education (CTE) systems today are transforming and evolving to meet the needs of diverse students and employers in the twenty-first century. The aim of career-technical training is to prepare youth and young adults for careers and successful entry into employment. Communities provide CTE through a variety of programs, including separate public schools devoted to specific occupational fields, county- or state-sponsored regional vocational training academies, and evening schools. Public school officials work closely with industries and trades in establishing curricula and guidance programs. The cooperative training approach, in which students study part time and work part time in the job for which they are preparing, is a common feature of public schools. Community colleges often provide vocational training courses. Many industries have instituted extensive vocational education programs for their employees, and today, virtually all trades require apprenticeship or on-the-job training.

Academic courses are provided so that workers who have not completed the public school requirements may do so while employed. In some communities, attendance in continuing education programs or schools is compulsory for those who are of school age.

What Is Career and Technical Education?

Career and technical education, also known as vocational education or training, prepares learners, with and without disabilities, for careers that are based in manual or practical activities. Traditionally, such preparation has been nonacademic and related to a specific trade, occupation, or vocation for which the learner is preparing. The term technical education refers to the learner's development of expertise in a particular group of techniques or technology associated with an occupation.

Generally, career education and vocational education are still used interchangeably today. Career and technical education, or vocational education, has traditionally been contrasted with academic education, which concentrates more heavily on theory and abstract conceptual knowledge. However, contemporary CTE reflects a broader educational goal of integrating academic and career-related education. Many states have already undertaken significant steps to promote the integration of academic content and CTE content. This typically involves matching up curriculum content tasks lists for CTE and the state's academic standards of learning (Association for Career and Technical Education [ACTE], 2006; Carnevale & Derochers, 2003; Castellano, Stone, Stringfield, Farley, & Wayman, 2004; CORD & Hull, 2005; Education Commission of the States, 2004).

Before the turn of the twenty-first century, vocational education focused on specific trades (e.g, automobile mechanic, welding, building trades), which critics claimed were occupations of lower social classes and carried a stigma. The business-industry and government sectors have had great influence on this shift in perspective on vocational education. As the labor market became more specialized and economies demanded higher levels of skill, governments and businesses invested more heavily in vocational education through publicly funded training and subsidized apprenticeship initiatives for businesses. At the postsecondary level, vocational education was typically provided by an institute of technology or by a local community college. A new name for vocational education was needed to reflect an emphasis on high-skill, high-technology occupations—*career and technical education.*

Career and technical education/vocational education became diversified through the twentieth century and now exists in industries such as retail, tourism, information technology, funeral services, and cosmetics, as well as in the traditional trades. Career and technical education is designed to help students, workers, and lifelong learners of all ages fulfill their working potential through high school and college education that provides them with

- Academic subject matter taught in relation to the real world (*contextual learning*).
- Employability skills, from job-related skills to workplace ethics.
- Education pathways that help students explore interests and careers in the process of progressing through school.

Career and technical education is also about

- Second-chance education and training for the unemployed and those seeking to upgrade their skills.
- Education to earn additional degrees, especially when related to career advancement.
- Corporate training, continuing education, skills upgrades, and refresher courses for those already in the workplace.

States have made significant progress in promoting the integration of academic content and CTE content, spurred by the continuing urgency of employment needs of youth and young adults.

Conditions for Youth with Disabilities and Need for Employment Preparation

Need for access to career-related course work. While more than half (56 percent) of students with disabilities had a goal of finding competitive employment after leaving high school, many who choose to enter directly into employment after completing high school are not adequately prepared to reach their goals (Wagner, Newman, Cameto, & Levine, 2006). Students with disabilities are less likely than students without disabilities to complete courses in high school that prepare them to succeed in skilled employment. Preparation must begin in the early school years to ensure that students participate in appropriate career-development courses. *Schools can bridge the gap* by providing work experiences, career and academic counseling, job coaching, and mentoring opportunities while encouraging students to enroll in the kinds of academic courses that will prepare them to succeed in work and college.

Need for work-based learning experiences in school. Over the past 15 years, work-based learning experiences have become more available to youth with disabilities (Wagner et al., 2003). According to parents' reports, almost 60 percent of youth with disabilities were employed during a one-year period in high school, some at work-study jobs, but the vast majority at non–school-related jobs (Cameto, Marder, Wagner, & Cardoso, 2003). Approximately 15 percent of youth with disabilities held work-study jobs in a given year (6 percentage points more than in 1987); increases of 14 to 18 percentage points were significant for youth with cognitive disabilities, emotional disturbance, or multiple disabilities. The most common work-study placements are at food service (19 percent), maintenance (16 percent), and clerical (15 percent) jobs.

More than 90 percent of youth in work-study jobs receive school credit or pay for their work. Older youth are more likely than younger youth to have work-study jobs. Work-study employment rates are approximately 10 percent for youth 15 years of age or younger, 15 percent for sixteen-year-olds, and 19 percent for seventeen-year-olds. The percentage of youth with work-study jobs varies for youth in different disability categories. Youth with speech impairments or learning disabilities are the least likely to have work-study jobs (7 percent and 10 percent, respectively). In contrast, approximately 30 percent of youth with mental retardation, autism, multiple disabilities, or deaf-blindness hold work-study jobs (Wagner & Cameto, 2004). Participation in work-based learning is associated with successful outcomes for youth with disabilities. The Individualized Education Plan (IEP) team can play a significant role in determining the appropriate contribution of work-based learning experiences in the student's education and transition plan.

Benefits of Career Preparatory Activities in Schools and Communities

Several positive academic and vocational effects for youth with disabilities are attributed to school-based career development—specifically, career advising and curriculum-based interventions such as computer-based career guidance. These positive effects include higher grades, better relationships with teachers, increased career planning, greater knowledge of careers, improved self-esteem, improved self-knowledge, and less career indecision (Hughes & Karp, 2004; Lapan, Gysbers, & Sun, 1997; National Collaborative on Workforce and Disability for Youth [NCWL], 2007).

Participating in CTE results in short- and medium-term earning benefits for most students at the secondary and postsecondary levels and increased academic course taking and achievement by students, including students with disabilities (Castellano, Stone, Stringfield, Farley, & Wayman, 2004; Plank, 2001; Stone & Aliaga, 2003). Those who complete both a strong academic curriculum and a vocational program of study (*dual enrollees or concentrators*) may have better outcomes than those who pursue one or the other (Silverberg, Warner, Fong, & Goodwin, 2004; Plank, 2001; Stone & Aliaga, 2003). Career and technical education participants are more likely to graduate from high school (Schargel & Smink, 2001; Smink & Schargel, 2004), be employed in higher paying jobs, and enroll in postsecondary education (Hughes, Bailey, & Mechur, 2001).

While work experiences are beneficial to all youth, they are particularly valuable for youth with disabilities. Youth who participate in occupational education and special education in integrated settings are more likely to be competitively employed than youth who have not participated in such activities (Luecking & Fabian, 2000; MacArthur Research Network, 2005; Mooney & Scholl, 2004; Wagner, Newman, Cameto, & Levine, 2006; Ward & Berry, 2005; Wehman, 2006). Reflecting these positive outcomes, current laws are reinforcing the need for career preparatory experiences for all youth.

FEDERAL LAWS AND ELIGIBILITY FOR CAREER-TECHNICAL EDUCATION

Federal funding of workforce development programs for youth in transition arises from three key pieces of federal legislation. Each has provisions regarding certain services for youth. The Individuals with Disabilities Education Act (IDEA) funds special education services in public schools. Title I of the Workforce Investment Act (WIA) addresses employment needs of traditionally underemployed groups such as high school dropouts, teen parents, the elderly, and people with disabilities. Title IV of WIA contains the Rehabilitation Act Amendments and reauthorizes Vocational Rehabilitation (VR) services for individuals with disabilities.

First, the IDEA Amendments of 2004 Eligibility Requirements define individuals who are eligible to receive special education services in secondary education. Transition services must begin at age sixteen or earlier if the IEP team determines there is a need for the individual student to begin earlier. Most states will end services at high school graduation or age twenty-one, whichever occurs earlier (Timmons, 2007). IDEA requires individualized assessment services, evaluations, and reevaluations to determine whether a student has a disability and the educational needs of that student. Transition services are based on identification of preferences, needs, and interests.

IDEA 2004 establishes the right of an eligible student to receive educational services, including classroom instruction, community experiences, mentoring, tutoring, and development of employment and independent living objectives. Furthermore, the IEP must address assessment, participation in general education and career-technical education, as appropriate, and transition service goals and supports. Transition services include preparation for postsecondary education, vocational training, integrated employment (including supported employment), continuing and adult education, adult services, independent living, or community participation (Timmons, Podmostko, Bremer, Lavin, & Wills, 2005).

The Workforce Investment Act, Title I—Provisions for All Eligible Youth, is aimed at assisting youth, including those with disabilities, who have barriers to employment. Transition-related services for youth can be provided from ages fourteen to twenty-one. The Workforce Investment Act also provides work-related assessments of academic levels, skill levels, and service needs, including basic and occupational skills, prior work experience, interests, aptitudes, employability, supportive services needs, and developmental needs. More intensive services for individuals may include comprehensive and specialized assessments of skill levels and service needs, which may include diagnostic testing, guidance and counseling, tutoring, study skills training, in-depth interviewing, evaluation to identify employment barriers and goals, summer employment opportunities related to academic and occupational learning, paid and unpaid work experiences, internships and job shadowing, adult mentoring, job search and placement assistance, follow-up services, and instruction leading to school completion or GED testing.

The Workforce Investment Act Title IV—The Rehabilitation Act—Vocational Rehabilitation Services for Youth with Disabilities—targets services to individuals who have a physical or mental impairment that constitutes or results in a substantial impediment to employment and who can benefit in terms of an employment outcome from VR services and needs assistance to prepare for, secure, retain, or regain employment. Depending on the state, services can begin as early as elementary school or junior high, and there is no upper age limit. Services provided include assessment for determining eligibility and vocational rehabilitation, including rehabilitation technology, review of existing data, identification of rehabilitation needs, development of an Individual Plan for Employment (IPE), and periodic assessments during trial work experiences to appraise the individual's capacity to work. Services also include assistance with accommodations and assistive technology if student is not eligible for services under IDEA. Career-related services include training to gain skills for employment or to adjust to work, college, or trade school tuition, funding for workplace adaptations, vocational counseling, interpreter services for people with hearing impairments, or reader services for people with visual impairments, placement services, job coaching, and supported employment. Other related services include transportation services, independent living skills training, and personal assistance services.

The Carl D. Perkins Career and Technical Education Improvement Act of 2006 provides funding for CTE programs in individual states. The Act provides grants to each state to help deliver career and technical education to youth and adults. These programs prepare individuals to enter directly into jobs that do not require a four-year degree. Funds are provided to individual states based on demographics and income of eligible participants, based on a set of criteria for distribution throughout the state. Specific career-planning and assessment services are not described in the Act; these are determined by state or local agencies. The Perkins Act also provides for transition from career and technical education programs to postsecondary programs or employment.

The Ticket to Work program is an amendment to the Social Security Act and is designed to provide Social Security Administration (SSA) beneficiaries with disabilities more choices for employment services, vocational rehabilitation services, and other support through the establishment of Employment Networks. The act assists individuals with disabilities (ages eighteen to sixty-four) to participate in CTE programs and, at the same time, provides incentives for employers to hire people with disabilities. The Employment Networks are government or community agencies, businesses, schools, or individuals who can provide employment services. These service providers receive compensation from the SSA after participants find employment. Although none are mandatory, services may include career planning, career plan development, vocational assessment, job training, placement, and follow-up services (NCWL, 2004).

The Adult Basic Skills and Family Literacy Education Act (Title II of the Workforce Investment Act) provides educational opportunities to (1) young people and adults who are out of the public school system but still need instruction in reading, writing, speaking, and math skills; (2) individuals who seek to complete their secondary education; and (3) parents to support the educational development of their children. Title II of WIA provides funding to states to administer educational programs for those eligible. Providers of these services may include local educational agencies, community-based or faith-based organizations, voluntary literacy organizations, colleges, libraries, and other organizations with the capacity to work with people who have these needs.

Federal Laws and Person-Centered Planning

Many youth with disabilities lack the same career opportunities as their nondisabled peers. In the past, youth with disabilities were not prepared to be active in the career-planning process and had little opportunity for choice and self-determination. Students' passive role in career preparation often resulted in the following results:

- Very few options being recommended or offered.
- Options that reflected the low expectations of advisors.

- Options that reflected perceived needs for protection and support.
- Options driven primarily by availability of community programs and opportunities rather than an individual's choices (Timmons et al., 2005).

Today, CTE programs focus on the skills, knowledge, and abilities that youth can contribute to the work place.

Most major federal workforce development legislation is now written with the assumption that individuals will obtain services based on an individualized plan of action that has been jointly developed by the individual and an organization acting on behalf of the government. These plans, referred to as "person-centered planning," are individualized and centered on the person's goals.

Person-centered planning processes are driven by an individual's needs and desires. In transition, person-centered planning focuses on the interests, aptitudes, knowledge, and skills of an individual, not on his or her perceived deficits. It also involves the people who are active in the life of a youth, including family members, educators, and community-service professionals. The purposes of person-centered planning are to identify desired outcomes that have meaning to the youth and to develop customized support plans to achieve them. The process closely examines the interests and abilities of each individual to establish a basis for identifying appropriate types of employment, training, and career development possibilities. A person-centered career plan identifies marketable job skills, articulates career choices, establishes individual outcomes, and maps specific action plans to achieve them (Timmons et al., 2005).

ORIGINS OF CAREER-TECHNICAL EDUCATION

Career, vocational, technologic, or practical arts education has a long history spanning centuries. Because it is impossible to chronicle all of the major contributors to CTE or significant events in its history, a few will be presented that had great influence on development in the United States. In Europe at the time of the onset of the Industrial Revolution in England, Denis Diderot (1713–1784) and Jean-Jacques Rousseau (1712–1778) began to stimulate a wider interest in the mechanical arts in France. In his *Discourse on the Sciences and Arts of 1750*, Rousseau criticized the arts and sciences (especially the arts in the luxury trades) for their undesirable effects on social values. His essay described the detrimental effects of the arts and sciences on civilization, criticizing urban high society and of its self-serving promotion of the arts and sciences. Diderot wanted to elevate the status of the mechanical arts by systematizing the arts and helping craftsmen work in a manner similar to the liberal arts and sciences. One of his purposes was to promote among the literate a better understanding and appreciation for craftsmen and their work and their contribution to technologic progress. He also believed that his work would benefit craftsmen by helping them to think more critically about their craft through more systematic and analytical reflection (Pannabecker, 1996). These two philosophers contributed greatly to the development of technologic education in Europe and the American Colonies. Elements of the differences between Diderot and Rousseau are still part of the mix in contemporary technologic education and will continue to be a part of future patterns in curriculum and instruction (p. 21).

Manual Arts Enters the Public School Curriculum

The shop system, based on the early theories of Rousseau, Diderot, and others, remains a central part of career-technical education today. In the United States, career and vocational education is rooted in the old apprenticeship system in which adolescents lived with their masters who would teach them a craft and how to be responsible members of society. In that system, career and life were intimately connected. The manual arts movement emerged in the late 1800s, as educators advocated making manual training available to all students within the public schools (Walter, 1993). Manual arts training signaled a shift away from the belief that college preparatory curriculum should be the sole purpose of high school to a belief that it should be broadened to prepare students for a variety of career options (Gordon, 1999).

Between the 1800s and 1900s, social and economic forces such as mass production, automation, and acceleration of technology led to an expansion of vocational and technical educational opportunities for youth. The Government Commission on National Aid to Vocational Education (1914) and passage of the Smith-Hughes Act (P.L. 64–347, 1917) provided the basis for the vocational education movement, with vocational rehabilitation programs for individuals with disabilities built in (Meers, 1980, p. 9). In 1937, the Fitzgerald Act was passed, which established a program of apprenticeship in the United States and the first standards for employing and training apprentices.

CAREER EDUCATION BECOMES A NATIONAL PRIORITY AND INCLUDES SPECIAL POPULATIONS

The career education movement gained additional momentum in the 1960s when it became a high priority of the then U.S. Office of Education's Bureau of Adult, Vocational, and Technical Education (Halpern, 1999). In

1963, the Vocational Education Act (P.L. 88–210) was passed to maintain, extend, and improve on existing programs of vocational education, as well as to use funds for persons who have academic, socioeconomic, or other disadvantages that prevent them from succeeding in regular vocational education (Gordon, 1999). In 1971, career education was proclaimed as a major educational reform by the U.S. Commissioner of Education, Sidney Marland, Jr. Marland believed that the high dropout rate in the United States was caused, in part, by the failure of the educational system to provide students with a "relevant" education that was aligned with their future goals and potentials (Kokaska & Brolin, 1985). Students with disabilities were not included in the initiative originally, but in 1977, the Career Education Implementation Incentive Act (P.L. 95–207) was passed to help states infuse career education into school curricula. Students with disabilities were included as a target population (Michaels, 1994). The Vocational Education Act of 1984 (P.L. 98–524) was named for House Representative Carl D. Perkins, a civil rights supporter, and still bears his name. Career development under the Perkins Act and transition systems under IDEA have remained enduring concepts and instruments in federal policy over the past half century to improve secondary education and postsecondary outcomes for youth with disabilities (Kochhar-Bryant & Greene, 2008).

Acquisition of Employability and Technical Skills, Knowledge, and Behaviors

As mentioned earlier, work-based learning has become an essential part of the academic curriculum, reinforcing academic and occupational skills learned in the classroom, providing opportunities for youth to explore and gain a broad understanding of an occupation, and in the process, motivating students and helping them to connect learning with future earning (American Youth Policy Forum & Center for Workforce Development, 2000). Working closely with employers allows schools to define the knowledge and skills necessary for graduates to successfully perform in college and the workplace (Achieve, Inc., 2004).

Through formal and informal work-based learning, students begin to apply academic knowledge within the workplace settings, gaining understanding and appreciation for the learning and skills required in the workplace. Knowledge, skills, and dispositions (attitudes and ethics) essential for success on the job, include (1) an understanding that links learning to a career goal, (2) understanding of the relationship between quality work and impacts on the job, (3) critical thinking, (4) a variety of problem-solving strategies, (5) understanding the value of immediate feedback for learning and improvement, (6) team skills, (7) appreciation of the importance of deadlines, and (8) motivation to explore a particular subject more deeply (Center for Workforce Development, 1998).

Students gain these skills and dispositions through direct instruction, assessments of career interests and abilities, exposure to expectations and conditions of the workplace, life skills instruction, development of self-determination, self-evaluation, planning, and social-behavioral skills. Career and technical education theorists embrace five central concepts related to the development of CTE competencies:

- All teaching within career and technical education must begin and end with an appreciation of the student's understanding.
- The student must be facile with a core set of currently accepted knowledge and skills within career and technical education.
- Career and technical knowledge and skills are dynamic; thus, students must have the skills necessary to adapt within work environments.
- Student's idiosyncratic understandings of career and technical knowledge and skills must be valued, as these understandings may lead to new discoveries, insights, and adaptations.
- The goal of career and technical education must be an occupationally self-regulated, self-mediated, and self-aware individual (Doolittle & Camp, 1999).

These five concepts provide a framework within career and technical education for blending career or occupation-specific knowledge, opportunities for innovation and change in occupation-specific knowledge, and the thoughts and perspectives of the individual student and teacher.

Options for Career and Technical Education

Many postsecondary options exist for youth with disabilities in the United States. *Career and technical colleges* offer a variety of options at the high school and postsecondary levels, including associate degrees, certificates, and work apprenticeships. States offer different kinds of opportunities to assist students to prepare for careers. In one mid-Atlantic state, for example, public education is provided through a combination of comprehensive high schools, specialized schools, and community and technical colleges. More than half of all recent high school graduates in the United States pursue some type of postsecondary education (Wagner, Newman, Cameto, Levine, & Marder, 2007). In many other countries, a smaller percentage of students go on for more schooling after high school.

High School Programs and Hybrid (Dual-Enrollment) Secondary-Postsecondary Programs

High school students are taking advantage of programs to earn college credits (National Center for Education Statistics [NCES], 2005b). Federal funds have been provided to the states to create dual-enrollment opportunities, particularly for at-risk students, so that high school students may earn college credits. National studies have found that 71 percent of public high schools offered programs in which students earned credit at both the high school and college levels for the same course, known as "dual credit." During the 2002–2003 school year, there were an estimated 1.2 million enrollments in courses for dual credit (Education Commission of the States, 2004; NCES, 2005b). Of the public high schools that offered courses for dual credit, 61 percent indicated that the courses were taught on a high school campus, 65 percent on the campus of a postsecondary institution, and 25 percent through distance education technologies. Schools could offer these courses at more than one location.

Studies also have found that more than half of all colleges and universities in the nation enrolled high school students in courses for college credit (2002–2003 academic year), which translates into about 813,000 or about 5 percent of high school students (NCES, 2005a).

Tech-prep program. Under the Perkins Act, a tech-prep program is a program of study that is carried out under an articulation agreement between the participant and the organization. It consist of at least two years of secondary school preceding graduation and two years or more of higher education, or an apprenticeship program of at least two years following secondary instruction. The program has a common core and required proficiency in mathematics, science, reading, writing, communications, and technologies designed to lead to an associate's degree or a postsecondary certificate in a specific career field. High-quality tech-prep programs

1. Meet academic standards developed by the state.

2. Build student competence in mathematics, science, reading, writing, communications, economics, and workplace skills through applied, contextual academics, and integrated instruction, in a coherent sequence of courses.

3. Lead to an associate or a baccalaureate degree or a postsecondary certificate in a specific career field.

4. Lead to placement in appropriate employment or to further education.

5. Link secondary schools and two-year postsecondary institutions, and if possible and practicable, four-year institutions of higher education through nonduplicative sequences of courses in career

fields, including the investigation of opportunities for tech-prep secondary students to enroll concurrently in secondary and post-secondary coursework.

6. Integrate academic and vocational and technical instruction, and utilize work-based and worksite learning where appropriate and available.

7. Provide technical preparation in a career field such as engineering technology, applied science, a mechanical, industrial, or practical art or trade, agriculture, health occupations, business, or applied economics.

8. Use educational technology and distance learning, as appropriate, to involve the consortium partners more fully in the development and operation of programs.

Tech-prep programs prepare vocational and technical education teach-ers to (1) effectively implement tech-prep programs; (2) remain current with the needs, expectations, and methods of business and all aspects of an industry; (3) prepare postsecondary education faculty in the use of con-textual and applied curricula and instruction; and (4) provide training in the use and application of technology.

Tech-prep programs include training designed to enable counselors to more effectively provide information to students about tech-prep educa-tion programs; support student progress in completing tech-prep pro-grams; provide information on related employment opportunities; ensure that such students are placed in appropriate employment; and stay current with the needs, expectations, and methods of business and all aspects of an industry.

Apprenticeship Programs

Apprenticeship is a system of training skilled crafts practitioners. Apprenticeships are typically geared toward those interested in working in industrial or service trades such as carpentry, plumbing, machining, or automotive maintenance) (ACTE, 2006). Training occurs on the job while working for an employer who helps the apprentice learn the trade. Through the Apprenticeship Agreement, an apprentice, as an employee, receives supervised, structured on-the-job training combined with related technical instruction. On-the-job training and related instruction provides the range of learning and practice opportunities needed to perform at a highly skilled level. Some apprenticeship programs also have dual accreditation through postsecondary institutions that apply credit for apprenticeship com-pletion toward an associate's degree. Upon completing a one- to four-year

(2,000 hours to 8,000 hours) apprenticeship, workers can earn apprenticeship completion certificates that recognize the individual as a qualified journey-worker nationwide. This Certificate is one of the oldest, most basic, and most highly portable industry credentials in use today and is issued by a federally approved State Apprenticeship Agency (U.S. Department of Labor, 2007).

Postsecondary Education Institutions

There are two basic types of postsecondary education institutions: (1) community, technical, and junior colleges and (2) four-year colleges and universities. Community, technical, and junior colleges offer programs that are fewer than four years in length and that can lead to a license, certificate, associate of arts (A.A.) degree, associate of science (A.S.) degree, or an associate of applied science (A.A.S.) degree. Associate degree programs prepare students for technical occupations such as accounting, dental hygiene, computer programming, or information technology. Technical diploma programs meet the needs of businesses and industry and provide employees with required certification for employment.

In most states students who earn two-year degrees may enter four-year schools and receive credit toward a bachelor of arts (B.A.) or a bachelor of science (B.S.) degree. Technical colleges generally have a special emphasis on education and training in technical fields. However, although some technical colleges offer academic courses and programs, not all technical colleges offer two-year programs that lead to an associate of arts or science degree. Many junior, community, and technical colleges offer technical programs in cooperation with local businesses, industry, public service agencies, or other organizations. Many programs are formally connected to education programs that students begin in high school, such as "tech-prep" or "school-to-career" programs.

Four-year colleges and universities usually offer a B.A. or B.S. degree. Some also offer graduate and professional degrees. Students who wish to pursue a general academic program usually choose a four-year college or university. Such a program lays the foundation for more advanced studies and professional work. These colleges and universities primarily offer B.A. and B.S. degrees in the arts and sciences. Common fields of study include biology, chemistry, economics, English literature, foreign languages, history, political science, and zoology.

A Career Preparation Framework

The National Collaborative on Workforce and Disability for Youth (NCWD) (NCWD/Youth, 2004) conducted an extensive literature review of research, demonstration projects, and effective practices related to transition and covering a wide range of programs and services (Timmons et al., 2005). The study revealed that no single institution or organization could provide the full range of services for successful transition, but rather, a systematic interagency coordination approach was needed to facilitate quality transition for all youth. Such quality transition for individuals with disabilities requires the following elements:

- A continuous, systematic planning, coordination, and decision-making process to define and achieve postsecondary goals.
- Curriculum options or pathways to accommodate students' needs and different postsecondary goals.
- IEP planning that defines a postsecondary goal and designs a course of study, supportive and supplemental services, and a variety of transition-related activities that support the postsecondary goal.
- Preparation to assist the student and family to take an active role in planning during high school and for the student to take responsibility for his or her own life (self-determination and self-advocacy) upon exit from high school.
- Access to high quality standards-based education regardless of the setting.
- Information about career options and exposure to the world of work, including structured internships.
- Opportunities to develop social, civic, and leadership skills.
- Strong connections to caring adults.
- Access to safe places to interact with their peers.
- Support services and specific accommodations to allow students to become independent adults.

The NCWD/Youth (2004) study defined five categories, referred to as *Guideposts for Success* (see Resource A), that can help navigate families, service providers, educators, government programs, mentoring organizations, and youth themselves through the transition processes. The five categories include: school-based preparation experiences, career preparation and work-based learning experiences, youth development and leadership, connecting activities, and family involvement and supports. These *Guideposts* are built on the following basic values:

1. Highest expectations for all youth, including youth with disabilities.

2. Equality of opportunity for everyone, including nondiscrimination, individualization, and inclusion and integration.

3. Full participation through self-determination, informed choice, and participation in decision making.

4. Independent living, including skill development and, if necessary, long-term supports and services.

5. Competitive employment and economic self-sufficiency, with or without supports.

6. Individualized transition-planning that is person-driven and culturally and linguistically appropriate (Timmons et al., 2005).

What Are Career Pathways?

Career clusters and *career pathways* are terms frequently used in relation to career-technical education. The Perkins Act of 2006 uses the term *programs of studies*. Another term sometimes used is *sequence of courses*. In general, the career clusters and career pathways are grounded in occupational and industrial areas and allow individuals to pursue a broad range of careers with considerable mobility (Alssid et al., 2002; ACTE, 2006). Career clusters help students investigate careers and design their courses of study to align with their career goals.

Box 5.1 — **A State Example: Career Pathways in Virginia**

The Office of Career and Technical Education in Virginia has adopted the nationally accepted structure of *career clusters, career pathways,* and sample *career specialties* or occupations. Within each career cluster, there are multiple career pathways that represent a common set of skills and knowledge, both academic and technical, necessary to pursue a full range of career opportunities for all students within that pathway—ranging from entry level to management, including technical and professional career specialties. Based on the skills sets taught, all CTE courses are aligned with one or more career clusters and career pathways.

From the list of prioritized pathways, the Virginia Community College System (VCCS) works with colleges to develop a core set of competencies at the postsecondary level for each identified pathway. These competencies will then become the foundation for a core or common set of foundation level courses for each selected pathway that will be uniform throughout the VCCS. This common core of foundation level courses could be offered not only by all VCCS colleges offering the identified career pathways, but would also serve as the core set of courses for apprentice-related instruction, dual-enrollment, and other education and training programs connected to the VCCS career pathways system. This common set of competency-based foundation courses represents a statewide set of dual-enrollment courses that allow for the creation of statewide career pathways from secondary to postsecondary career and technical education programs. Table 5.1 lists the sixteen career clusters and associated pathways.

Table 5.1   Sixteen Career Clusters and Their Pathways

Agriculture, Food, and Natural Resources	**Hospitality and Tourism**
Food Products and Processing Systems	Restaurants and Food/Beverage Services
Plant Systems	Lodging
Animal Systems	Travel and Tourism
Power, Structural, and Technical Systems	Recreation, Amusements, and Attractions
Natural Resources Systems	
Environmental Service Systems	**Human Services**
AgriBusiness Systems	Early Childhood Development and Services
	Counseling and Mental Health Services
Architecture and Construction	Family and Community Services
Design/Preconstruction	Personal Care Services
Construction	Consumer Services
Maintenance/Operations	
	Information Technology
Arts, Audio/Video Technology, and Communications	Network Systems
	Information Support and Services
Audio and Video Technology and Film	Interactive Media
Printing Technology	Programming and Software Development
Visual Arts	
Performing Arts	**Law, Public Safety, Corrections, and Security**
Journalism and Broadcasting	Correction Services
Telecommunications	Emergency and Fire Management Services
	Security and Protective Services
	Law Enforcement Services
	Legal Services
Business, Management, and Administration	
Management	**Manufacturing**
Business Financial Mgmt. and Accounting	Production
Human Resources	Manufacturing Production Process Development

(Continued)

Table 5.1 (Continued)

Business Analysis	Maintenance, Installation, and Repair
Marketing	Quality Assurance
Administrative and Information Support	Logistics and Inventory Control
	Health, Safety, and Environmental Assurance

Education and Training

Administration and Administrative Support

Professional Support Services

Teaching/Training

Marketing, Sales, and Service

Management and Entrepreneurship

Professional Sales and Marketing

Buying and Merchandising

Marketing Communications and Promotion

Marketing Information Management and Research

Distribution and Logistics

E-Marketing

Finance

Financial and Investment Planning

Business Financial Management

Banking and Related Services

Insurance Services

Government and Public Administration

Governance

National Security

Foreign Service

Planning

Revenue and Taxation

Regulation

Public Management and Administration

Science, Technology, Engineering, and Mathematics

Engineering and Technology

Science and Math

Transportation, Distribution, and Logistics

Transportation Operations

Logistics Planning and Management Services

Warehousing and Distribution Center Operations

Facility and Mobile Equipment Maintenance

Transportation Systems/Infrastructure Planning, Management, and Regulation

Health, Safety, and Environmental Management

Sales and Service

Health Science

Therapeutic Services

Diagnostic Services

Health Informatics

Support Services

Biotechnology Research and Development

Integration of Academic and Career-Technical Education Standards

Many states have taken steps to integrate academic content and CTE content, matching up the objectives and tasks for their CTE secondary courses with Academic Standards of Learning.

High School Industry Certification. High School Industry Credentialing initiatives encourage students to work toward a selected industry credential or state license while concurrently pursuing a high school diploma. Students who earn a credential by passing a certification or licensure examination may earn up to two student-selected credits to meet graduation requirements. A credential is defined as follows:

- A complete industry certification program, for example, certified nursing assistant (CNA).
- A pathway examination that leads to a completed industry certification, for example, automotive technician examinations from the National Institute for Automotive Service Excellence.
- A state-issued professional license, for example, Cosmetology.
- An occupational competency examination, for example, skill assessments from the National Occupational Competency Institute (National Occupational Competency Testing Institute [NOCTI], 2006).

Industry credentials provide the following benefits to students:

- Evidence that the student has completed advanced educational preparation by verifying competency in career and technical education skill areas that are in demand by business and industry.
- Student-selected credit(s) and added value to a student's resume for obtaining entry-level positions in the job market.
- Increased job opportunities for advancement in a chosen career path.
- Enhanced self-esteem for students through achieving national occupational competency standards recognized by business and industry.

In some states, students who complete a career and technical education program sequence and pass an examination or occupational competency assessment in a career and technical education field that confers certification are often permitted to substitute the certification or credential for a science, history, or social science credit. The examination or occupational competency assessment must be approved by the states' Boards of Education as an additional test to verify student achievement. Table 5.2 illustrates a single career cluster for a medical assistant and the credentialing requirements in one state.

PLANNING FOR TRANSITION
FOR STUDENTS WITH DISABILITIES

The success of students with disabilities in CTE programs depends on the care with which the transition plan is developed and implemented.

Table 5.2   Career Cluster

Medical Assistant I 8345

Grade Level: 11 (suggested) (36 weeks, double-period)

Prerequisites: None—Introduction to Health and Medical Sciences is strongly recommended.

Students develop basic skills and techniques to assist the physician in the following areas: receptionist duties, patient examinations, cardiopulmonary resuscitation, and simple laboratory tests. On-the-job clinical instruction may occur in physicians' offices or clinics and is coordinated by the Health and Medical Sciences teacher.

Medical Assistant II 8346

Grade Level: 12 (suggested) (36 weeks, triple period)

Prerequisites: Medical Assistant I

Students further develop medical-assisting skills and techniques learned in Medical Assistant I. They also learn medical economics; assembly and maintenance of patient records; care of equipment; special diagnostic testing such as EKG, visual, and audio testing machines; and assistance with office therapy. Advanced on-the-job clinical experience in physicians' offices or clinics is a part of the course. Successful completion of the program leads to employment in physicians' offices or clinics. Keyboarding is recommended.

Available upon completion of Medical Assistant II 8346:

- Medical Assisting Assessment (NOCTI)

- NRDA Certification (National Allied Health Registry/National Association for Health Professionals)

Credential Title/ Description/Entity	How to Earn Credential	Implementation Data	Possible Preparatory Courses/Career Cluster
Medical Assisting Assessment Occupational competency assessment of skills and knowledge covered in a medical assisting instructional program National Occupational Competency Testing Institute (NOCTI)	Pass the NOCTI knowledge-based exam (3055) consisting of 198 test items. Test includes general office procedures, general laboratory procedures and diagnostics, clinical procedures, patient instruction and foundations of health care	**No Virginia students have taken this assessment** **848 tests were taken nationally with a 60.3 national norm**	Medical Assistant II 8346 Health Science

Credential Title/ Description/Entity	How to Earn Credential	Implementation Data	Possible Preparatory Courses/Career Cluster
NRDA Certification (Medical Assisting) One of several certifications in the health sciences field offered by the National Association for Health Professionals National Allied Health Registry/ National Association for Health Professionals	Complete a state-approved medical assisting program Pass a knowledge-based examination pertaining to common requirements and job functions of a medical assistant	**No Virginia students have achieved this certification**	Medical Assistant 8346 Health Science

Source: Virginia Department of Education, Office of Career and Technical Education Services, Richmond, VA.

Quality CTE programs are designed for all students who are expected to be ready for employment or for postsecondary education in their fields of study. Students with disabilities should be represented in any CTE program proportionate to their representation in the total school population of the particular district (Office of Civil Rights, 2007). Identified content standards and learning objectives are based on national industry recognized accreditation and credentialing standards.

To successfully make the transition from school to adult life and the world of work, adolescents and young adults need guidance and encouragement from caring, supportive adults. The best decisions and choices made by transitioning youth are based on sound information, including appropriate assessments that focus on the talents, knowledge, skills, interests, values, and aptitudes of each individual (Timmons et al., 2005). They provide equal access to the full range of technical preparation programs to individuals who are members of special populations, including the development of tech-prep program services appropriate to the needs of special populations; and provide for preparatory services that assist participants in tech-prep programs.

When discussing enrollment of students in a career-technical course, the team should consider the following items: career interest inventory results, student performance, safety, student's abilities, behavior plan, student's physical limitations, student's strengths, and CTE course competencies. All students must be given the opportunity to take the entrance, or "gateway," tests for entry into the course or program, unless the IEP team determines that the student is eligible for alternative assessments.

Career and Technical Education Courses and Students with Disabilities

Career and technical education courses are electives available to all students at the high school level. The purpose is to provide students with training so they may enter the workforce immediately following high school or pursue further training at a technical or community college. Students generally earn three or more CTE credits in a single program area to be a CTE major or concentrator.

Special needs students select areas of career interest in the same way that all other students do, assisted by school counselors who are knowledgeable about career-assessment tools. Special education services are available to all students who qualify through certification. Students who enroll in CTE courses should be eligible for the same services as those provided in any other classroom.

Career and technical education provides programs to prepare students for occupations that require extended training rather than short-term on-the-job training. Students with disabilities whose postsecondary transition goals require CTE training should also explore supplemental or adjunct supports such as vocational evaluation, CTE program visits, interviews, and team planning sessions. Students considering a CTE program are typically required to meet the same eligibility criteria that apply to all students. As part of the transition planning process, vocational evaluation data can be valuable to the IEP team and the student for determining the student's career interests, aptitudes, and needs.

Career-Technical Education Participation and the Individualized Education Plan

The IEP team determines modifications to be made for CTE classes in the same way they are determined for other classes. Special consideration should be given to the student's interest, ability level, maturity level, and ability to pass a safety test if the course involves a lab/shop component. Accommodations might include extended time, having material read, oral testing, abbreviated assignments, etc. The safety test can be read to students, but they must understand the questions and answer correctly. Table 5.3 presents common accommodations in classrooms and work settings.

Table 5.3   Common Accommodations in Classrooms, Assessment Settings, and Workplaces

Presentation Accommodations	Information read aloud
	Sign language
	Braille
	Large print
	Directions clarified
	Assistance from another person
Presentation Equipment Accommodations	Magnification
	Amplification
	Noise buffer
	Templates
	Audio/video cassettes
	Lighting/acoustics
	Computer or other machinery
Response Accommodations	Communication device (symbol boards, talking boards)
	Computer or other machinery
	Spell checker
	Brailler
	Tape recorder
	Calculator
Scheduling Accommodations	Extended time
	Extra breaks
	Multiple sessions
	Time beneficial to individual (such as around medication schedule)
Setting Accommodations	Number (individual may work better alone or in small groups)
	Place (individual may work better at home or offsite setting)
	Proximity (individual may need to be closer to instructor, blackboard, restrooms, etc.)

Source: Adapted from *State Participation and Accommodation Policies for Students with Disabilities: 1999 update (Synthesis Report No. 33)* by M. Thurlow, A. House, C. Boys, D. Scott, and J. Ysseldyke, 2000. Retrieved January 16, 2004, from the University of Minnesota, National Center on Educational Outcomes Web site: http://www.education.umn.edu/NCEO/OnlinePubs/Synthesis33.html

If students are working toward attainment of a regular high school diploma, they often are required to pass a "gateway" exam in certain core academic areas (e.g., English, biology, or algebra). If students do not pass all required exams, they are generally eligible to receive a special education diploma if they meet the requirements of their IEP. Standard diploma alternatives are known by many names, including IEP diploma, certificate of achievement, certificate of attendance, occupational diploma, or modified diploma. Alternatives to the special education diploma are now under discussion in many states, since nonstandard diplomas are often viewed as substandard by employers and may hinder entry into employment (Krentz, Thurlow, Shyyan, & Scott, 2005; Thurlow, 2005).

When developing the IEP and postsecondary goals for a high school student, career and technical courses may be considered as part of the student's education plan. These courses provide essential knowledge and skills to enter the workforce or pursue postsecondary training or education. Appropriate placement for the student is very important to ensure both success and satisfaction of the student in the program. When considering a career and technical education program, the following steps are important to consider in IEP development.

1. Determine the student's interests, career goals, and plans after graduation.

2. Determine the ability level of the student. Career and technical education courses involve both hands-on activities and a certain level of reading, math, and technology.

3. Have someone on the IEP team (career and technical instructor, school counselor, special education teacher) who can adequately describe the course that is being considered for the student and the competencies that are taught.

4. Once the course is determined, the IEP team reviews the competencies and determines which ones will be included in the student's IEP.

5. The IEP team determines the modifications that should be made for the student based on the competencies the student will be working toward mastering.

The career-technical education instructor is encouraged to attend the IEP meeting and should be prepared to do the following:

- Provide a course description.
- Describe the program of study (sequence of courses).

- Review the course competencies.
- Discuss and document any occupational hazards that exist in the course.
- Discuss the safety test for the course.
- Participate in the discussion to determine the best placement for the student, appropriate modifications and accommodations, and determine which competencies the student will be accountable for mastering.

A word on safety. Liability issues exist for students when they are placed into classes with dangerous equipment. For example, in some classes students use saws, milling machines, lathes, lifts, and electrical circuits. Safety procedures and training are vital to the success of the student in a CTE program, and the program as a whole. Consideration should be given to students' level of maturity and need for supervision with regard to safety issues. The IEP team should choose the most appropriate program for the student based on interest, ability, and readiness of the student not only to master the safety requirements, but to participate in the class without compromising the safety of the student and other members of the class. General safety guidelines should be available and should be a part of the instruction for all students. Special consideration should be given by the IEP team to assessing potential safety issues for students with disabilities in CTE programs. However, safety considerations should not serve as a gatekeeping or exclusionary function by which any student with a disability is considered "at-risk" in a CTE program. Often the term "behavior risk" is associated with students with disabilities (when there has been no history of such risk), and safety issues may serve to exclude rather than include.

CAREER AND TECHNICAL COURSE ACCOMMODATIONS/MODIFICATIONS

When an IEP team determines that a student with a disability can master the content standards and learning objectives required to complete the program, and that such a program meets the transition needs, then the student should be identified for CTE programs. The IEP team must also specify the support services, aids, and accommodations that will be provided to enable the student to be involved and progress in the general CTE curriculum. Accommodations provide different strategies to help students learn information and communicate their knowledge back to the instructor. The changes do not lower standards or expectations for learning. Table 5.4 outlines some common accommodations.

Table 5.4   Career and Technical Course Accommodations/Modifications

Accommodations	Person Responsible (example)
1. Extended time	CTE instructor
2. Shortened assignments	CTE instructor
3. Alternative materials	Special education (SE) resource coordinator
4. Preferential seating	CTE instructor
5. Notes taken by designated person(s)	SE resource coordinator
6. Tape recording of lecture	SE resource coordinator
7. Study guides	SE resource coordinator
8. Tests taken in alternative settings	SE resource coordinator
9. Oral examinations	CTE instructor
10. Retake tests	SE resource coordinator

A preplanning meeting with the CTE instructor before the IEP may help to resolve concerns and issues related to a student's placement into a CTE program. Once the Team recommends participation in a CTE program, the IEP is developed to identify support services, aids, and modifications that will be provided to assist the student with participation and progress in the program.

When a student needs extra support to succeed. Occasionally students may experience challenges in the career and technical class. The career-technical teacher should consult with the special education teacher for assistance in providing additional services and supports for the student. If the student continues to be unsuccessful, the teacher may request an IEP Team Meeting to review the student's placement in the course. The IEP should also address Functional Behavior Assessment of behavioral issues if needed, and prescribe remedies in the form of specific objectives. The team must agree on the contents of the plan.

Collaboration. Collaboration is essential for supporting successful participation of students in CTE programs. Career center staff, school staff, and district level administrators should work together to resolve issues and problems related to the participation of students with disabilities. Networking, planning, and continuous communication are essential for coordinated services for students with disabilities. All personnel involved should have understanding of each other's programs and should clearly understand the transition planning process.

The role of family members. Family members have very important roles in supporting and preparing youth for adulthood. As youth make this transition, there is a natural tendency to seek independence and to gradually rely less on parents and other family members (Jeynes, 2005; Kreider, Caspe, Kennedy, & Weiss, 2007). Parents and youth may have different expectations of schools and workforce development programs as well as different levels of access to information about transition and career planning (NCWD/Youth, 2004). Professionals need to encourage parents of high school students to do the following:

- Understand the demands of entering career-technical college or employment for their child.
- Understand the process of independence and decision making.
- Help to identify goals for the IEP process.
- Investigate possible career paths with their child.
- Help to ensure an environment that promotes good study skills, time management, and wise choice making and decision making.
- Investigate postsecondary options with their child.
- Investigate Disability Support Centers.
- Investigate sources of funding (NCWD/Youth, 2004).

Youth with no family or from nontraditional family settings may not have adults in their lives who can give guidance and support. In these cases, extra effort must be made to ensure that the youth has access to caring adults to help make decisions (and sometimes share responsibilities) that are customarily handled by parents or other family members (Annunziata, Hogue, Faw, & Liddell, 2006; Timmons et al., 2005).

ASSESSMENT FOR PLANNING AND TRANSITION

The transition from youth to adulthood is a lengthy process. Career development is one aspect of transition that often involves a few false starts as youth explore multiple options. For youth with disabilities who explore careers through structured programs, the process of transition may involve transferring from one program or service provider to another. Each time a youth begins working in a new program, the need for assessment should be revisited.

Assessment defined. Assessment is defined as "the process of collecting data for the purpose of making decisions" (Salvia & Ysseldyke, 2004, p. 5). The assessment process can be complex, and a deep understanding of assessment dynamics is essential, particularly when working with youth with disabilities. Adults who work with youth need to have a solid understanding of the purpose, benefits, and limitations of assessment if they are to provide effective guidance. Assessment is not an end unto itself. The following principles should guide each step of the assessment process:

- Self-determination based on informed choices should be an overriding goal of assessment.
- Assessment is a dynamic intervention process.

- Assessment facilitates self-discovery of talents, goals, strengths, and needs.
- The purposes and goals of assessment should be clear.
- Assessment should be integrated into a larger plan of individualized services.
- Assessment should consider environmental factors affecting the individual.
- Formal assessment instruments should be carefully chosen with attention to their documented reliability and validity.
- Formal assessments should be administered and interpreted by qualified personnel.
- Assessment reports should be written in easily understandable language.
- Assessment activities should be positive and lead to self-empowerment (Timmons et al., 2005).

Screening. A youth's assessment data may suggest previously unidentified or undiagnosed problems that may affect career planning and career development. These problems may include low literacy levels, inconsistent academic performance, limited vocabulary, or lack of proficiency in English. Learning disabilities, behavior disorders, mental and physical health problems, or other hidden (nonapparent) disabilities may be present. A screening process may be needed to determine whether further diagnostic assessment (usually conducted by a specialist) should be provided (National Institute for Literacy, 2007).

The four domains of assessment for transition. Assessment of transition-age youth falls into four major domains—educational, vocational, psychological, and medical (Timmons et al., 2005). In these domains, there is quite a bit of overlap, and assessment in one domain will often lead to useful information or understanding in another. In the educational and vocational domains, assessments measure achievement, aptitudes, skill levels, interests, physical and functional capacities, and cognition. These data are then used to form educational, training, or employment plans specific to the individual's situation. Individuals who use English as a second language or are English language learners are also tested to measure skills in reading, writing, and speaking. No assessment outcome stands alone, and data from all four domains are needed to have complete and well-documented plans in place for the individual.

In testing and performance reviews, there are seven areas commonly considered when working with transition-age youth: academic performance or achievement; cognitive abilities; behavioral, social, and emotional considerations; vocational interests; job aptitudes and skills; occupation specific certification; and physical and functional capacities. Cognitive abilities may fall under the educational or psychological domain. Physical and functional capacities may fall under the vocational or medical domain (Timmons et al., 2005).

Accommodations and Supports from Career Assessment to Transition

The following person-centered planning process is outlined within six career development stages.

1. *Career Assessment and Interpretation*
   a. Identify and describe assessments that contribute to career planning.
      - basic achievement skills
      - vocational aptitudes and abilities
      - employability skills
      - work-related social skills, personality types, and learning styles
      - career interests and preferences
   b. Interpret assessment results and analyze and summarize assessment information to formulate a comprehensive personal profile.
   c. Select and complete assessments to fill information gaps for effective career planning.

2. *Career Information*
   a. Investigate career clusters and the continuum of occupations within each cluster.
   b. Explore options for education and job training during high school and in the postsecondary setting.
   c. Self-assess beliefs and attitudes toward work.
   d. Explore and analyze education and training requirements of specific areas of interest.
   e. Discuss and reflect upon environmental factors and employment projections related to specific career interests.
   f. Develop an in-depth knowledge of specific careers of interest.

3. *Career Exploration*
   a. Explore labor market information.
   b. Explore occupations related to careers of interest.
   c. Explore training and education options for occupations related to careers of interest.
   d. Collect, organize, and analyze information from a variety of sources to develop a plan for achieving personal career goals.
   e. Make decisions and develop a timeline to achieve long-term career goals.

4. *Career Planning*
   a. Recognize and illustrate the concept of a lifelong learner, relating personal considerations about learning.
   b. Analyze the impact of education on lifestyle projections.
   c. Compare and contrast pathway options for careers of choice.
   d. Develop and evaluate personal options for career preparation and propose a plan for achieving goals for adult living, learning, and work.
   e. Develop adult living and lifelong learning goals after considering and exploring pertinent factors.

5. *Work and Training Readiness*
   a. Synthesize skills needed for work and specific job training in the twenty-first-century workplace.
   b. Recognize and self-evaluate learning skills acquisition.
   c. Develop transferable skills (hard skills—include basic academic and technology skills; soft skills—include problem solving, reliability, team work, customer service) to improve marketability in the workplace.
   e. Self-evaluate interpersonal and intrapersonal skills, establishing targets for improvement.
   f. Acquire personal skills in areas, including (1) goal setting, (2) time management, (3) communication, (4) decision making, (5) problem solving, (6) intrapersonal (self) communication, (7) workplace ethics, (8) respectfulness, (9) wellness and safety, (10) ability to accept criticism and praise, (11) basic financial literacy, and (12) personal safety.
   g. Develop a personal skills profile of work and training readiness.

6. *Skill Building*
   a. Explore and document current achievement in basic skills areas of reading, mathematics, and locating information.
   b. Establish goals for gaining basic skills required for occupations related to careers of interest.
   c. Utilize technology tools required to perform job duties for occupations related to careers of interest.
   d. Pursue basic skills that support efforts to seek, obtain, or maintain a specific job.

The six stages from assessment and planning to transition help prepare youth with disabilities for in postsecondary academic or employment settings. School professionals can enhance career-building opportunities for youth by working closely with local postsecondary institutions.

POSTSECONDARY AND WORKPLACE ACCOMMODATIONS

Many vocational-technical colleges, community colleges, and four-year colleges and universities employ disability specialists who support post-secondary students. They provide customized accommodations and adjustments to instructional materials, strategies for adjusting teaching or learning methods, tutoring, counseling, or other accommodations that aid students in completing academic classes or degree programs (Dare, 2006; Timmons et al., 2005). The level of assistance available in postsecondary settings varies widely. Some independent postsecondary schools and other providers of training or education (such as trade schools or craft apprenticeships) typically do not have staff familiar with accommodations and may have limited success in helping young people with disabilities. Section 504 of the Rehabilitation Act and the Americans with Disabilities Act provide the basis for these services in postsecondary programs if the student has recent documentation of a disability. Students, however, have a much greater level of responsibility for requesting accommodations than they had in secondary settings (Shaw, 2005, 2006).

Vocational assessments can also greatly inform job accommodations with training programs and employers. An effective vocational assessment should examine potential needs for accommodations that will enable a youth to perform the essential functions of a chosen job. Onsite and offsite accommodations that might improve the job placement success of youth with disabilities include modifications to a job, restructuring of tasks, use of job coaches to assist with training, or use of American Sign Language interpreters (Timmons et al., 2005).

The Job Accommodation Network (JAN) (Job Accommodation Network [JAN], 2008) is a free consulting service that provides information about workplace accommodations, the Americans with Disabilities Act, and the employability of people with disabilities. The Job Accommodation Network has information for employers and people with disabilities.

Accommodations and advising. Advisors should consider the environmental factors that can help a youth succeed in a challenging setting. For example, youth who have learning disabilities can often succeed in college and other postsecondary education or training options with appropriate learning accommodations. Youth with emotional or behavioral disabilities may succeed in competitive employment when carefully screened for selected jobs and when well-defined job support services are in place. Employers may be willing to make environmental work site changes or task accommodations so a youth with complex physical disabilities can perform the essential functions of a desired job. Coworkers can be trained as peer mentors for youths with intellectual disabilities or attention deficit hyperactivity disorder. Youth who are considered vulnerable to exploitation may be successfully placed into safe and nurturing competitive job settings with adequate levels of job supervision. To test the viability of some vocational options, agencies need to be willing to work with youth to help address issues of access and accommodation (Thompson, Morse, Sharpe, & Hall, 2005; Timmons et al., 2005). It should be noted that most workplace accommodations are inexpensive and not difficult to put into place.

Key Roles of School Personnel

Several key personnel are essential to students' success in career-technical education.

School Guidance Counselor

At the high school level, guidance counselors are concerned with educational and career guidance while they also focus on the personal development of the students. He or she is responsible for the administration of career assessment inventories, development of individual plans, and appropriate placement of the student in a career-technical program and creation of a schedule for the student. The counselor must also be directly involved in the development of the student's Transition Plan within the IEP. High school counselors help students choose school courses and activities that relate to their interests and that will prepare them for life after high school. They also show students how to apply for college or for job-training programs. At the postsecondary level, academic advisors provide information about college entrance requirements, financial-aid programs, and entry-level job opportunities in the areas where they might be attending school.

Special Education Teacher

The special education teacher is responsible for scheduling and conducting the IEP meeting, developing the IEP with the IEP team, maintaining the student's records, and providing or coordinating whatever services are needed for the child. The parent/guardian is invited to participate in the IEP meeting and in development of the IEP. Consent of the parent/guardian is required for initial evaluation and change of placement of the student unless the student has reached the age of eighteen.

Vocational Rehabilitation Specialist (Counselor)

The Vocational Rehabilitation (VR) specialist is often involved in a student's transition planning while the student is still in school. Upon graduation, the VR specialist works with the student to assist with access to and support in employment or postsecondary education. The rehabilitation specialist typically works for the state's VR agency, helping people with disabilities prepare for and find employment. For students who are eligible for VR, services may include evaluation of the person's interests, capabilities, and limitations; job training; transportation; aids and devices; job placement; support to begin postsecondary education; and job follow-up. Priority in services is given to individuals with the most significant disabilities. The term "specialist" is becoming more widely used today because, as one state VR director shared, the traditional term "counselor" connotes a person who sits behind a desk that separates him or her from the client and they just "talk." The new specialist is active, mobile, working with youth in schools, and meeting students where they are in a variety of contexts.

Job Development Specialist

A job development specialist works for either a school system or an adult service agency such as the VR agency or a supported employment agency. As the job title suggests, the primary role is to find jobs for people with disabilities. The job development specialist identifies the need for and assists in the development of supportive services that can help the individual become job ready. He or she informs business, labor, and the public about training programs and may instruct applicants in resume writing, job search, and interviewing. The job developer visits employers to inquire about available positions and may offer the employer services such as placement of individuals into jobs, training the employee on job tasks and appropriate workplace behavior, talking with supervisor(s) and coworkers about disability awareness, providing long-term support to the employee on the job, and helping to promote interaction between the employee and his or her coworkers. The job development specialist demonstrates to employers the effectiveness and profitability of employing individuals with disabilities by identifying the tasks that they can perform (Thuli & Hong, 1998; U.S. Department of Labor, 2007).

The School Administrator

The school administrator is generally the Local Education Agency (LEA) designee representing the local system in IEP team decisions. He or she is responsible for obligating the LEA's resources to implement the IEP.

Choosing a Career-Technical School

Students with disabilities can achieve great success in CTE programs. The National Longitudinal Transition Study-2 (NLTS-2) of more than

8,000 students with disabilities, ages thirteen to twenty-one, found that students who took concentrated coursework in CTE were less likely to drop out of school and had average annual earnings of approximately $6,200 more than nonvocational students. This is an important finding because students with disabilities typically have the highest dropout rate, the highest unemployment rate, and the highest underemployment rate when compared with same-age nondisabled peers. Students should investigate and compare training alternatives, such as community colleges, which have lower tuition than private schools. Also, some businesses offer education programs through apprenticeships or on-the-job training. Students should ask several important questions before enrolling in any program:

- What kind of diploma will I receive when I complete the program—a certificate in the chosen field or eligibility for a clinical or other externship?
- Are licensing credits earned transferable?
- If I decide to pursue additional training and education, will two- or four-year colleges accept credits from the vocational or correspondence school?
- What kinds of facilities are there at the school—computers and tools, for example, that students use for training and supplies? What kinds of accommodations are there for students with disabilities?
- Can I visit the school in advance to see the classrooms and workshops? Can I sit in on a class?
- What are the instructors' qualifications and the size of classes? Sit in on a class. Are the students engaged? Is the teacher interesting?
- What is the program's success rate? How many students complete the program?
- How many graduates find jobs in their chosen field? What is the average starting salary?
- How much will the program cost, and are books, equipment, uniforms, and lab fees included in the overall fee or are they extra?

There are many Web-based and print resources on CTE and career pathways that are available to students in their state and local districts. For example, students can find information through Web-based state career and technical education resource networks, local district CTE resource networks, career planning guides, community college Web sites, career technical school Web sites, and through career counselors in the school.

6 Focus on the Year After High School

INTRODUCTION

Students whose plans include graduation from high school and enrollment in postsecondary education are faced with a new configuration of challenges, many of which they may or may not be aware (Gil, 2007). Although more students are accessing colleges and universities, many of them may not have the preparation, knowledge, or skills they need to make the shift to higher education. Students with disabilities face the typical developmental tasks of moving away from a familiar high school, but they have the additional burden of finding and maintaining education supports that were so readily available to them during their secondary years (Chiba & Low, 2007). As a result of these dramatic changes, students, their families, teachers, and counselors need to pay greater attention to the requirements for a successful transition to postsecondary education (Sitlington, Clark, & Kolstoe, 2000).

Recent researchers have reported that students have not received adequate information and subsequent preparation for the transition to college (Eckes & Ochoa, 2005; Harris & Robertson, 2001; Janiga & Costenbader, 2002). Current literature about the transition to postsecondary education reveals that many students with disabilities are unaware of the differences between high school and college settings (Madaus, 2005; Madaus & Shaw, 2004; Mull, Sitlington, & Alper, 2001; Thoma & Wehmeyer, 2005). This evidence is not surprising because the process is complex and demands collaborative effort among the team of the student's transition partners. This chapter divides this process into sections that include transitions to (1) self-determined choices, (2) self-advocacy, (3) college services, and (4) college learning.

In addition to this information, two students will share their transition paths to postsecondary settings. ReKeisha and Paul have communicated their postsecondary education desires with their transition Individualized Education Plan (IEP) teams, but each of these students has planned and prepared for this transition in a different manner. Throughout the chapter, seniors ReKeisha and Paul will share how they dealt with planning and preparing for the myriad decisions and actions that are necessary for enrollment in college.

TRANSITION TO SELF-DETERMINED DECISIONS

As students express a desire to attend postsecondary education after high school completion, strategies that teach evidence-based practices and self-determination skills should be taught by their teachers (Konrad, Fowler, Walker, Test, & Wood, 2007; Raskind, Goldberg, Higgins, & Herman, 1999). In Chapter 3, components, practices, and characteristics of self-determined individuals were described and discussed. In this section, self-determination practices will be applied to the transition from high school to the first years in a college setting.

A crucial step in student's role as a decision maker is active engagement and leadership in preparation for, and participation in, IEP meetings. Students who direct their IEPs and engage in transition planning improve academically and increase the likelihood of successful postsecondary outcomes (Konrad et al., 2007; Wehmeyer, Palmer, Agran, Mithaug, & Martin, 2000). Read the steps ReKeisha and Paul completed to inform their IEP teams about their intentions to attend college.

| Box 6.1 | ReKeisha and Paul: Transition to Self-Determined Decisions |

ReKeisha has been an active participant during her Transition IEP meetings for the four years she has spent in high school. She has assumed a leadership role in her meetings for several years. As she plans for her upcoming meeting, ReKeisha will lead her team through a discussion about the progress she has made on her postsecondary education annual goal and the Summary of Performance. She has used a portfolio to organize college information, and she has analyzed evidence she has collected for her college pursuits. ReKeisha's postsecondary goal to attend a four-year public university or college has remained the same; however, her annual goal has been broken down into objectives that have been adapted and modified as she learned additional information.

Paul also attends and participates in his Transition IEP meetings. His desired postschool outcome statement and his postsecondary education annual goal on his IEP include his aspirations to attend college. Paul's siblings have attended a local university and Paul announced his intention to attend the same university during his IEP meeting at the end of his junior year. He shared that he visits this campus frequently and "knows his way around."

Reflection About IEP Participation and Engagement:

1. List the positive steps both students have taken as they prepare for their transitions to college.

2. Describe how both students could strengthen their leadership roles in the IEP meetings. What information and actions steps could ReKeisha and Paul include in their meetings?

An abundance of literature describes how self-determined students are better equipped to make successful transitions to adult outcomes (see Chapter 3 for comprehensive information about self-determination). Only a few studies have investigated the self-determination skills of college-bound students with disabilities (Thoma & Wehmeyer, 2005); however, the process of engaging students in self-determined decisions and choices can be addressed during self-directed IEP meetings during which the student leads the team as he or she plans goals and action steps, identifies strengths and preferences, and assesses needs. This section will list grade-appropriate activities for all college-bound students in the left-hand columns. Right-hand columns will feature tasks and activities for students to direct during IEP meetings and learning environments.

Middle school is an optimal time for students to direct their IEP meetings, voice their preferences, and explore new interests and talents through exploratory elective classes and extracurricular activities (Repetto, Webb, Neubert, & Curran, 2006). "The preadolescent's strong desire to be independent can be fostered in exploratory programs. The ability to weigh multiple options and make wise choices reinforces students' real-life decision-making processes" (Queen, 1999, p. 195). The decision to go to college, or explore the possibility of going to college, can be an important discussion with the middle school student and his or her IEP team (Webster, Clary, & Griffith, 2001). Other activities and discussion topics about college preparation can be found in the following list of suggested middle school activities and IEP decisions. Several components found in the respective grade lists will be discussed in greater detail in other sections of this chapter.

Middle School List

Activities	Student-Directed IEP Decisions
Explore interests/careers	Identify strengths and needs
Participate in extracurricular activities	Identify preferences
Read books from a summer reading list	Identify accommodations
Enroll in a variety of exploratory classes and clubs	Decide diploma option (if applicable)

As students move from middle school to high school, they need to work closely with their IEP team members and counselors to identify a diploma track and college preparatory classes. Hitchings, Retish, and Horvath (2005) urged students and their support teams to develop a rigorous four-year plan of study in preparation for college. Their research supports active engagement in career development during early years in high school, a time when students gain understanding about the connections between school performance and career choices.

Data from the National Longitudinal Transition Study-2 indicated that many of postsecondary students with disabilities who were interviewed were not using accommodations in college and did not see themselves as having disabilities (Wagner, Newman, Cameto, Garza, & Levine, 2005). Clearly, many students do not have ongoing assessments and experiences with accommodations, or they may not comprehend the links between their needs and warranted academic adjustments or accommodations. Selecting appropriate accommodations and monitoring their effectiveness within rigorous high school classes give students occasion to practice using accommodations and gaining access to essential content. Honest discussions among freshmen and their support teams will assist students in identifying strengths, learning about their disabilities, and developing skills in weak areas. The Freshman List suggests activities and decisions that may increase the likelihood that students will build a level of comfort with their accommodations and assistive technology and, subsequently, develop strategies to meet demands of challenging classes.

The sophomore year of high school represents a critical time that will steer students toward successful transitions to postsecondary education.

Freshman List

Activities	Student-Directed IEP Decisions
• Meet with counselor to develop plan of study	• Update report of strengths and needs
• Enroll in college preparatory classes	• Remediate areas of need
• Participate in extracurricular activities	• Update report of preferences
• Attend college fairs	• Review and evaluate current accommodations
• Determine college costs	• Determine effective assistive technology
• Volunteer or job-shadow during summer	• Develop an annual goal for postsecondary education
• Read books from a summer reading list	• Determine agencies to attend future IEP meetings
	• Collect data and evidence to share with IEP team and SOP

Among the topics with which a student should lead discussions are (1) the status of his or her disability documentation, (2) foreign language requirements and, if applicable, exemptions to this requirement, and (3) appropriate accommodations for college entrance exams. Current documentation of the student's disability and the related topic of appropriate accommodations will be discussed in detail later in this chapter and in other chapters of this book.

Students and their IEP teams should carefully consider the student's ability to successfully complete a foreign language requirement (DiFino & Lombardino, 2004). Although many colleges require two years of foreign language from high school, others allow students to complete the language requirement during college, and other universities permit student to waive the foreign language requirement. Madaus (2003) cautioned that if students and their teams decide to waive foreign language requirements for a student, then this decision should be based on a well-documented language or processing disability rather the possible harmful effect of foreign language courses on a student's grade point average. Madaus has compiled a list of helpful ideas for students and their teams to discuss when they deliberate about foreign language requirements. This discussion should take place during the freshman or sophomore year so the student will have ample opportunities to take foreign language courses before high school graduation. Students may share with their IEP teams that growing numbers of colleges and universities accept American Sign Language as an acceptable foreign language study. With the help of high school counselors, students should investigate the foreign language requirements of the colleges or universities to which they may eventually apply. The following list suggests activities and ideas for students with disabilities who are sophomores in high school.

Sophomore List

Activities	Student-Directed IEP Decisions
• Meet with counselor to review program of study	• Update report of strengths and needs
• Prepare a long-range calendar with important dates	• Remediate areas of need
	• Update report of preferences
• Visit colleges, narrow search	• Review and evaluate current accommodations
• Review college costs	• Review assistive technology usage
• Take PSAT exam	• Review annual goal for postsecondary education
• Volunteer or job-shadow during summer	
• Read books from a summer reading list	• Discuss disability documentation for postsecondary education
	• Collect data and evidence to share with IEP team and SOP
	• Discuss future internships with committee
	• Check on foreign language requirements for colleges (if applicable)

At this point in their academic lives, juniors in high school (1) have developed a sense of their learning needs, (2) practiced, evaluated, and refined their accommodations, (3) know their areas of talents and strengths, and (4) understand their disabilities. This knowledge will serve students well as they begin to evaluate colleges and the support for students with disabilities on each campus. West and Taymans (2001) advise students to investigate various types of colleges that include two-year and community colleges, private junior colleges, and four-year colleges. In addition to these postsecondary options, Webb (2000) urges students also to consider education offered by military branches, trade and technical schools, and online choices.

Among the activities listed for juniors is a search for scholarships and other financial aid options. Suggestions for scholarships and other forms of financial aid can be found on Web sites sponsored by the National Center for Education Statistics (http://nces.ed.gov/collegenavigator) and the National Council for Support of Disability Issues (http://www.ncsd .org/scholar/scholarship.htm). During this year, students will spend considerable time preparing for college entrance exams, including compiling appropriate information and documentation for any special administration they may need. Students and their counselors may find the following Web sites helpful as they arrange to take the SAT (http://www.college-board.com/ssd/student/index.html) or ACT (http://www.act.org/aap/disab/index.html). The following Junior List illustrates activities and associated student-directed IEP decisions.

Junior List

Activities	Student-Directed IEP Decisions
• Participate in internship during summer	• Update report of strengths and needs
• Take PSAT or ACT and SAT exams	• Remediate areas of need
• Narrow college choices to five to ten	• Review annual goal for postsecondary education
• Visit chosen colleges	
• Investigate scholarships and financial aid	• Identify career goals
• Obtain sample applications from chosen colleges	• Contact Disability Support Services for information about eligibility
• Update calendar of deadlines	• Determine and use appropriate college accommodations
• Participate in internship during summer	• Determine and use appropriate assistive technology for college
• Read books from a summer reading list	
	• Ensure disability documentation is current for college
	• Collect data and evidence to share with IEP team and SOP
	• Continue discussions with support agencies

Students' senior years are filled with opportunities for organization, a practice that will be essential in college. The final year of high school is filled with endings and beginnings, coupled with deadlines and decisions. Students' compliance with deadlines provides excellent practice for their future college assignments (e.g., housing contracts, long-term assignments, and loan and scholarship paperwork). Students may need support and strategies as they plan their time, identify deadlines, determine preparation time for college admission applications and essays, set realistic goals, and determine reasonable procedures for monitoring their progress (Hong, Ivy, Gonzalez, & Ehrensberger, 2007).

Although students and their IEP teams should be compiling and reviewing information for the Summary of academic and functional Performance (SOP) throughout high school (see right-hand columns of freshman, sophomore, and junior lists), the senior year represents a time for students to review progress, summarize results of goals, and demonstrate understanding of their strengths and disabilities. Martin, Van Dycke, D'Ottavio, and Nickerson (2007) urge educators to use a student-directed SOP to "give students opportunities to learn about their disability, compile their transition assessment information, identify useful accommodations, and detail their post-high school goals" (p. 15). The SOP can be a useful tool, especially if students direct and organize the material for future postsecondary education support and other transition areas. Martin and colleagues have developed instructions for the Student-Directed Summary of Performance that include these sections (pp. 18–19):

Instructions: Summary of Performance

Section 1: My Summary of Performance

My Postschool Goals for One Year after Exiting High School

My Postschool Goals for Five Years after Exiting High School

Section 2: My Perceptions of My Disability

Section 3: School's Perspective on My Disability

Section 4: School-Produced Summary of My Academic Achievement and Functional Performance

In addition to the student-directed tool, templates of SOP models are available from several sources. School personnel should first investigate templates recommended by state departments of education or local school districts. The National Transition Documentation Summit SOP model template (2005) may be downloaded from the Council for Exceptional Children (www.cec.sped.org). Among the states that have developed a state SOP or adapted the National Transition Documentation Summit are the Departments of Education in Colorado, Connecticut, Georgia, Kansas, New Hampshire, Oregon, and Virginia; transition educators and administrators may find formats or templates about SOPs on these states' Web sites. A template for a Student Directed SOP from the Albuquerque Public Schools (New Mexico) is found in the article by Martin et al. (2007). The following Senior

Senior List

Activities	Student-Directed IEP Decisions
• Update calendar for deadlines	• Update report of strengths and needs
• Obtain financial aid forms from colleges	• Remediate areas of need
• Ask for letters of recommendation	• Review and refine annual goal for postsecondary education
• Prepare and review admission essay	
• Complete admission applications to final choices	• Review career goal
	• Maintain contact with Disability Support Services at chosen colleges
• Arrange for high school transcripts to be sent	
	• Review use of appropriate college accommodations
• Ask high school to send final transcript to college	
	• Review use of appropriate assistive technology for college
	• Double-check that disability documentation is current for college
	• Direct development of SOP
	• Finalize plans with support agencies
	• Attend a summer program for college-bound students with disabilities

List illustrates activities and associated student-directed IEP decisions.

TRANSITION TO SELF-ADVOCACY

Students who are informed, aware, and engaged participants in their transition to higher education have a higher likelihood of successful outcomes. Reiff (2007) warns that individuals who are not effective self-advocates may be headed for a grim and unfulfilled life. "Adult life tends to be much more satisfying for individuals who have a sense of themselves as independent and autonomous. A lack of self-advocacy skills may lead to feelings of dependence and insufficiency" (p. 174). Reiff further encourages people with disabilities "to hold their heads up high. They are not being helpless. They are taking care of themselves—independently. And that's the whole idea" (p. 177). How can self-advocacy be promoted early in high school so students are prepared to self-advocate when they embark on a postsecondary education path?

As they do with other skill sets, students need to rehearse self-advocacy skills in environments where they are able to get constructive feedback from teachers, peers, and their families. Role plays and practice sessions can assist students as they prepare to meet with college advisors, confer with their professors about accommodations, meet with medical personnel, interview for a job, or interact with agency personnel (West, Corbey, Boyer-Stephens, Jones, Miller, & Sarkees-Wircenski, 1999). West and her colleagues suggest that IEP teams incorporate self-advocacy tasks into IEP goals; this action would ensure students and their support team actively engage in building skills in self-advocacy.

Under the Americans with Disabilities Act (1990), students must take responsibility for providing the college disability service office with documentation that describes a considerable limitation of a major life activity. Without this documentation, the college is not responsible for providing accommodations. Further, if the student has a clear understanding of her disability and the documentation that provides evidence of her disability, she will be an active voice when she meets with disability service office staff to make decisions about appropriate and reasonable accommodations.

The Family Educational Rights and Privacy Act (FERPA) (1974) or the Buckley Act allows parents to access their children's school records as long as they have not reached the age of eighteen. FERPA guarantees privacy to students enrolled in postsecondary education, and that means institutions must have written consent from the student before they release information about grades, transcripts, fines, notes from advisory or counseling meetings, and other college documents (Department of Education, 2005). Getzel (2005) cautions that family members may be frustrated by the seemingly unresponsive attitude of the postsecondary education institution when parents or family members ask for specific information. FERPA, however, mandates that the responsibility of managing educational issues shifts from family members to students. If high school students and their families grasp the legal responsibilities of FERPA and other legal mandates, this information may help them realize the necessity of developing self-advocacy skills.

College student representatives on the National Council on Disability advised students to investigate linkages with agencies to assist them with the transition from the full array of supports through high school to adult services that require application (Moore, 2003). Early identification of these agencies will allow students to familiarize themselves with available services and appropriate supports, establish relationships with agency personnel, and enlist agency assistance during the transition to postsecondary education. The ability to self-advocate for services from adult agencies such as Vocational Rehabilitation, Division of Blind Services, or community transportation during the transition to postsecondary education will bode well for students as they transition from college to career opportunities. The text box illustrates the importance of gaining self-advocacy skills.

Paul: Transition to Self-Advocacy

When Paul's IEP team developed his twelfth grade IEP and compiled data for his Summary of Performance, they asked Paul how he planned to ask for warranted accommodations when he enrolled in college. He turned to his mother and asked if she would make the same arrangements for college accommodations that she had made for Paul during high school. When his English teacher asked him to name accommodations that had helped him succeed in school, Paul shrugged and said, "I guess more time on tests and stuff."

Reflections About Self-advocacy:

1. If you were on Paul's IEP team, how would you advise him about the opinions he voiced during his IEP meeting?

2. What instruction or information does Paul seem to need?

TRANSITION TO COLLEGE SERVICES

For countless students, disclosing their disabilities and connecting with disability support services on the college they attend will be crucial to their postsecondary success. To receive services, students must first disclose their disabilities and deliver current and complete documentation to verify their disabilities and related need for accommodations (National Joint Committee on Learning Disabilities [NJCLD], 2007). Documentation standards may vary from college to college because institutions establish their own requirements within the broad guidelines of Section 504 and the Americans with Disabilities Act (Gregg, Scott, McPeek, & Ferri, 1999). Documentation must indicate that the student has a disability that significantly limits a major life activity and supports the need for an academic accommodation (Office of Civil Rights, 2007). Without documentation of the disability and justification for accommodations, students will not receive accommodations or services at the postsecondary level.

Early in high school, students and their IEP teams must be aware that (1) students must be willing to self-disclose their disabilities, (2) most colleges and universities will not accept IEPs and SOPs as the sole source of documentation, (3) colleges and universities require professional evaluations from three to five years prior to college enrollment, and (4) school systems may be reluctant to administer complete psychological evaluations during the last part of high school. All of these issues have the potential to be insurmountable roadblocks if the student has not discussed these ideas during IEP meetings, counseling appointments, and other planning sessions in school.

Disclose or Not Disclose?

The decision to disclose a disability is faced by countless high school students with disabilities, and if a student decides to self-disclose, he or she takes on the responsibility of demonstrating that the disability limits them in a major life activity (Duffy & Gugerty, 2005). Students ultimately make choices to disclose their disabilities to colleges and universities, but these decisions should be made based on investigation and consideration. Among the ideas on the student-friendly Web site developed by the Postsecondary Innovative Transition Technology (Post-ITT) (2007) are suggestions for students to consider as they make important decisions about disclosure. "You choose to disclose your disability or not to disclose your disability. Whether or not you disclose is entirely up to you. The college will not ask you and will not provide support services unless you choose to disclose. If you do choose to disclose, you can expect that all discussions about your disability will be held in confidence" (Post-ITT, 2007, 1).

Once the student reveals his disability, the college or university coordinates appropriate and reasonable accommodations for him. Students and their families need to be aware that all information about the disability is handled in a confidential manner in compliance with FERPA (1974), a federal law that protects the privacy of student education records. Further, any information about the student is shared on a limited basis (e.g., warranted accommodations with student's professors). Additional information about disclosure and other transition to postsecondary education information can be accessed on the Post-ITT Web site (http://www.postitt.org).

Documentation

Receiving support services in college settings is vitally important for rapidly increasing numbers of college-bound students with disabilities. Documentation for K–12 students is required for eligibility in special education, under which many students receive academic interventions and specialized instruction. When students transfer to college, documentation is used to verify evidence of a disability and thus ensure a fair and equal admission decision. If students are admitted, proper documentation will assure access to education and use of warranted accommodations (NJCLD, 2007).

The Association on Higher Education and Disability (AHEAD) (2004) has identified two fundamental functions of disability documentation. The first function is to establish protection for the individual from discrimination that he or she may encounter as a result of a disability. The second purpose is to determine the accommodations to which the individual is entitled. Once delivered to the college or university, staff of the disability support services will partner with the student to identify appropriate services and accommodations. By the time students graduate, they should be on familiar terms with the purpose of the documentation: to prevent discrimination and to provide evidence of a current disability that justifies and explains the need for services.

According to documentation guidelines offered by AHEAD (2004), "Disability documentation for the purpose of providing accommodations must both establish disability and provide adequate information on the functional impact of the disability so that effective accommodations can be identified" (p. 2). As they confer with their IEP teams, psychologists, or other diagnostic professionals, students must insist that all disability documentation meets college requirements and can be easily understood by college support services personnel. Unlike K–12 students' school-subsidized evaluations, very few colleges or universities are willing or able to pay for evaluations that document disabilities and need for accommodations.

The Office of Civil Rights (2007) states, "School districts are not required under Section 504 or Title II to conduct evaluations that are for the purpose of obtaining academic adjustments once a student graduates and goes on to postsecondary education" (p. 1). As K–12 schools experience frequent and deeper budget deficits, school personnel may be reluctant to administer evaluations for students in the last years of high school. Further, high schools are not required to supply the type of disability documentation that many colleges and universities require, thus causing a significant disconnect (NJCLD, 2007). Students and their families are urged to begin early planning to avoid documentation roadblocks after high school.

Students who are eligible for services through their state Vocational Rehabilitation (VR) programs can investigate local VR offices and arrange to have evaluations at no cost. Vocational rehabilitation is a state-supported agency that assists individuals with disabilities who are pursuing meaningful careers, including training or education to attain careers. Active involvement of VR counselors in the transition planning process has been frequently mentioned in best transition practices (Lamb, 2007) and throughout this book. The possibility of this agency paying for the evaluation the student must have to be eligible for postsecondary services only strengthens the need for VR counselors to be engaged stakeholders in the transition process. The Office of Special Education and Rehabilitative Services refers students to the following Web site to find state VR offices and links to area offices: http://www.jan.wvu.edu/SBSES/VOCREHAB .htm. Students who do not receive evaluation through their high school or are not eligible for VR evaluation must pay for evaluation costs.

Although IEPs and SOPs may be valuable resources for students to provide as they collaborate with postsecondary education service providers, these documents are not sufficient documentation for most four-year colleges and universities. College-bound students who have 504 Plans usually have the same difficulties when they submit their plans as proof of a disability. Some junior and community colleges and technical institutions may accept a student's 504 Plan, IEP, or SOP as evidence of a disability, and because these documents often include a history about the use of accommodations or auxiliary aids, they may satisfy documentation requirements for these institutions. Data from high school documents may provide useful information about the student's strengths, needs, disability, and accommodations, but this information is supplemental for college instead of the blueprint these documents represented in high school.

A medical diagnosis from a student's physician usually is not sufficient documentation for college support service requirements. Most colleges and universities require a description of the functional impact of the condition, the effect of the condition in an academic environment, and suggestions for academic adjustments (Office of Civil Rights, 2007). Some vocational, technical, or two-year institutions may not require the same levels of documentation. Students' early inquiries about requirements from the school they plan to attend will help them devise plans to obtain appropriate documentation.

ReKeisha: Transition to College Services

ReKeisha is updating her transition portfolio as she prepares for her IEP meeting. She has compiled evidence of the steps she took to complete her annual goal in postsecondary education, and she is working with her guidance counselor and teachers to put the finishing touches on her Summary of Performance. Because she had worked diligently to complete her annual IEP goals and Summary of Performance, ReKeisha believed these documents would be sufficient evidence of her disability and her history of accommodations. When she telephoned the disability support center of the college she chose to attend, she found she needed current documentation of her disability. This particular college required an evaluation that was administered during the last three years. ReKeisha was alarmed because her last diagnostic evaluation had been done in the sixth grade. She felt like the hard work she had completed on her annual goal had been in vain. ReKeisha's school district would not administer the evaluation because she was so close to graduation. In desperation, ReKeisha decided to attend the college without affiliation with the disability support office, and hope for the best.

Reflections About Transition to College Services:

1. What steps could ReKeisha take to remedy her issue with documentation of her disability?

2. Do you believe ReKeisha should rethink her decision about attending college without support from the disability support office? Explain your reasons as if you were addressing ReKeisha.

TRANSITION TO COLLEGE LEARNING

Effective transition planning includes activities, discussions, and experiences that will give students a glimpse of college learning. This section will highlight practices that will help students meet the rigors of higher education. Students' success in general education classes as a predictor of college success is a theme consistently found in transition and postsecondary education literature, but few students with disabilities formulate four-year plans that promote the type of skills and knowledge required in college (Hitchings, Retish, & Horvath, 2005). Over two decades ago, Dalke and Schmitt (1987) were among the professionals who began discussions about the differences between high school and college settings for college-bound students with disabilities. As a result of these efforts, information about high school and college differences began to appear in journal articles, books, college Web sites, brochures, and other publications that offered advice to college-bound students with disabilities. This section will feature a list of the differences between high school and college that combines and summarizes information from several sources (Getzel & Wehman, 2005; Murray State University, 2005; Southern Methodist University, 2007; Syracuse University, 2004; Webb, 2000). The information about differences has been categorized into two sections found in Table 6.1: (1) differences between the institutions and (2) differences over which the student has control. After considering if a difference will impact transition, students and their support teams can use the Action Steps to plan and prepare for postsecondary differences.

Table 6.1 Differences Between High School and College: Institutional

Level of Competition	
High School	**College**
• Students compete against the entire study body.	• College students compete with students who did reasonably well in high school.
• Students with lower GPAs will probably not attend college.	• Students compete with other students in career majors and for employment placements.

*Student **Action Steps** to prepare for this difference:*

Level of Responsibility	
High School	**College**
• School personnel frequently tell students what they should do.	• Students develop self-discipline by developing ways to remind themselves of assignments and responsibilities.
• Teachers and administration follow up with students who do not complete tasks.	• Professors typically do not remind students about incomplete work.
• Students count on teachers, parents, and administrators to remind them of assignments and other requirements.	• Students maintain a calendar of deadlines for assignments and class responsibilities.
• Unless a student attended a private school, his or her education is required and free.	• College attendance is a choice and students are required to pay tuition, either their own funds, loans, or scholarships.

*Student **Action Steps** to prepare for this difference:*

Campus and Class Size	
High School	**College**
• High school campus is housed in a few buildings.	• College campus is much larger.
• The main office at the high school handles many operations.	• Separate buildings house departments or colleges, the library, student residents, technology labs, and other campus offices.
• Classes consist of twenty-five to forty students.	• Students visit an array of offices (e.g., pay fees and fines, sign up for advising, arrange for disability parking). Many of these functions can be completed via online services.

- Students know most of their classmates.
- Depending on the size of the college, class size can be several hundred students, especially in required general education courses taken during the first two years.

Student **Action Steps** to prepare for this difference:

Advisement and Counseling	
High School	**College**
- Students must pass high school exit exams to graduate.	- Advising about a student's program of study is usually handled by a designated advisement office, or designated faculty members in the student's major study area.
- Students must complete Carnegie units in required classes and a few electives.	
- School arranges students' schedules.	- Students take required courses for general education requirements and core courses in their majors but usually have a wide array of choices for electives.
- Guidance Counselors advise students on four-year plans of study and students may not be aware of requirements to graduate.	
- Guidance Counselors may serve as personal counselors as well.	- A wide variety of times for the same class gives students the ability to match class times with preferred learning times.
- Guidance Counselors may help students with learning issues in their classes.	- Personal Counselors are usually available on campus.
- Guidance Counselors offer students information about career options.	- Career Counselors are usually available to help students with career options and choices.
- Students depend on parents and teachers for advisement and counseling.	

Student **Action Steps** to prepare for this difference:

Class Format	
High School	**College**
- Class periods are about forty to fifty minutes or ninety minutes in block schedules.	- Classes may be two to three hours once a week, an hour and thirty minutes twice a week, or one hour three times per week.
- Classes equal one credit per class.	- College classes are comprised of credit hours per class (e.g., one course = three credit hours).
- Class sessions may include in-class reading and writing, checking papers, and hands-on materials.	
- Teachers check to see if students have completed homework.	- Professors may lecture for the majority of class time.

(Continued)

Table 6.1 (Continued)

- Teachers may include activities to ensure students understand the assigned readings.

- Teachers write study notes on the board for students.

- Many teachers engage students at the basic knowledge level.

- When students are absent, the teacher provides information about missed work.

- The high school provides textbooks.

- Students typically have one book per class.

- Professors may not collect homework but expect students to learn from doing it.

- Professors expect students to seek help if they do not understand assigned readings.

- Although some professors may provide notes or presentations to students through an electronic or paper format, students are expected to generate their notes during class.

- Professors expect students to think independently and critically, and apply knowledge they have learned.

- When they miss class, students must ask for missed work from the professor or another student.

- Students buy their own textbooks and may have several textbooks for each class.

*Student **Action Steps** to prepare for this difference:*

Assignments	
High School	**College**
• Students may not know class assignments for the entire semester.	• Professors provide a syllabus that details work, assignments, expectations, due dates, and resources students will need for the entire semester.
• Teachers remind students of assignments.	
• Assignments tend to be frequent and short in length.	• Assignments may be long-term and lengthy.
• Students are asked to read short assignments that are discussed and taught again in class.	• Students are assigned extensive reading sections or complete books that may not be discussed in class but material is on exams.
• Students involved in school-related activities may turn in work later.	• Students must turn in work on the due date stated on the syllabus, regardless of their involvement in school-related activities.
• Students may not be required to read a complete book.	

*Student **Action Steps** to prepare for this difference:*

Faculty Interaction	
High School	**College**
• Teachers are certified (or in progress to be certified) educators.	• Professors are experts in the content of the subjects they teach and may not have prior teaching experience.
• Teachers notify students who need assistance.	• Students must initiate communication with the professor if they require help.
• Teachers are available before, during, or after school for assistance.	• Professors are available during office hours posted on the syllabus.
• Students usually address teachers as Miss, Ms., Mrs., or Mr.	• Students make appointments to see the professor.
• Teachers often support or attend students' extracurricular activities.	• Students address professors as Professor or Dr.
	• Within their departments of major study, students may find mentors among professors.
	• Students may engage in research and professional organizations with faculty.

*Student **Action Steps** to prepare for this difference:*

Exams and Quizzes	
High School	**College**
• Students take tests frequently in classes.	• Professors may test infrequently, sometimes only twice each semester.
• Students are tested over small portions of material.	• Exams tend to be cumulative and cover large segments of material.
• Teachers give students study guides that match the information on exams.	• Students must organize and review all class materials for exams.
• Make-up tests are readily available for students and arranged by teachers.	• Students must request make-up exams, and professors determine if missed exam can be rescheduled.

*Student **Action Steps** to prepare for this difference:*

Grades	
High School	**College**
• Students receive grades for all class work.	• Students may complete assignments to learn material, but not receive a grade.

(Continued)

Table 6.1 (Continued)

• Students can earn extra credit points to raise final grades.	• Many professors do not award extra credit work.
• Students can earn homework points.	• Professors may not give homework grades.
• Teachers may adjust low grades on exams when determining final grades.	• All grades are averaged when calculating final grades.

*Student **Action Steps** to prepare for this difference:*

Resources and Support

High School	College
• Teachers develop learning strategies for students to use.	• Students choose or develop strategies based on their learning needs.
• Teachers provide assistive technology and other technology within the classroom.	• Students choose and use assistive technology and other technology in many campus venues.
• Teachers evaluate the effectiveness of accommodations and assistive technology.	• Students evaluate the effectiveness of accommodations and assistive technology.
• Teachers and parents make appointments with various resources and support services.	• Students are responsible for finding resources and support services on campus.
• High school personnel walk students through resources (e.g., the library or class enrollment).	• Students make appointments for support services.
	• Students must sign up for information sessions about resources (e.g., library resources, study skills class).

*Student **Action Steps** to prepare for this difference:*

Differences: Students Have Choices

Study Time

High School	College
• Students may study about two hours per week.	• Students need to spend three hours outside of class for each credit hour of class (e.g., three hours of credit = nine hours of study).
• Students may not need to read an assignment more than once.	
• Students may graduate without reading their textbooks.	• Students need to review class notes and reading assignments regularly.

- Students may not write or highlight in textbooks.

- Students own their books and can write notes or highlight texts.

*Student **Action Steps** to prepare for this difference:*

Attendance	
High School	**College**
Teachers take attendance every period, every day.	Many professors do not take roll so students choose to attend classes.
Lack of attendance is reported to parents.	Many professors award participation points during class.
School administrators may take punitive action against students who miss classes.	

*Student **Action Steps** to prepare for this difference:*

Critical and Independent Thinking	
High School	**College**
Students receive information about basic concepts from listening in class.	Students are expected to comprehend and apply information from classes and readings.
Most exams are based on basic knowledge levels of learning, or giving back exactly what the teacher taught in class.	Students are expected to evaluate, synthesize, and analyze information.
	Diverse thinking is accepted and valued.

*Student **Action Steps** to prepare for this difference:*

Behavior	
High School	**College**
Students are punished for breaking rules and may be sent to an administrator.	Students who break rules in a residence hall may appear before a housing administrator, conduct officer, or police officer.
Students are reprimanded for inappropriate behavior in class.	Parents are not informed of behavior issues unless the severity of the incident warrants further intervention.
Students are reprimanded for inappropriate behavior on campus.	Students who break parking or traffic rules may receive tickets from campus police.

(Continued)

Table 6.1 (Continued)

• Behavior incidents are reported to parents.	• A student must take responsibility for compiling information in his or her own defense if the student goes before a disciplinary board or council.

*Student **Action Steps** to prepare for this difference:*

Time Management	
High School	**College**
• Students' time is structured by teachers and parents.	• Students manage their own time and schedules.
• Students attend classes every weekday and have five to ten minutes between classes.	• Students may have two classes for three days each week, an evening class one night per week, and a Saturday class every two weeks. Class times vary according to students' schedules.
• Students take classes for one year or 36 weeks.	• Students enroll for classes each semester (fifteen weeks + finals week).
• Students may have time in class to complete assignments.	• Students must plan time in their schedules to study.

*Student **Action Steps** to prepare for this difference:*

Motivation	
High School	**College**
• Students perform to meet family expectations.	• Students are eager to learn information in a major they choose.
• Students perform to maintain grades for sports or activity participation.	• Students perform to maintain a scholarship.
• Students maintain GPAs that are acceptable for college.	• Students perform to maintain their GPAs and degree requirements in their majors.
	• Students see linkages between successful degree completion and lucrative careers.
	• Students pay tuition, books, and fees.

*Student **Action Steps** to prepare for this difference:*

Activities	
High School	**College**
• Students may need parental permission or school approval to participate in activities.	• Students choose to participate in activities on campus.
• Activities are viewed as social events.	• Activities are often linked to career or leisure interests.

CLOSING THOUGHTS

"Planning is bringing the future into the present so that you can do something about it now"

—Alan Lakein

Countless students like ReKeisha and Paul will express their interest in attending colleges or universities. To accomplish these goals, students must be prepared as self-determined choice makers, advocates, seekers, and learners. Preparations and practice in these essential skills and dispositions help students gain confidence during high school and will help pave the way to postsecondary education success and completion. By bringing their futures "into the present," students and the people who support their transitions can truly "do something about it now"!

7 Role of Community Agencies in Supporting the Transition to Postsecondary Education

INTRODUCTION

In education and human services, a systematic approach to transition service delivery means developing goals, activities, and approaches to address the holistic needs of children and youth with disabilities in a coordinated manner. The individual is viewed as having complex and interconnected needs that often require coordinated responses from services within the school and between school and community agencies (e.g., vocational rehabilitation, mental health, adult services, public health, social services, juvenile services, and family services). Coordination is about connecting people within systems and the extraordinary commitment that is required to accomplish it.

The Individuals with Disabilities Education Act (IDEA) 2004 holds schools responsible for ensuring that students with disabilities receive appropriate transition services and planning. But reflecting the understanding that *schools cannot do it alone, IDEA and No Child Left Behind (NCLB) Act also require that schools establish linkages with community and postsecondary agencies and share the responsibility for transition services.*

Furthermore, IDEA requires states to have interagency agreements among state and local education agencies and public agencies. Planning for systematic transition services cannot be done in isolation but must reach beyond the school boundaries into the community. After several decades of mandates for "interagency collaboration," research shows that the concept of collaboration for transition services is not well understood at state and local levels nor has it been widely tested and adopted (Research and Training Center on Service Coordination, 2001). Further development of models and best practices for school–community coordination is needed for transition services for youth with disabilities.

Since approximately half of all students with disabilities (2003 to 2004) spend 80 percent or more of their day in a regular classroom (National Center for Education Statistics, 2005c), there is a growing interest in linking the educational and community-based human service systems to provide comprehensive supports for children in general education (U.S. Government Accountability Office, 2004; Hart, Zimbrich, & Whelley, 2002). Such an approach requires that schools reach out beyond their boundaries and seek a shared responsibility with agencies that provide services for students.

The President's Commission on Excellence in Special Education (2002) found that "the overriding barrier preventing a smooth transition from high school to adult living for individuals with disabilities is the fundamental failure of federal policies and programs to facilitate smooth movement for students from secondary school to competitive employment and higher education" (U.S. Department of Education, 2001). Congressional and federal leaders now recognize the compelling national need to strengthen transition programs and to coordinate services for youth with disabilities among secondary transition programs, postsecondary services for students with disabilities, and vocational rehabilitation agencies. New efforts to align education and disability related laws are under way.

Chapter 2 discussed the changes in legal entitlements under IDEA 2004 and educational services as the accomplished student moves from the secondary to postsecondary setting. This chapter addresses the role of community agencies and the variety of professionals with responsibility for providing services that support transition for youth and young adults who have exited high school. Case examples illustrate how agencies can work together to support postsecondary planning. This chapter responds to the following questions:

- What is the role of community agencies in supporting transition to postsecondary?
- What agencies or services are available to assist students to make a successful transition to postsecondary education?
- What services do they provide, and who are the professionals who provide them?
- How does the student access these services?
- How does the postsecondary student work with Vocational Rehabilitation?

WHAT IS THE ROLE OF COMMUNITY AGENCIES IN SUPPORTING TRANSITION TO POSTSECONDARY?

In the past few decades, the successes and benefits of service coordination in health care, mental health, and mental retardation services have gained the attention of educators and policy makers. Because virtually all individuals with disabilities are being served by the public education system, there is a growing interest in learning from the successes of these service systems as examples for use within that system. Keen interest exists in linking community-based services with education to provide a comprehensive system of educational options for capable youth and young adults moving into the postsecondary system.

The requirement for interagency collaboration and shared responsibility means that (1) schools must develop a seamless system of supports to assist the student to make a successful transition to postsecondary life, (2) the student and family must be engaged in transition planning well before graduation, and (3) schools and cooperating agencies must have formal interagency agreements. Studies of best practices indicate that effective transition requires structured interagency coordination, such as interagency agreements or memoranda of understanding among agencies (Luecking & Certo, 2002; National Center on Secondary Education and Transition [NCSET], 2002, 2004a, 2004b). Both IDEA and NCLB encourage strategic partnerships and structured agreements among schools and community service agencies.

Despite federal mandates, more work needs to be done to create smooth transitions for youth (Hart et al., 2002). For example, teachers responding to a national survey by the U.S. Department of Education reported that in the area of youth transition, more than half rarely, if ever, coordinate referrals to adult service providers (Study of Personnel Needs in Special Education, SPeNSE, 2002). Data from the National Longitudinal Transition Study-2 (Wagner, Newman, Cameto, & Levine, 2005) show that more than 85 percent of secondary special education students were unable to receive services from communities agencies until after high school, even though IDEA legislation requires that a student's IEP include a statement of interagency responsibilities or any needed linkages, if appropriate, to ensure that IDEA youth will receive the services needed to achieve their postsecondary education or career goals.

All states are taking some action to provide direction and resources for improving linkages between schools and service providers. Ten states reported that they have passed legislation or regulations specifically providing for greater coordination between schools and services providers. In addition, while less than half of school districts reported having a transition coordinator at each high school, all but three states reported hiring state transition coordinators who can assist teachers in their efforts to link students with providers after high school. All states reported providing technical assistance to local educational agencies on interagency coordination (U.S. Government Accountability Office, 2003a).

State and Local Communities
Recognize the Value of School-Linked Services

Recent arguments for implementing coordinated school-linked services rest on six basic premises. First, educators and policy makers have come to recognize that all facets of a child's well-being impact his or her potential for academic success and successful transition. Second, demographic trends indicate that an increasing number of American school-age children can be considered placed at-risk for school failure and social problems such as substance abuse and delinquency. Third, prevention is more cost-effective for society than correction or remediation. Hodgkinson (2003) reports, for example, that there is an established relationship between dropping out of school and the probability of committing a crime and that dropout prevention is cheaper in the long run than the cost of incarceration.

Fourth, at-risk children come to school with multiple problems that cut across conventional health, social, and education systems boundaries, problems that schools are ill-equipped to handle alone. Fifth, the current system of child-related service delivery is fragmented, often characterized by duplication, waste, and lack of coordination (Timmons, 2007). Finally, because schools have sustained, long-term contact with children, they are the logical gateway for providing multiple services to children (Adelman & Taylor, 1997).

What Is a Systematic Approach to Service Coordination for Transition?

A "systematic" approach to transition services means developing strategies to address the support needs of youth with disabilities in an organized and coordinated manner to support access and success in the postsecondary setting. A *coordinated interagency service system* is a systematic, comprehensive, and coordinated system of secondary education and transition for individuals with disabilities, which is provided in their communities in the most integrated settings possible and in a manner that promotes individual choice and decision making (Kochhar-Bryant, 2008). *Interagency service coordination* may also be defined as a strategy for mobilizing and organizing all of the appropriate resources to link the individual with needed services to achieve Individualized Education Plan (IEP) goals and successful transition outcomes. Transition, therefore, is not a single passage or "bridge" between school and adult life for students with disabilities. It is a comprehensive and coordinated planning process that provides ample time and support to prepare the youth to successfully complete a secondary program of study and to achieve postschool goals.

In applying this definition, a coordinated interagency service system for transition includes the following items:

- Includes activities, goals, and strategies to improve the availability of and access to needed services by individuals and groups.
- Includes systematic strategies explicitly designed to restructure and improve education or community services.
- Uses both local and statewide system change strategies to assist local education and community-service organizations to develop interagency collaboration.
- Values student/consumer-centered goal setting that focuses the coordination efforts on (1) end results expected for the individual and (2) on maximizing the individual's level of potential and capacity for personal decision making (self-determination).

The general goal of service coordination is to ensure that students who may need services from both school and community agencies receive the services they need in a timely manner—to do whatever it takes (Friesen & Poertner, 1997; National Center on Outcomes Research, 2001; National Center on Secondary Education and Transition, 2002).

More than 25 years ago, Intagliata & Willer (1982) defined the purposes of service coordination as (1) ensuring continuity of care (continuity),

(2) ensuring that services will be responsible to the person's full range of needs (comprehensiveness and flexibility), (3) assisting individuals to overcome obstacles and gain access to services (accessibility), and (4) ensuring that services match clients' needs (appropriateness). Service coordination also helps overcome the rigidity of the system, fragmentation of services, inaccessibility, and inappropriate use of services. This definition remains relevant today.

Functions of Service Coordination

Several functions or tasks make up the process of agency coordination for students progressing through and transitioning into postsecondary settings, including the following:

- Information and referral
- Identification and preparation
- Assessment and evaluation
- IEP/transition planning and development
- Service coordination/linking
- Service monitoring and follow-along
- Individual and interagency advocacy
- Service evaluation and follow-up (Kochhar, 2002)

School districts are not expected to work alone in developing and delivering transition services. As required under IDEA 2004, NCLB, the Vocational Rehabilitation Act, and the Higher Education Act, school districts are encouraged to coordinate with other service systems and formalize relationships through interagency agreements for providing services. Through these agreements, school and agencies define the expected results of their collaboration (*outcomes*) for students and families involved in transition services. Examples of outcomes include the following:

- Increased participation in community-based work experiences.
- Greater percentage of students with disabilities who receive the general education diploma.
- Increased enrollment of students with disabilities in two- and four-year colleges.
- Increased rate of entry into employment after graduation.
- Greater percentage of students living independently.
- Greater percentage of seniors who access needed adult services.

Such a coordinated approach requires that schools reach out beyond their boundaries and seek a shared responsibility from the many agencies in a community that provide services that support students in transition.

Parents as Partners: The Role of Families in Interagency Service Coordination

Recent legislation establishing service coordination for children and families has resulted in an expansion of family-centered service coordination that is unique in law and in practice. Recent change in education legislation is reaffirming the role of parents in education. The IDEA of 1997 and 2004, NCLB 2001, and the Higher Education Act Amendments of 1998 all strengthened the role of parents in their children's IEPs and transition plans, in school decision making, and in teacher preparation.

Together, the IDEA 2004 and NCLB set expectations for parent–professional partnerships that are unprecedented for the public school system. Parents were given important roles in identifying and evaluating their children with disabilities, and in the development, implementation, and revision of their educational programs. IDEA 2004 encouraged parents to become more involved in their children's education and, additionally, to work in other ways as partners with educators and policy makers (Abrams & Gibbs, 2000; Christie, 2005; Henderson et al., 2003). Parents are encouraged to be involved in policymaking at the state and local levels as members of the Advisory Panels and in developing school improvement plans.

In summary, IDEA and NCLB convey three messages to parents, teachers, and service providers: (1) the importance of the parent–professional partnership in service delivery and improving educational outcomes for children and youth, (2) the inclusion of the family unit (system) as the target for intervention and support by the schools and community agencies, and (3) the importance of strengthening the families' role in decision making and educational improvement. IDEA 2004 and NCLB require schools to transform the traditional notions of parent involvement from signing report cards, reading newsletters, and chaperoning holiday parties to include activities such as participating in school decision-making processes, providing input to teachers about how to assist their children, and forming genuine partnerships with the school community.

WHAT AGENCIES OR SERVICES ARE AVAILABLE TO ASSIST STUDENTS IN MAKING A SUCCESSFUL TRANSITION TO POSTSECONDARY EDUCATION?

Adult service agencies in a county or district provide a comprehensive system of services responsive to the needs of individuals with disabilities who have postsecondary education as their postsecondary goal, including those with emotional disabilities, learning disabilities, cognitive disabilities, physical disabilities, or multiple disabilities. Types of services typically include vocational rehabilitation assessments and supportive services, counseling and mental health services, independent living services, postsecondary accommodations, social services, legal services, and health services.

IDEA 2004 requires school-linked human service agencies to support students' transition from school to postsecondary education and employment. While the school system is required by law to provide the services that are written into the IEP/ITP, organizations that provide supportive services are expected to share the responsibility for transition support services. For example, if the student needs medical services, they can be sought and provided from Medicaid, public health agencies, private insurance, early periodic screening, and diagnosis and treatment programs. If transition support services are needed, they may be sought and provided from vocational rehabilitation agencies, employment services, adult service agencies, job training programs, Workforce Investment Act programs, or supported employment projects.

The student's IEP should contain a *statement of interagency responsibilities* or any linkages required to ensure that the student has the transition services needed from outside agencies and that representatives from those agencies are invited to attend IEP meetings. This requirement for interagency services means that there must be formal interagency agreements between schools and cooperating agencies.

IDEA 2004 requires school-linked human service agencies to support students' transition from school to postsecondary education and employment. A wide array of support services exists in local communities. By blending community supports and resources, transition programs can better assist students to achieve their postsecondary goals. Examples of such community services are provided in Table 7.1.

WHAT AGENCY SERVICES ARE PROVIDED AND WHO ARE THE PROFESSIONALS WHO PROVIDE THEM?

The following sections describe several service coordination roles that assist youth to successfully navigate a transition from high school to postsecondary settings.

Secondary Transition Coordinator: Bridge to the postsecondary world. Secondary transition specialists typically begin work with students when they reach the age at which they are eligible for services and planning (sixteen under IDEA 2004, with option to begin earlier if needed). The coordinator works with the student to identify preferences and goals. He or she collaborates with general educators to recommend a course of study through high school to prepare for careers and independent living in

Table 7.1   Community Agencies and the Shared Responsibility for the Service System

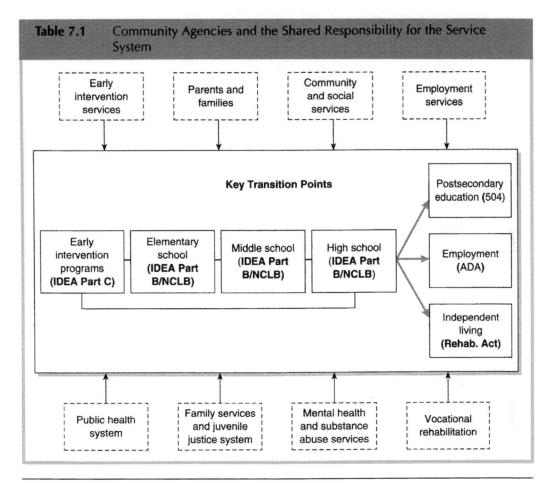

Source: From Kochhar, Carol A., Et Al. Successful Inclusion: Practical Strategies For A Shared Responsibilty, 2e. Published by Allyn and Bacon, Boston, MA. Copyright © 2000 by Pearson Education. Adapted by permission of the publisher.

either college or employment settings. The coordinator arranges opportunities for the student (or a group of students) to learn about different careers through videos, job shadowing, visits to work environments, and hands-on work activities that allow the student(s) to try out a job. Finally, the coordinator makes connections with the adult service system, identifies the support services or accommodations the student may need in the postsecondary setting, assists students to assemble portfolios of academic records, job experiences, resumes, and postsecondary recommendations. Transition coordinators may follow up with the student and continue their support services for a period of time after the student has graduated. Recent research on the role of transition coordinators shows that 94 percent of states also employ one or more at the state level (Jackson, 2003; Schiller et al., 2003; U.S. Department of Education, 2001).

School Counselor. At the high school level, guidance counselors are concerned with educational and career guidance while they also focus on the personal development of the students. High school counselors help students choose school courses and activities that relate to their interests and that will prepare them for life after high school. They also show students how to apply for college or for job-training programs. At the postsecondary level, academic advisors provide information about college entrance requirements, financial-aid programs, and entry-level job opportunities in the areas where they might be attending school.

Disability Support Specialist. The Disability Support Specialist (DSS) provides consultation and ongoing support to enable students to make full use of opportunities at the college or university. The DSS Director often serves as liaison with college faculty, staff and administrators, vocational rehabilitation counselors, and other social service agencies. The DSS serves as the central point of contact for information on physical and programmatic access, specific accommodations, resolution of complaints and problems, faculty and staff concerns, and identification of available services. In addition, the office of Disability Support Services, or Disability Support Center, can provide training, consultation, and information regarding disability issues. The Coordinator of the Disability Resource Center also fulfills the role of 504 Coordinator and helps provide for reasonable accommodations.

Vocational Rehabilitation Counselor. The Vocational Rehabilitation (VR) counselor is often involved in a student's transition planning while the student is still in school. Upon graduation, the VR counselor works with the student to assist with access to and support in employment or postsecondary education. The rehabilitation counselor typically works for the state's VR agency, helping people with disabilities prepare for and find employment. For students who are eligible for VR, services may include evaluation of the person's interests, capabilities, and limitations; job training; transportation; aids and devices; job placement; support to begin postsecondary education; and job follow-up. Priority in services is given to individuals with significant disabilities.

Social Security Administration. The Social Security Administration operates the federally funded program that provides benefits for people of any age who are unable to do substantial work and have a severe mental or physical disability. Several programs are offered for people with disabilities, including Social Security Disability Insurance, Supplemental Security Income, Plans to Achieve Self-Support, Medicaid, and Medicare. Examples of employment services include cash benefits while working (e.g., student-earned income), Medicare or Medicaid while working, help with extra work expenses the individual has as a result of the disability, and assistance to start a new line of work. Postsecondary services generally include financial incentives for further education and training.

HOW DO STUDENTS ACCESS AGENCY SERVICES?

While the school system is required by law to provide the services that are written into the IEP, organizations that provide supportive services are expected to share the responsibility for transition support services. For example, if the student needs medical services, they can be sought and provided from Medicaid, public health agencies, private insurance, early periodic screening, and diagnosis and treatment programs. If transition support services are needed, they may be sought and provided from vocational rehabilitation agencies, employment services, adult service agencies, job training programs, Workforce Investment Act programs, or supported employment projects.

Access Through the Individualized Education Plan. The student's IEP should contain a statement of interagency responsibilities or any linkages required to ensure that the student has the transition services needed from outside agencies and that representatives from those agencies are invited to attend IEP meetings. For example, if the IEP indicates that the student needs an assessment for vocational rehabilitation services by the VR agency, but that agency cannot provide such an assessment, then the local educational agency is required to reconvene the IEP Team to identify alternative ways to meet the transition objectives. The transition coordinator must invite representatives from those agencies to attend the meetings.

Postsecondary Planning in the Last Year of High School. IDEA legislation mandates transition provisions for youth preparing for graduation. Information about the requirements for entering postsecondary institutions or employment should be obtained and that information used through "backward planning" to map students' secondary course of study. The classes that secondary students take in their final years—both academic and career-technical—should not only meet requirements for graduating from secondary school, but also for entering postsecondary education or employment. The IEP team identifies and explores supports and accommodations that the student will need in postsecondary environments and plan for ways to prepare the student to transition to these supports (National Center on Secondary Education and Transition [NCSET], 2003).

In the final year of high school, the student, in consultation with parents and guidance counselors, should identify potential colleges that (1) they can qualify for, (2) have programs that match their interests and abilities, (3) have student support services available, and (4) have a strong record of supporting students with disabilities. If the student is planning to enroll in a two- or four-year college or technical school, he or she can ask the guidance counselor to help them select colleges, apply and negotiate for support services, find information on how to access campus resources, discuss interview techniques, discuss self-advocacy techniques and ways to promote one's strengths, and the advantages and disadvantages of self-disclosure of the disability. Students with disabilities need to be aware of several important questions that they should ask when preparing to apply for Disability Support Services.

- Who is responsible for coordinating services for students with disabilities? Is this a full-time, permanent position?
- What documentation of my disability will the college need? What should I make sure I take with me from high school?
- Is there anyone to help me coordinate academic and other support services? Will I have an advocate or mentor?
- Is there ongoing professional supervision of tutors (i.e., peers, educators, mentors, educational therapists, special education teachers) and counselors (social workers)?
- What is the ratio of professionals to students?
- Is a program representative available to answer all your questions clearly and thoroughly?
- How many students are served by the DSS office?
- What do students pay for support services? Are these charges considered in the school's financial aid packet?

In the last year of high school, with the support and involvement of the family and transition team, each student should make sure the IEP includes transition plans and a *summary of performance* (SOP), now required under IDEA 2004. Finally, students should learn to speak about their disability and to describe accommodations that are necessary or helpful. If appropriate, they should contact the VR agency or the Social Security Administration at age eighteen or in the last year of school to determine eligibility for benefits (Kochhar-Bryant, 2002).

HOW DOES THE POSTSECONDARY STUDENT ACCESS SERVICES FROM VOCATIONAL REHABILITATION?

The 1998 Rehabilitation Amendments (P.L. 102–569) strengthened the collaboration and coordination among secondary schools, postsecondary schools, and rehabilitation agencies to support transition to employment or postsecondary settings. Interagency agreements were required in every state that transferred responsibility for transitioning students from the

State Education Agency to the State Unit providing VR services. This provision links the IEP and the Individual Written Rehabilitation Plan (IWRP) in accomplishing rehabilitation goals prior to high school graduation.

Vocational Rehabilitation provides funds for eligible students with disabilities to attend postsecondary education or technical education programs. Vocational Rehabilitation assists persons with cognitive, sensory, physical, or emotional disabilities to attain employment, postsecondary education, and increased independence. Students with disabilities are entitled to accommodations to help them succeed in the postsecondary program, but students are responsible for disclosing their disabilities and asking for the accommodations they need. Vocational Rehabilitation services typically last for a limited period of time and are based on an individual's rehabilitation plan.

The 1998 Amendments to the Rehabilitation Act also required rehabilitation agencies to make information about services and providers available to students in their final two years of high school. Rehabilitation services such as early assessment for eligibility for services, vocational assessments, and counseling in work behaviors are now available to students in their final years of high school and after graduation. Close collaboration between secondary personnel and rehabilitation counselors after the student reaches age sixteen is vital to linking the student with VR services and engaging parents in planning.

The Summary of Performance Helps Students Access Vocational Rehabilitation Services. What information needs to be included in the SOP to assist VR counselors in determining the eligibility for VR services and in writing the Individual Plan for Employment (IPE)? section 504 of the Rehabilitation Act of 1973 requires students to self-identify but also to provide documentation of their disability to become eligible for services. The required documentation may include one or more of the following: (1) the date and diagnosis of the disability, (2) how the diagnosis was determined, (3) the credentials of the professional, (4) how the disability affects a major life activity, and (5) academic and functional limitations that are caused by the disability. Students with disabilities are eligible for VR services if (1) their physical or mental impairment constitutes or results in a substantial impediment to employment, (2) they can benefit from VR services in terms of employment outcome, and (3) they require VR services to prepare for, secure, retain, or regain employment. Based on these requirements the most important consideration for VR counselors is whether the SOP provides them with a diagnosis signed by a credentialed professional and enough current information about how the disability affects major life activities.

Examples of these life activities include mobility, communication, graduation from high school, and the academic and functional limitations of the disability as it applies to postsecondary education/training or employment. The SOP will be most valuable to VR counselors if it contains enough detailed information to develop a comprehensive plan of services in the students' IPE. The IPE is required for every customer eligible for VR services within 90 days of eligibility and is written by the counselor and the customer together. The major focus of the IPE is the individual's employment goal and the tentative date for reaching the goal. The counselor must also list the services needed by the individual to reach the goal as well as who will provide and pay for the services, and include the start and end dates. These components of the IPE are developed through a comprehensive discussion with the youth customer in conjunction with any reports, evaluations, or records the school or the customer provides. Consequently, the more comprehensive the SOP is, the more valuable it will be in assisting the VR counselor and their youth customers in developing the IPE. In addition, given that the majority of states operate under Order of Selection (serving individuals with most severe disabilities first) the more detailed the SOP, the better the VR counselor can develop a comprehensive IPE allowing these students to be served more expeditiously.

The SOP could be especially helpful in providing comprehensive background information on their school performance if a youth customer accesses VR services several years after high school and finds it difficult to remember much information about their academic and functional skill levels. It is essential that the SOP include detailed, current information to assist VR counselors and their young customers with the necessary information to develop a more personalized and realistic employment goal and the essential services and programs to ensure a successful employment outcome (Lamb, 2007).

Services Provided by Vocational Rehabilitation Agencies. The value of the supports provided by VR counselors has been documented by Lamb (2003) in a case study on the role of the VR counselor in transitioning youth with disabilities to postsecondary education and employment. In this study, ten students with disabilities who had completed postsecondary college and training programs were interviewed to determine which supports provided by their VR counselor were most critical to their success. Seven of the ten students reported that monetary support for tuition and books was essential for the completion of their degree. Similarly, seven out of ten reported that the purchase of assistive technology and software programs was essential for their success in completing their degree or training program. Four of the ten students indicated that specialized tutoring in reading, writing, mathematics, and study skills were necessary for their academic success.

WHAT IS THE ROLE OF THE LOCAL INTERAGENCY TRANSITION PLANNING COUNCIL?

In the course of planning with individual students, it may become clear that adult services, related services, or vocational education are unavailable or are fraught with barriers. Often such barriers must be overcome through an interagency coordination strategy. Typically, a school level collaboration involves a variety of transition-related personnel who discuss the barriers and issues facing transition-age youth and then develop a plan to address these issues. These stakeholders include educators, adult service providers, parents, students, employers, administrators, vocational educators, general educators, and related service providers.

An interagency transition planning council is one mechanism for increasing the availability, access, and quality of transition services. Such a council achieves this by developing and improving policies, procedures, systems, and funding for providing services to youth with disabilities and their families (Baer & Kochhar-Bryant, 2008). The local transition planning council may have different names in different communities, including "community transition team," "interagency community council," "interagency planning team," or "local transition advisory group." The planning council may be purely advisory or have decision-making authority. As a decision-making body, the council may decide on the direction and operation of the interagency partnership, its goals and objectives, its management and staff, the use of resources, distribution of resources, and target populations.

The goals of a Transition Planning Council typically include (1) coordination of services to ensure nonduplication and cost-effectiveness; (2) sharing responsibility for assisting students and families to link with community services; (3) providing a quality, local service delivery system to support transition; (4) anticipating current and future needs for services and developing plans to build capacity to meet those needs; (5) improving student outcomes in adult living, learning, and employment roles; (6) developing a registry of adult service agency representatives who can attend IEP/Transition planning meetings and act as resources to the transition process; and (7) developing formal interagency agreements in which information about eligibility can be shared, needs assessed, gaps in services identified, and service capacity strengthened.

Developing the Local Advisory Council Team. The local advisory council should include a relatively small group of concerned, knowledgeable, and committed individuals. A small group is often more effective in directing and monitoring interagency coordination than a large assembly.

The local council should include a balance in representation among school and community agencies, individuals with disabilities, and parent representatives. Local councils typically include representatives from special education, general education, career-technical education, two- and four-year colleges, vocational-technical training institutions, adults with disabilities (particularly those who have received transition services), parents of youth with disabilities, local business or industry, VR services, community-service agencies, adult service providers, and additional public and private service providers.

A council chair should be designated to serve as the lead interagency coordinator or liaison. The council should (a) develop a long-range plan of two to five years to sustain the program; (b) define short- and long-range goals within an established timetable; (c) assess the transition needs of youth in the system; and (d) define expected outcomes or impacts on youth and families. It is important that the council has the authority to determine the direction of the interagency partnership and review its accomplishments on a regular basis.

GETTING STARTED BUILDING A COMMUNITY TRANSITION TEAM

To find out if your community has a transition team and how you can get involved, contact your school district's special education department or office of student service. Ask who directs transition services for students with disabilities in the district. You may also contact the local Parent Training and Information Center at the state or local level, or the regional special education resource center. If a local transition team does not exist in your community, then collaborate with others to create one. The following steps may be useful:

1. *Do your homework.* Explore what your community is already doing to provide transition services to youth. Explore the range of transition services provided in your school and community by talking with school professionals, student, parents, and community and parent groups, or search district and state Web sites.

2. *Identify areas that need improvement.* Decide what transition services are of the highest priority and which of the service gaps you want to address. Talk with others to gain some consensus on the priorities for action. Locate any available needs assessments, special education improvement reports, parent or student satisfaction summaries, and similar documents that might address transition needs.

3. *Create an action plan.* Talk with school professionals, parents, community and parent groups, and others about strategies to address these service gaps. Share your assessment information with others and enlist them to examine transition services in other districts. Create an inquiry group to conduct research.

4. *Evaluate your plan.* Define how you will measure the "success" of your efforts. What results or outcomes are you expecting and how will you know when you have achieved them? Agree on what you will use to determine if your efforts are successful (adapted from National Dissemination Center for Children with Disabilities, 2002).

Box 7.1 **Successful Interagency Coordination for Transition**

While in high school, Bill participated in community-based nonpaid work experience at a local hospital and at a hotel through his high school's Occupational Work Experience program. Upon completion of these experiences, Bill, his parents, and the work-study coordinator agreed that he needed a job in the community. He was referred to the Rehabilitative Services Commission's Pathways program for VR support services in a community-based work experience. In discussing Bill's employment options with his Pathways VR counselor and his parent, a referral was made to the Ladders to Success employment program for job development in Bill's senior year.

With the Ladders' help, Bill secured a job as a houseman at a hotel. Rehabilitative Services purchased job coaching services. Just before graduation, Bill was determined to be eligible for County Board of Mental Health Services. Rehabilitative Services made Bill's mental-health case manager aware of his need for supported employment services. One month after graduation, a meeting was held with Bill, his father, the job coach, the Ladders job developer, the mental-health case manager, and the employer to assure there were no unaddressed issues. Two months later, the Pathways VR counselor closed Bill's case, confident that support services were in place.

8 Student Voices

A voice cannot carry the tongue and the lips that gave it wings. Alone must it seek the ether. And alone and without its nest shall the eagle fly across the sun.

—*The Prophet*, Khalil Gibran

INTRODUCTION

Demands for performance and outcomes have obligated professionals who facilitate transition to take notice of longitudinal studies, graduation rates, measures of skill acquisition, and other empirical data about college-bound high school students. Although those data are essential for program planning and curricula, teachers, counselors, parents, and certainly students can gain insight from the individuals who are currently enrolled in colleges or universities as they discuss their transitions to postsecondary education settings. Chapter 8 will provide information from a number of studies in which individuals with disabilities have shared their experiences in colleges and universities and offered advice to enhance postsecondary education services. In addition to these studies, current students with disabilities will answer questions and offer suggestions based on their unique transitions to postsecondary education.

Over a decade ago, Greenbaum, Graham, and Scales (1995) interviewed forty-nine successful adults with learning disabilities about their postsecondary education experiences. Study participants reported that although they had received considerable support from their families, they believed social support was missing throughout their college years. The participants were able to describe their disabilities and were determined and motivated. Further, the interviewees expressed a strong sense of goals and direction, a finding similar to a 1990 study of successful adults with learning disabilities completed by Gerber and his associates. The adults who participated in the Greenbaum et al. study (1995) recommended that students need to obtain information on both the postsecondary school's academic program and disability services. The adults urged high school students to have well-developed skills in self-determination, advice echoed by students in a study conducted by Hennessey, Roessler, Cook, Unger, and Rumrill (2006). A total of two hundred and eight college students with disabilities were surveyed to determine their postgraduation concerns; the study participants urged college students to become self-advocates and promote involvement of their stakeholders or support personnel. Webb (1995) found that college students with disabilities wanted more extensive career preparation and college information from school counselors and transition personnel in their high schools. Rather than formal job exploration or career counseling during their transitions to college, the students had gathered career information from previous jobs, volunteer work, and discussions with friends and family.

A case study approach was used with high-ability students with learning disabilities who were successful at the college level (Reis, Neu, & McGuire, 1997). Throughout their K–12 schooling, many of the participants had difficulties in reading and writing and experienced negative interactions with some instructors and peers. Participants attributed their success to their abilities to incorporate compensatory and learning strategies and executive functions into their college experience. As a result of these findings, Reis and her colleagues urged professionals to help students "learn how to learn and how to develop a personal system that enables them to achieve" (p. 477).

Stodden, Whelley, Chang, and Harding (2001) reported that although most postsecondary institutions offered advocacy assistance, students with disabilities in their study believed that more emphasis needed to be placed on the development and enhancement of advocacy skills. These students described great difficulty with study, communication, and organization skills. They reported that institutions offered them some assistance with these skills, but the students implored support professionals to provide extensive training and comprehensive coordination of these skills in their personal, educational, and social lives.

Box 8.1 — **Reflection About Research**

After reading the brief review of student voices in published research, what messages are the students in the studies conveying to secondary teachers?
  To parents of college-bound students with disabilities?
  To students with disabilities who want to enroll in postsecondary education?

VOICES FROM CURRENT STUDENTS

In addition to published research that focuses on students' opinions, Chapter 8 features the expert voices of students with disabilities who currently attend a midsized university. The students are enrolled in traditional programs of study on a campus of a four-year public university. The challenges their disabilities present are as diverse as the students themselves (see Table 8.1). These experts volunteered in response to a request

Table 8.1   Meet the Experts

Jeremy is a sophomore with a burning interest in sports. He has taking a combination of on-line and campus classes during his time at the university. Jeremy is African American and uses a wheelchair with a mouthpiece.

Julie is a Caucasian woman who has low vision. She is older than traditional college students and is a senior with an interest in public relations.

Lisette is a Caucasian woman in her junior year who uses a motorized scooter for mobility on campus. She is actively involved in campus activities and is pursuing a career in business.

John Frederick is a sophomore who lives on campus and actively participates in university activities. He has a learning disability and is African American.

LeTicia is a senior who is slightly older than her peers. She is committed to completing her university studies and is eager to graduate. LeTicia has a learning disability and is African American.

Samuel is a recent college graduate who has physical disabilities and traumatic brain injury. He is Caucasian and is working in the community.

John is an articulate student who is hard of hearing and is Caucasian. He has an avid interest in writing.

Jade is a junior in college who is African American. She is a student with anxiety and depression.

Avory is a Caucasian female student who has a learning disability. She expects to graduate soon with a degree in education.

Sherwood is close to the end of his college career, and he will graduate with a degree in business. He is Caucasian and has a learning disability.

Elinora is a sophomore who is an outstanding student. She is a Caucasian who has low vision.

Emma is a junior who is female, Caucasian, and deaf. She is committed to her plan of becoming a teacher.

Miguel is a male sophomore who has low vision. He is a successful student who has plans for further education.

Lauren is a Caucasian graduate student who has cerebral palsy. She is an active advocate for individuals with disabilities.

Jordyn is a sophomore who plans to be a teacher. She is Caucasian and has a learning disability.

made through the disability resource center on campus and were willing to share their thoughts and ideas with prospective students, their parents, teachers, and resource personnel. Students chose fictitious names and either participated in an interview or submitted written answers to questions that were sent to them electronically.

The process of making a transition to postsecondary education from high school can be challenging for students and the parents, teachers, and other stakeholders who support their transitions. To assist students and facilitators as they traveled the path to postsecondary education, Webb (2000) developed the OPEN model (Opportunities in Postsecondary Education through Networking). The steps of the OPEN model, Deciding, Planning, Preparing, Exploring, Selecting, and Enrolling, are used to organize the expert commentary from the students who offered advice about transition to postsecondary education.

DECIDING

The first step in the transition to postsecondary education is *Deciding*, a two-pronged step of (1) identifying a career path and the necessary education and training for this career, and (2) identifying a postsecondary education path that matches career choice and student preferences and abilities (Webb, 2000). The students who were interviewed about this step had the following thoughts about the Deciding Process.

What age were you when you decided you wanted to go to college?

Miguel: I always thought I would go to college. Everybody does. My brother went to college and I followed in his footsteps. The next step is college.

John Frederick: Since my years in primary school, I've always wanted to attend college.

Samuel: I really feel I came out wanting to be a doctor, or at least go to college. I was given medical books at a young age. They fascinated me enough to want more. We always had books around that contained great knowledge so I began looking at the pictures and understanding what I was looking at. Once I was able to read I knew I enjoyed learning so I kept looking for things to learn.

Elinora: Honestly? I've always known I would go, but probably around ten or eleven, I became conscious of "college" and what that meant.

Sherwood:	Probably when I was about three years old and that's because we would always go to college games and I would see the college and I just wanted to go there. I was about eleven and helped my cousin move in to the dorm. I just wanted to experience the same thing, like learning the experiences of college life.
Jade:	My mom. She always stressed to me the importance of a good education.
Jordyn:	My whole life.

Who influenced your decision to attend college? How did this person or situation influence your decision to attend college?

Avory:	My mom. My parents got divorced when I was in eighth grade and I never wanted to be stuck like my mom. She had no college so she has had the kind of job to just support us. She's always wanted to be a teacher too.
Julie:	There were many influences for me to want to go to college. The first thing that comes to mind is my parents. They were immigrants from Europe and they always emphasized education. They did not complete high school when arriving in the states at twelve and nine. I guess my siblings and myself were expected to further our education.
Samuel:	My father has always had a knack for knowledge, mostly in medicine, so I figured I would continue where he left off. He didn't have the money to go to college for med school, just enough to be a paramedic on the fire department. He has always inspired me to want to know everything. I knew then I wanted to know everything he knew and more, so he gave me the itch to learn.
LeTicia:	My child. I realized that I wanted him to be proud of my successes and to show him that I can complete a positive goal.
Emma:	I was going through a real hard time with myself when I was a junior in high school. My mom was really concerned about me so she decided to have me to see my school counselor. Before I got to see my school counselor, I did not want to go to college; I was going to settle for a minimum wage job for the rest of

my life. I already made a decision that college was going to be too hard for me and that I was not going to make it. It was not until I got to talk to my school counselor about that. She really opened my eyes to see how important it is to go to college so I can be successful and have a better life. She believes in me so much and really cares about me. She is very blunt and is very honest with me. She wanted me to see the reality about things and understand better about the real world. It did help me to see things differently and help make my life better.

Jordyn: My parents. It's been something I grew up knowing. It was the next step after high school.

John Frederick: With all honesty, no one influenced me to go to college. I didn't choose to attend a university because my parents are college graduates, but because I knew it was best for me and my future endeavors. With me wanting to become an Editorial Director for a magazine, it's crucial and beneficiary that I obtain both an undergraduate and graduate degree.

Sherwood: I'd be my dad, yeah, and my grandfather. My dad always used to watch our grades, when I was growing up. And then when I turned 18, I remember we sat there and talked about different colleges and I turned in applications to a few colleges. My grandfather went to college back in the twenties. When I was growing up, he would always help me with homework. I always wanted to be like my grandfather.

Miguel: It was more like I wanted to be successful. What more of a way can somebody be successful or have more opportunities?

Lisette: I have pushed myself to attend college; however, my family and teachers have helped pave the way too.

What advice would you offer to students who are deciding whether or not to attend college?

Emma: Giving advice to a student, friend, or even your child about what they want to do in their life is a hard thing to do. You can only do so much for that person, but at the end, it is really their decision about what they want to do with their life.

Avory: That's a hard one because I don't think it's anyone's decision besides yours. If they don't want to go, they won't do well. If you're motivated to go, you'll do well—with some extra support.

Elinora: Unless you aren't academically strong, I would say "GO TO COLLEGE!!!" It's a fun experience. You learn discipline, networking skills, and independence, not to mention whatever information you pick up in class. It can only help you. Obviously there are people who aren't cut out for college, but with such diverse programs these days, I think that'd be a small group.

Lauren: College is a wonderful learning and growing experience. You can learn about yourself and the different subject areas you would like to learn about. College can help you learn how you can be influential in your community/society.

John Frederick: My only advice is to go with what your instincts say and to determine whether or not your future career requires a college education.

Samuel: It's not a quick fix. If you want to be a leader and invest in yourself and make a difference, go to college, change the world.

What advice would you offer to teachers, counselors, or agency personnel as they help students who are deciding whether or not to attend college?

Lauren: To be supportive in the students' decision and let them be instrumental in deciding what they want to major in or study. Keep an open mind when reviewing their cases. You never know what they are capable of unless you try.

Sherwood: To teachers, first off, do not have your students read out loud. It's really embarrassing. It's not the fact that the student can't read, it's just that you put them on the spot. (It) makes everyone in the class think the student can't read. The words get all jumbled up in your head. It's not fair. Counselors, be more understanding. I've dealt with a few counselors and there's one in particular who I honestly felt bad about myself leaving her office, like pond scum, and this is after telling her I had a disability. I would not treat her like that if she was in the same boat.

Lisette: Do not lecture students/people to go to college. You should be positive and help "pave" the way. If you nag, the student or person will only grow that much farther way.

Jordyn: To be patient and help the student. Understand how much it can help their future. Never make them feel like they're doing it for anyone but themselves, not their parents. They should end up doing it for themselves.

Jeremy: To let the student know this is something to take serious because they have to do this for themselves and no one else.

Julie: It is important that the student knows what direction they want to move towards. If students are unsure of this, it would help if teachers, agencies and families expose the youth to what may help with this decision.

Jade: Have kids who are in college talk to them about their great experiences. Also, refer them to the Students In Free Enterprise (SIFE) Web site for knowledge about college.

Elinora: So much of college is focusing on your "career." I think people don't elaborate on how much you grow as a college student or how much fun it really is. It's about the EXPERIENCE, not the results. It's a journey. I know that when I went to the college visits at my high school, all we talked about were numbers (test scores, GPAs, and costs). No one mentions that college is a unique time in your life where you get to know yourself.

Samuel: First hear their dreams and allow them to reach those dreams. If the student really wants to be something that requires a degree, explain that there are steps to get to their goal. My mother always told me it is called delayed gratification. That is, give up the short term useless materialistic things in life to enjoy great things later in life.

Emma: I always believe that it is best to experience something before you make a life decision for yourself. For example, I was not sure if I wanted to go to college. It was not until my high school counselor encouraged me to attend this summer program at a college. I got the chance to live in the dorm for a week, meet the teachers, have a group session, meet my own peers, and learn about different programs and about different majors that the college had to offer.

Box 8.2   **Reflections About Deciding**

When did these students decide to pursue postsecondary education? How does this information impact the transition process?

As the students described who or what influenced their college decision, did their answers suggest themes? How could these themes guide students with disabilities, their teachers and counselors, and their parents?

Once a student chooses a postsecondary education path, the steps of Planning and Preparation begin. These areas involve planning and preparing for the academic rigors of postsecondary education, the social and emotional changes this transition creates, and practical aspects such as financial support, agency collaboration, transportation and housing, college entrance exams, and admission requirements (Webb, 2000).

PLANNING

From preschool to high school, accommodation and success have been students' dominant frameworks, rather than the self-determination, self-advocacy, and individual development required by postsecondary education institutions (McCarthy, 2007). During the planning process, students must actively participate, engage, and make decisions that will impact their enrollment in postsecondary settings governed by Section 504 and the Americans with Disabilities Act. Field and Hoffman (2002) found that many secondary schools relied on the preferences and directions of parents and educators as Individualized Education Plan (IEP) teams planned for future education. As students make decisions to attend postsecondary education institutions, it is critical that they take the helm of this transition planning. Students shared the following ideas about the planning process.

What do you wish you had done differently as you planned your transition to college?

Jordyn: Read more books in high school. I don't think you get enough books in high school. Challenge myself more. In high school, you take classes with your friends instead of classes that will challenge you.

Jade: I wish that I would have learned to stay focused on my studies in the beginning but I partied, dropped out, and later went back to college.

Samuel: I wish I had given up focusing on the world and girls and focused on learning and networking.

Jeremy: Wrote better papers because that's one of the things college professors take really seriously.

Elinora: I wish I had spent more time learning the campus. I regret needing an escort to/from class.

Avory: I was more afraid to start my junior year because I transferred from a junior college to a university.

LeTicia: I wish I would have been taught about different methods of learning.

Lauren: I wish have been more open-minded to going to the community college because when I applied and got the scholarship to go there, but then I realized that was the best learning experience for me. It gave me more time to prepare for the university setting.

Describe how college is different from high school.

Avory: The freedom . . . it was really different, the professors were different. They weren't as personal as it was in high school. Because of my learning disability the first year, they kind of discouraged me but at the end, they were impressed by how motivated I was and how well I did. I get that feeling from most professors. Because I have a disability, they think I'm not an A student, and at the end they are really shocked.

Sherwood: Oh, I see differences, and I see things that are very alike (laugh)! High school, you can get away with getting a C. In college, you really can't. You are in the big world now. You have to force yourself to go to class, even though sometimes, you can skip a class and not worry about it like you did in high school.

Emma: You get to live in the dorm or an apartment on campus with a roommate, you get to be involved on campus with different clubs, sports, organizations, or even work on campus.

Lauren: College is different from high school because with the flexibility of classes, you can pick the classes you would like to take. You have classes with a diverse group of people that you may have not met otherwise. And the professors that are teaching the classes want to help the students learn and love the subject material they are teaching, at least most of them.

Jordyn: You need to be independent in college. You need to know that if you don't study, it's not going to get done. I had to grow up. I had to study because I wanted to study, not because someone told me to.

Elinora: No one is standing over your shoulder, reminding you that you have assignments due. The college sees you as an adult; they mail you bills and expect you to handle your own affairs. It's your job to make a name for yourself, to make yourself exceptional. There are no hordes of students to hide behind. You compete with yourself.

Lisette: You need to learn to manage your own time. You are taking care of yourself now and for some people that is a very scary thought.

LeTicia: You become more focused on your classroom performance and you start to interact with various people from many diverse backgrounds.

Samuel: Most everyone wants to be there. Almost everyone is an adult. Most importantly, it is more about application than memorization.

John Frederick: In college, your class schedule is more flexible than high school. You may have one class on Tuesdays and Thursdays only. You may also encounter things you thought you never would experience. However, don't let it scare you. It only shows that you have more brains than others who would rather make bad choices than good.

Jeremy: The whole transition is because in high school, the teacher basically baby sits you but not in college.

What elements in college came as a complete surprise to you?

Sherwood: Nothing really shocked me. Take that back . . . the girls! My freshman year of college, the girls shocked me. High school had all these rules, college—short shorts, miniskirts! And the amount of papers you had to write. It just bogged you down.

Avory: The amount of work—holy moley! I never expected it would be so hard. I expected it to be hard but never to consume my life. I'm an overachiever!

Samuel: The ability to make your own schedule and be responsible for yourself was a complete surprise to me.

Lauren: Everything was so open with the freedom of speech, and professors and students expressing their beliefs, the professors wanted to make sure you understood the material. They were more accessible and able to help during office hours that they set aside to meet with you.

Jordyn: I guess it was the lecture classes. There are a million people sitting around you. That was the biggest thing. The essays we had to write were so much longer than high school.

Miguel: Sometimes you have to teach yourself. Teachers can only do so much. When it comes down to it, it's about how much you want to learn.

Jade: Some of the classes were not as hard as I thought they would be and some were harder, but professors are willing to help and they have tutors.

Elinora: The helpfulness of my teachers. From what I'd heard, college professors were cold, indifferent people who didn't care if you sank or swam. But every professor I had was eager to help me and see me succeed. And they weren't afraid to get involved with my personal life. Several teachers were great confidantes and gave me excellent advice.

John Frederick: Last-minute studying! Never study for finals or midterms at the last minute!

What advice would you offer to students about planning transitions to college?

John Frederick: Prepare financially, mentally, and academically. Take college courses in high school or your local junior college to save you from taking general education courses.

Sherwood: Don't get a job your first few years of college. It will really stress you out with a job and college.

Lauren: Check out all the schools that you would like to attend and different majors that you would like to study, then you will have some idea when you get to that university.

Jade: Be dedicated to succeeding!

Elinora: Be prepared to be on your own, even if you're living at home. College is YOUR journey; you are no longer viewed as a CLASS but an individual.

What advice would you offer to teachers, counselors, or agency personnel as they assist students in college planning?

Samuel: Teach them fundamentals like time management and money management. Basically teach them how to take on responsibility or how to prepare for it.

Elinora: Begin to treat students as they will be treated in college. Learn to balance holding their hand and letting them fly alone.

Box 8.3 — **Reflections About Planning**

Which students seemed to be self-determined about planning their transition to post-secondary education?

Some of the students seemed aware of postsecondary education and others were not aware of college expectations. Discuss these differences and particular comments that support your perceptions.

Based on the students' comments, summarize their message to students who are planning to attend postsecondary education.

PREPARING

Data from the National Longitudinal Transition Studys-2 indicates that students with disabilities are less likely to attend postsecondary education institutions (Wagner, Newman, Cameto, Garza, & Levine, 2005). The minimal participation of individuals with disabilities may be because of poor academic performance in high school, little access to general education classes (Newman, 2006), or fragmented preparation to ensure successful transitions to postsecondary education (Gregg, 2007; Madaus, 2005). Further, another key component of planning is preparation to use accommodations in a postsecondary education setting. Students who enter postsecondary education institutions need a well-documented history of experiences with accommodations and evidence of their effectiveness (Madaus & Shaw, 2004). As you read the students' commentary about their transitions to postsecondary education, note the areas in which they chose to comment and their specific paths of preparation.

As a student in high school, how did you prepare to attend college? What specific preparation did you do?

Jeremy: I really started organizing my time and work ethic.

Sherwood: I had a teacher in high school who was always very positive and we would always talk about political issues. With me wanting to be a political science major, he prepared me—American government, European history, sociology, economics helped as well. I could see doing this another four or five years. Then when I started taking the classes in college, all of the stuff I learned in high school helped me out. I was in student government and I liked how the process of our student government ran.

Lauren: I applied for scholarships to the local universities. I met with Vocational Rehabilitation to see if they could help pay for school. I also took dual-enrollment classes at a community college as a high school student. It helped prepare me for the work load that was expected in college.

Jade: I took college prep courses, and I checked out different schools via their Web sites and visits to their campuses.

Miguel: Start taking school a little more seriously. You do ACT and all that stuff.

John Frederick: My first year of high school, I was a student in the International Baccalaureate Diploma Program and then I transferred back to my local high school where I enrolled in Honors and Advance Placement (AP) courses. I participated in an array of honorary clubs and organizations as well. I also consulted with my guidance counselor every month as well.

Who help you in this preparation? What helped the most?

Miguel: My family. They are my support, teachers whom I bonded with, guidance counselors.

Jordyn: My parents. . . . They helped me with the applications, organizing them so I had everything prepared and documented.

Avory: My best friend has similar disabilities to myself and we studied together. We took all of our classes together. My strengths are her weaknesses, and my weaknesses are her strengths. It was awesome!

Emma: When I started my senior year in high school, I had to take a life skill class where my teacher and counselor helped my senior class to apply for a college and take the SAT test that was required for the college we wanted to apply for. My mother had to help me fill out all the paperwork for the college like my health information, dorm information, financial aid, and the other forms because I did not have much time for it since I was in school. My mother did sit down with me and explained the forms she filled out. She wanted me to have a clear understanding of what the forms were about and what I needed to do with them.

Elinora: The teachers at my high school were amazing. I learned excellent writing skills from them. I've noticed that my peers in my college classes are clueless about effective writing and I'm glad that I paid attention in my high school English classes.

What classes helped you to prepare for college? Why?

Lauren: Probably the English and math, probably the general education courses. Mostly the dual-enrollment classes I took my senior year.

Jeremy: Mostly my English and math classes because they were the classes you put most of your time into and that helps with all classes in college.

Elinora: I took about 6 AP courses and they helped me a lot because they were structured similarly to college classes.

Jordyn: A study skills class that offers organization, tips for study, and talking with other students.

Avory: I have to say, all of my college preparation classes. They had a college preparation program in the high school and we were able to be a part of it. We learned how to be creative. It was a really great experience for me.

What experience with accommodations did you have in high school?

Jordyn: My IEP coordinator helped me find the accommodations that worked the best. Extra time gave me time not to panic. A tape recorder did not do much, but teacher's notes worked well for me. Each time we tried a new thing, we would discuss it.

Elinora: Everyone was compliant, but I also went to a private school. At the beginning of each school year I had a meeting with my teachers and passed out copies of a letter I'd written, describing the basic accommodations I needed. As long as teachers knew what I needed, they were happy to help. Most were surprised I didn't ask for more assistance.

Avory: I always had an hour out of my day that I could go and get specific help, like with homework, or specific help that I needed. I took all my tests in a room with a reader. Just the support of the teacher, my case manager, was helpful. By my sophomore year, I was all on my own and took all regular education courses.

Miguel: Extended test-taking time, copies of notes, preferred seating.

Lauren: They were nonexistent until I took the SAT. I missed school to take it and sat in the front office to take it. I had extended time and a scribe. In high school, I had extended time to get to my classes so I wouldn't get trampled in the hallway.

Jeremy: I received a note taker.

Sherwood: I had extra time on the ACT and I had extra time on the SAT, and I was allowed a calculator as well. I also had extended time on tests in high school. I had a note taker in high school as well. Once a week, I had to go to this class about how to study.

Did you use assistive technology during high school?

Lauren: No, they didn't offer me an Alpha Smart until the last semester of my senior year.

Avory: I got books on tape and that really helped, especially for my literature classes where I had to read a whole bunch.

Sherwood: I used a tape recorder and I had one of those little spell-check things. The spell-check I used when I was taking tests, essay tests. Tape recorder, I used to tape all my classes. Oh, and I was allowed to use a word processor on all my tests in high school.

Elinora: Yes, I used a Jordy headset to view the projector screens, dry-erase boards, and chalk boards. Other than handheld magnifiers at home, the Jordy was my only tool. I used a cane for walking.

What advice would you offer to students about preparing for college?

Elinora: Learn to speak for yourself. It will be your job to tell professors and administrators what you need. Nothing looks more unprofessional than using a parent or friend as a mouthpiece. Also, learn to take responsibility for your actions. Accountability is key. Excuses are pointless.

Emma: First, I would like to encourage them to fill out the application for the college, find out what it is required for them to get accepted into the college like taking the SAT test or whatever test they are required to take. They have to know how to prepare for those tests and what to study.

Avory: Make sure you have a great support system at home. Make sure that you're entering a college that has a good support system.

Jordyn: To take high school seriously and realize that if you used to studying now, you will be better prepared and used to having the accommodations. Take time to learn to study and learn accommodations. Don't slack off especially during your senior year.

LeTicia: Do your own research and don't rely on other people to help you with questions. Invest time in preparing for your own future.

Sherwood: Do not get a serious job! If I could go back in time, I would not work as much as I have, because honestly, it's going to hold you back, collegewise. The little amount of money that you make when you're in college is not worth your future. If I was not so serious about the job I'm currently in, I probably would have graduated maybe a year ago.

What advice would you offer to teachers, counselors, or agency personnel as they prepare students for college?

John Frederick: Enroll in courses that benefit your need for college, enroll in SAT/ACT preparation courses, research for scholarships, consult with your guidance counselor and parents, talk to current college students, and visit a list of colleges and universities where you desire to attend.

Sherwood: Guidance counselors, tell them about the major that they're looking at and what they can do with that major once they have finished. I know a lot of people who don't know what their major is and they've changed their major over and over again. You really need to research that major to see if it's good for you. Talk to people who are knowledgeable about that major. See if it's something you want to do for the rest of your life.

Avory: Give them positive supports and preparation so they feel like they can do it. Encourage them during this preparation. When I went to college, I wasn't scared of it.

Lauren: To be encouraging—because if the student has one person that helps them achieve their goals for going to college, they will never forget that person, for helping them achieve their goal.

Elinora: Teach students to speak for themselves, think for themselves, and be utterly and completely responsible for their actions. Teach them to know exactly why they did something, to be decisive, and to manage their time.

Jordyn: Continue to challenge them and prepare them. They should be able to hear about an assignment and take responsibility. That's how it is in college. In college, they give you a syllabus and when it's due, it's due. High school teachers should not write assignments and reminders up on the board everyday if they want to prepare their students.

Box 8.4 **Reflections About Preparing**

Which students commented about the academic preparation they completed in anticipation of attending postsecondary education?

What other areas or domains of preparation did they mention?

Based on the students' commentary, how can teachers, counselors, parents, and agency personnel support transitions to postsecondary education?

EXPLORING

When students begin to explore postsecondary education options, they gather and review information about institutions, view Web sites, and interview students and campus personnel (Webb, 2000). Throughout the Exploring phase, students determine if and how each campus characteristic is compatible with their academic, social, and life preferences or needs (Webb & Peller, 2004).

The pressure on high schools to decrease drop-out rates and increase graduation rates may result in transition teams who offer little or no assistance to students as they explore postsecondary education options (Kochhar-Bryant & Bassett, 2002). This scenario, coupled with the reality that colleges and universities offer little outreach to students with disabilities (Hong, Ivy, Gonzalez, & Ehrensberger, 2007; Mellard & Berry, 2001), may impact the breadth and depth of exploration students complete before selecting a postsecondary education institution. As you read the students' thoughts about the exploration they completed, think about the support they received, the effort they applied to the process, and support systems that may have been helpful to them.

What activities or tasks did you do to investigate different colleges?

Emma:	I would wait to hear from the college in the mail. When I finally got something in the mail, I would get all these brochures and the catalogs about the college. I would read them over and fill out different forms for the college.
Avory:	Which college had a good education program. And had a good disability resource center which could help me get the extra support I needed—my comfort zone. I've been really lucky to live around colleges that have good education departments.

Lisette:	I talked a lot with different people about the colleges they went to. I also visited the campuses.
LeTicia:	I went to the office to find out what type of assistance was available to students that had learning disabilities. I didn't realize that learning problems were considered valid disabilities until I had been in school for almost three years.
Jeremy:	My high school college counselor helped me a lot through the process.
John Frederick:	I participated in college fairs at my high school and other local schools in my county. I also did a lot online research as well.
Jordyn:	Other than just visiting the schools, I talked with my high school college advisor in the college help center. They had books that had facts about the colleges. My IEP coordinator helped go through different schools with me.

What advice would you offer students who are investigating colleges or universities?

Lisette:	Do not just go to a college where your best friend of boyfriend/girlfriend is going. Go to a college that you truly see yourself at. If there is a hesitation, then that is probably not the school for you.
John Frederick:	My advice is to research universities who comply to your needs financially, academically, socially, and who ensures development for your future. Every school has its own distinction. Smaller schools offer better opportunities as opposed to larger universities.
Avory:	Check out the opinion of people on campus, how they feel, how they act.
Elinora:	Make sure they have what you want, and if they don't, make sure you can live without it. A good student resource center is ideal. I never thought I'd be at the Disability Resource Center as often as I am. Sometimes it's the personal interaction, not the enlarging of tests or note takers that makes a school hospitable.
Jordyn:	To go to a school that makes you comfortable. Not to look at sports teams or social things, but look to see if the school has enough academic support to make you succeed. You can walk around the library, feel comfortable,

and know that you could sit down and study somewhere. You could succeed academically, not just socially.

Sherwood: Look at the school and look at what they offer major-
wise. Honestly, look at the different life styles on campus. Look at Greek life or intramural sports because
honestly, that does help you out a lot. Look at the per-
centages of students who do graduate.

Julie: From experience, I would encourage them to find out if
there is a disabilities center on campus and visit it as
soon as possible. Taking courses at a community college
and this university, I have learned how important the
disabilities center can be with the success you will have
in a college.

*What advice would you offer teachers, counselors, or agency personnel as they
assist students who are exploring different colleges?*

Sherwood: This one is really hard. I think teachers should sit down
with students and give their honest advice about a
school. Students really do listen to what teachers have
to say. I pretended that I didn't, but I really did. Teachers
have been to school, and they know this student. With
the help of teachers, I mean, our decision can be made.

Lauren: Let them discuss their interests or their fields of study
would be. Help guide them into the right college setting
for them, whether it would be a community college or a
university. Being instrumental in helping the students
find scholarships that are available would be an added
bonus.

Lisette: Do not pressure the students into a school. Help them
by leading the way. Show them different choices. Take
them to different schools. The best advice I can give to
an agency is watch the body language and attitude of
the student and the college atmosphere itself. Are people friendly? Are the employees too pushy? It should be
a calm atmosphere that should be inviting.

Jordyn: Help students make pros and cons of each school.

Julie: I would be sure to inform these people that more opportunities must be experienced by the student. Furthermore, a longer time of linkages to agencies would be
good. They can monitor and offer needed help a college
student may ask for.

Emma: I would suggest the teachers, counselors, or agency personnel talk to their students to see what they want to do in their future. If the students are not sure of what they want to be in the future, they should be encouraged to take a career test to find what career option would be best for them.

Miguel: Just show them the many opportunities. Some kids don't know what's available, what's out there.

Elinora: Every student is different. I think sometimes that counselors try to fit students into groups (the honors kids, the disabled kids, the kids who don't do well in school . . .). Recognize and appreciate the differences in each student and help that student find a university that will challenge and accommodate him/her. Be open to questions. Research. Don't just send the student home with a fact sheet after your five-minute appointment and expect them to do everything on their own.

Avory: To be as honest as possible. Give them all the information that they need. Tell specifically what support is available at college.

John Frederick: The advice I would give to mentors is to gather all information from the student's needs and perspectives, and match them with the various university profiles who meet their needs.

Box 8.5 **Reflections About Exploring**

Which students may have conducted a search for postsecondary education institutions that matched their preferences and needs? Who did not?

In what ways do the students' comments signal that they realized the necessity for a good match between their own preferences and needs and the characteristics of the institution?

School personnel, along with students and their parents, focus on retaining students in school, passing high school competency exams, and graduating. Although these aims are essential building blocks to postsecondary education, what advice do the student voices offer to high school students and their stakeholders?

SELECTING

After students compile and review materials and information about postsecondary education possibilities, they may be prepared to select which school is commensurate with their interests, abilities, and needs. Historically, factors such as location, cost, student's academic record, the institution's reputation, and family tradition also have been influential to students with and without disabilities (Kinzie et al., 2004; Mooney, 2007; Pitre, 2006; Sander, 1992; Stewart & Post, 1990). The college choice is a complicated process that impacts the student, family members, and the receiving institution. Read the students' ideas about influences in their lives and consider how their ideas could impact future students, their families, and their support personnel.

What or who influenced the actual college you chose to attend?

Emma: My counselor told me about a college that is for both deaf and hearing students. She told me about this summer program they had there. It is called Explore Your Future program that is specifically for the high school students who are deaf and hard of hearing. I thought I could not go because of other circumstances, but my counselor strongly encouraged me to attend to this program. I was really glad I got to go to this program because I needed to see what a real college was like and make a decision about what I want to do with my life.

Elinora: Money and family. My siblings were all happy with the college and it was close enough to home so that I would be comfortable on campus (or rather, my PARENTS would be comfortable).

Miguel: I picked this school, my parents didn't pick it out for me.

Lisette: I was going to a private college; however, it was not as accessible as I needed it to be. The Director at this school made things possible and without her I probably would still be attending my old school.

Jordyn: I decided to go because of a specific major. It was a smaller school with smaller class sizes. It's a smaller learning environment. I wanted teachers to know who I was and not a number.

Sherwood: What really influenced me was living in my hometown, where my family is.

Avory: I chose to go to a community college for the extra support and smaller classes because of my learning disability. And I got to live at home and that helps.

What activities or tasks did you do to investigate the support for students with disabilities?

John Frederick: I did a lot of online research and consulting with my guidance department to see what university takes the actual time to provide full-time services to students with disabilities.

Elinora: I had friends who'd had a great experience and my vision and mobility teachers told me there were a lot of resources on campus. I also went to campus myself to check out the Disability Resource Center.

Lauren: I talked to the Disability Resource Center director to see what services I would be eligible for. I went to the schools myself. I was very self-directed.

Avory: I was mainstreamed so I had, I don't know what to call her, a case manager. She really helped me get in contact with the school's disability support center.

Lisette: You need to talk to someone in the disability department. I have learned just to speak what you need. There are so many people in colleges and your voice must be heard.

Jordyn: Before I considered a school, I looked at the disability center at the school. I made sure that there was free tutoring, and other things were available. It was important to me. You need that office for people to talk to when you need it.

Julie: I was linked with Division of Blind Services (DBS) through high school and entering college. I did not consider such an office was in existence. I believe my DBS councilor was somewhere in the background during that time.

Box 8.6 — **Reflections About Selecting**

What factors seemed to influence the students' decisions about the colleges they attended?

Which students described an investigative process of the colleges they ultimately chose?

What characteristics of disability support services did the students mention as they discussed the importance of this office on campus?

APPLYING

Mounting numbers of students with disabilities are entering postsecondary education; however, according to findings from the National Longitudinal Transition Study-2, many of them do not receive postsecondary accommodations because they do not self-disclose their disabilities (Wagner et al., 2005). Skinner and Lindstrom (2003) encouraged students to self-identify and seek appropriate assistance as one of ten essential strategies for successful transition to college. The students' comments reflected a range of comfort with disclosing information about their disabilities and other related admissions information.

To how many colleges did you apply?

Jordyn:	Four.
Sherwood:	Five and got into three.
Lauren:	I applied to three.
Jade:	Four.
Julie:	I applied to five colleges, two out of state and three in the state.
Jeremy:	About seven.
Lisette:	Two.
John Frederick:	I applied to seven universities; however, this college met my needs.

Some college applications offer an option to disclose a disability. What are your thoughts about this option?

Jeremy:	I don't think that's right because people can't help the fact they have a disability.
LeTicia:	I believe that helps the faculty with making the best educational choices for specific students.
Elinora:	I don't remember if I disclosed mine. I would advise it though. It's a part of you that the college will have to acknowledge. If you hide it from them, then it shows that you are trying to hide it from yourself. And a college that discriminates against you for being disabled isn't a place you'd want to go anyway.
Jordyn:	I think it important to know you have a disability.
Sherwood:	My feelings for that are on every application I filled out, I put my disability. I don't think that had any bearing on

	whether I got in or not. I'm kinda comfortable with it. Mainly everyone knows I'm dyslexic.
Jade:	I am fine with it because it gave me the ability to get the help that I needed to succeed in life—like my paid internship with the federal government.
John Frederick:	The disclosure to reference a disability is an excellent option. It gives students who have struggled with college entrance exams the opportunity to fall back on other admission considerations.
Miguel:	Does it help in the admissions process? It's a good thing, isn't it?
Lisette:	I think it is a good idea to disclose your disability because you need to make them aware of it. However, I could see why some people think they got into college because they have a disability, because of needing a minority stature. My thoughts go both ways. However, colleges base your acceptance on much more than your disability so for me I do not find it an issue.

What advice would you offer to students as they begin the application process?

Elinora:	Stay on top of the dates! Don't let time get away from you. Plan out what you're going to do as each month approaches. Stay on top of scholarship applications. Collect your information. DON'T PROCRASTINATE!!!
John Frederick:	Fill the application out correctly and have your counselor or parents review them before mailing or sending out. Also, pick three individuals who are willingly to write references (choose those who know you well).
Lauren:	The application process can be long and time-filling. Just go at them one at a time.
Sherwood:	Do it real soon. Do not wait—the faster the better, and go over it a lot. Make sure you go over your application.

Box 8.7 ——— **Reflections About Applying**

Which students seemed to have some level of comfort about disclosing their disabilities? What advice would you give to students as they begin the application process?

ENROLLING

The final stage of the OPEN model is *Enrolling* at a postsecondary education institution (Webb, 2000). In the closing segment of Chapter 8, the students share both the triumphs and their challenges of their postsecondary education careers.

Describe your accommodations in college. Are they different from what you received in high school?

Jordyn: In high school, I got the actual teacher's notes, now I use student's notes. In high school, [I took] all the time I need for tests, in college time and a half for exams.

Lisette: Yes. I have an apartment that is customized for a wheelchair and I also go to the Disability Center to take tests, which makes it easier.

Julie: The technology has helped tremendously. I believe the lack of technology and textbooks on CD were a big reason for my poor grades at another college.

Jeremy: I receive a note taker and no they really aren't much different.

Describe your proudest moment of college.

Lisette: My proudest moment would be finishing each semester. One of my professors really helped me getting through one of my classes and without her motivation and support I probably would have failed. Thanks, Professor!

LeTicia: The day I realized this would be my last semester as an undergraduate.

Elinora: Hmmm there's a toughie. Probably when I was taking a class with a professor, and she wanted to read some of my writing aloud. It was a piece on my opinion of "community"; I wrote about how I don't like the idea of community because, often, when a bunch of people get together to do work, I have to stand on the sidelines. Very few people can think of a way to incorporate my abilities—they assume I'm useless. I was proud because she acknowledged my point as a valid one and an entire discussion spiraled off what I'd written. It was amazing how people gained new perspective about my situation.

Sherwood: I have a few. The one that is the proudest, and this is gonna sound kind of crazy, joining the same fraternity that my dad, my uncle, and cousin are in. There was a class I knew I was going to fail, and I turned out with a B in a class. I was actually very proud of myself. I talked to the professor and he told me I aced the final. I was so proud. I got a little tear in my eye.

Julie: Enrolling eleven years later as a returning student was good, but I was also proud about making two A's in the courses I had taken. I knew I was going to do it.

Jeremy: The first day knowing I was officially a college student!

Jordyn: Getting an A in math!

Describe the challenges you face.

Julie: The challenges I face are juggling work and school. Some other things are materials for classes in proper format so that is readable. The last thing is keeping up with the speed of classes.

Sherwood: Sitting down and reading a textbook, I get frustrated to the point that I jumble stuff up and I just end up sitting the book down and not reading it. I sit down at my desk and try to write a paper or do some kind of assignment like that, I have to get up and move things around on my desk, check Facebook, or cook food. I have to say that I make the best omelet around during those times!

Elinora: Traveling across campus, answering tactless questions, explaining to people that I'm not lost or just waiting for someone. Trying to show people that I'm a competent person when they already have a preconceived notion of what I "should" be as a "disabled" student.

John Frederick: The challenges I face are worrying about not doing well on a final or midterm, understanding certain material, and not meeting my goals.

Jordyn: Having teachers that don't accept disabilities. Having the students ask you about getting notes, facing peers that don't understand and think you are taking the easy way out. She has attention deficit disorder, maybe I can get that!

LeTicia: Trying to overcome my struggles with computing mathematical problems.

Emma: My challenge was taking harder classes, having to study and work so hard, meeting the teachers' expectations and doing the best I can with school. It has not been easy for me, especially for anyone who goes to college.

Jeremy: Mostly not being able to take my own notes and relying on other people for that.

If you could change one element of the college environment, what would you change?

Miguel: Prices in the bookstore. Parking, maybe. Public transportation system.

Jordyn: I wish professors could be more informed. They need to understand that every disability is different. They think every disability is the same.

LeTicia: The way class schedules are geared towards the nonworking student and lack of online classes available.

What advice would you give students at the beginning of their college careers?

Emma: If I had to give advice to the students who are starting out college, I would tell them to stay focused, stay positive, work hard, do the best they can, make wise choices, make right friends, study hard, manage things better, and continue to work on their goals no matter what.

Sherwood: My advice—don't worry about what other people think, first off, when it comes to your disability. Like you might be in a class, and you might have to leave to take a test. The rest of your class looks at you with a weird look and the next day when you get back to class they ask you, where were you when we took the test. The first few times, I answered, I just left. But in honesty, I went to the disability center to take my test. By the end of the term, everyone thinks I'm going to fail because I haven't taken the test. Tell them, because they will be jealous. Dude, you get extra time when you take your tests? How do we do that? You have to have a psychological evaluation and you have to have a problem, but then you also get jealous of them because they don't have problems. Just don't get down on yourself.

John Frederick: As an experienced high school student, take your college preparatory courses with serious work ethics. These courses will benefit and prepare you for college. Always stay positive through hard times as well; we all face tribulations in high school. Motivate yourself to join every club and organization offered at your school who commands your interests and needs. RESEARCH UNIVERSITIES THAT MATCH WITH WHAT YOU WANT!

Jeremy: To work hard but to enjoy this wonderful experience.

Box 8.8 — **Reflections About Enrolling**

As the students described their proudest time in college, in what ways did they take ownership of this moment?
  What important advice have the students shared with students?
  With parents? With teachers and counselors?

The American historian James Truslow Adams advised us to "seek out that particular mental attribute which makes you feel most deeply and vitally alive, along with which comes the inner voice which says, 'This is the real me,' and when you have found that attitude, follow it." As the students shared their opinions about postsecondary education, heed their words, nourish their self-growth, seek continually for other voices, and follow their wisdom.

9 Considerations for Students with Specific Disabilities

INTRODUCTION

Transition to college and the path students with disabilities take to achieve this goal are discussed throughout this book. Chapter 6 details how evidenced-based practices have improved outcomes for other college-bound students with disabilities. Other chapters offer suggestions for topics such as learning about legal rights, building skills in self-determination, or finding a career path that matches students' needs. Chapter 9 provides ideas for students with specific disabilities. Each section features a student who shares that disability, along with a transition checklist tailored for many students who have the specific disability. Information from this chapter connects with all other chapters, but the purpose of each section is to help students build insight and awareness about their disabilities.

Of course, their disabilities are not the only component of students' lives. Indeed, their gender, sexual orientation, culture, ethnicity, race, socioeconomic status, and educational background influence the choices they make and the manner in which they approach opportunities and challenges. For example, Hogansen, Powers, Geenen, Gil-Kashiwabara, and Powers (2008) found that girls had different types of transition goals and that self-perception, mentors, peers, family, and exposure to opportunities were all factors in shaping the goals. Further, they reported that females had different experiences related to their sources of support and contextual matters such as cultural and linguistic diversity. Trainor (2007) found that girls were missing key skills in self-determination, and many in her study had difficulty projecting details about paths they believed their lives would take.

Race and ethnicity have impacted students' transition plans in areas of academic achievement, family expectations, and household income (Wagner, Newman, Cameto, & Levine, 2005). Leake and Black (2005) urged educators and transition partners to incorporate cultural competence in their practice; services and supports are appropriately provided in ways that are sensitive to the cultural mores and expectations of the students and their families. Ferri and Connor (2005) argue that the entanglement of race and disability has worked to create and maintain new mechanisms of exclusion. Consequently, the practice of racially segregating schools and segregating students into special education has resulted in patterns of underrepresented groups not choosing postsecondary education as an adult option. It stands to reason that all components of diversity impact students' transition planning. The ways in which students are members of diverse groups should be constantly considered, and practices to respect their diversity should be woven into all transition planning, regardless of a specific disability.

STUDENTS WITH LEARNING DISABILITIES

Students with learning disabilities who are college-bound or are engaged in postsecondary education have been subjects of research for the past three decades. Indeed, the number of scholarly articles and books probably outnumber those publications for other disabilities. Much of the information used to prepare students with disabilities for postsecondary education enrollment can be traced to early work in programs for students with learning disabilities. In spite of extensive work and allocation of resources, far too many students with learning disabilities are not completing high school, making seamless transitions to postsecondary education, or successfully completing college degrees. Granted, students with learning disabilities are gaining access to postsecondary education at higher numbers than any previous decade, but their educational attainment lags below their peers without disabilities, about one tenth the rate of students in the general population (Wagner et al., 2005). Once they are enrolled, they often need consistent support to stay in college and graduate (McGuire, 1997).

Most public and many private colleges and universities offer programs or services for students with disabilities, including learning disabilities. The explosion of disability support programs on college campuses during the last thirty to forty years opens options to students, but the sheer numbers may be confusing to the students and families trying to make college choices. In light of the many options, it is especially important for the student to have a voice in developing preferences, goodness-of-fit choices, and learning about appropriate accommodations. During Individualized Education Plan (IEP) meetings, students should create goals and objectives that will help them learn about their disabilities, their individualized needs, and programs and strategies to enhance academic progress. Kozminsky (2003) described this process as four interrelated stages in changing one's attitude about disability before making the transition to adulthood: recognizing the learning disability, deciding to whom to disclose the disability, understanding unique issues, and developing an action plan.

Many students with learning disabilities exit high school without the ability to monitor their own work and time, make accurate predictions about academic outcomes, or change their approaches to academic tasks that will help them succeed in postsecondary education (Brinckerhoff, McGuire, & Shaw, 2002). This advice was apparent as the college students in Chapter 8 urged high school students to learn independent study strategies and time management during their high school years. Establishing skills in time management and learning approaches or strategies are complicated, and it takes time to match strategies with unique needs. It makes sense that these concepts are woven into IEP planning and high school instruction.

For students with learning disabilities, "accommodations must be individually determined and based on the functional impact of the condition and its likely interaction with the environment (e.g., course assignments, program requirements, academic setting, etc.)" (Lindstrom, 2007, p. 230). The Summary of Performance (SOP) can be an excellent format to document the determination of accommodations and under what condition the accommodations were effective and appropriate. If written in collaboration with the student, the SOP can provide college support providers with critical information about the history of use, when the students used the accommodation, how well the accommodation worked, and instruction that was provided to the student. This evidence and information may be useful if students need to have accommodations in areas such as classes with extensive reading or writing, math, science, and foreign language that may present challenges in college (Lindstrom, 2007; Ofiesh, 2007). Students with learning disabilities need to include the use of and practice with assistive technology to expand independent learning. In preparation for this use of technology, students should discuss having an assistive technology evaluation with their IEP teams and teachers.

Students with learning disabilities may experience social or interpersonal challenges through college on to adulthood (Price, 2002). For example, if these students live in a residence hall or apartment, they may have difficulty comprehending verbal or nonverbal social cues in groups or with a roommate. These challenges may influence their conversations with college faculty as they discuss accommodations or ask for clarification about class expectations or materials. Practice sessions with high school teachers and role-playing with friends and family are among instructional techniques in which students can engage while in high school. Other suggestions for practice can be found in the following checklist for students with learning disabilities.

Checklist for Students with Learning Disabilities

Steps	Partners	Done!
Understand your learning disability and know under what conditions you have difficulty.		
Know your strengths and skills you use to compensate for your disability.		
Match your needs with the disability support service at colleges to determine the most appropriate college choice for you.		
Practice your accommodations in rigorous high school classes.		
Discuss assistive technology with your IEP team.		
Practice using assistive technology in your high school classes and monitor effectiveness for you.		
Practice self-monitoring your time on task and task completion on high school assignments.		
Plan how you will explain your needs and accommodations to the college disability support service.		
Summarize your accommodation history in your SOP.		
Role-play professor meetings when you describe your accommodations.		
Work with high school counselor to improve social interactions.		
Request a comprehensive vocational evaluation to help confirm career interests.		
Seek summer jobs or internships that will develop your strengths, help with needs, and strengthen social skills.		

STUDENTS WITH ATTENTION DEFICIT HYPERACTIVITY DISORDER OR ATTENTION DEFICIT DISORDER

Between 3 percent and 7.5 percent of the school-age population is identified as having attention deficit disorder (ADD) or attention deficit hyperactivity disorder (ADHD) (National Resource Center on AD/HD, 2002; Salend & Rohena, 2003), and a sizeable portion of these students may choose to attend college. Students with ADD or ADHD may have attention problems, difficulty shifting focus or sustaining attention, disorganization, distractibility, and procrastination. Other symptoms may include problems with time management, sleep disorders, impulsivity, mood changes, or hyperactivity (Association on Higher Education and Disabilities [AHEAD], 2002; Quinn, 2001).

A review of current research and evidence-based practices will give educators ideas about how they can facilitate the transition of their students with ADHD. A primary task for high school students with ADHD would be to identify strategies that use their strengths and circumvent their shortfalls in executive functioning (National Resource Center on AD/HD, 2002). Skills in executive functioning include planning, organizing, strategizing, and paying attention to or remembering details (Horowitz, 2007), a skill set that is valuable in postsecondary education and adult settings. Allsopp, Minskoff, and Bolt (2005) found that students with ADHD who were able to independently choose and use strategies, along with those who experienced strong instructor-student relationships, had higher levels of academic success.

Mentoring holds promise for students with ADHD, whether it manifests in the strong instructor-student relationships mentioned previously or the practice of matching students with ADHD with older or experienced mentors who have similar personal characteristics (Glomb, Buckley, Minskoff, & Rogers, 2006). Mentorship may also come through tutoring in high school or college. Hock (2005) urges students with ADHD to work with tutors who are trained in strategic tutoring. Tutors trained in the Hock's Strategic Tutoring Instructional Model organize content into a form that is easily managed by the student, while carefully considering strategies students need and can easily learn.

Effective time management skills and freedom from financial stress were predictors of the academic success of college students with ADHD (Kaminski, Turnock, Rosen, & Laster, 2006). Although the ability to manage time in college will benefit all students, skills and practice in time management for students with ADHD is critical. Many colleges offer workshops or classes for students who want to improve time-management skills. Academic advisors, counselors, and therapists provide valuable resources about managing classes, free time, social time, and study periods. Students with ADHD may find the subsequent list a helpful framework as they plan their transitions to college.

Checklist for Students with ADHD

Steps	Partners	Done!
Assess skills and areas of need in executive functioning (planning, organizing, strategizing, and paying attention to or remembering details).		
Identify and practice strategies to assist student with executive functioning.		
Choose appropriate strategies for tasks.		
Practice building faculty–student relationships with high school teachers.		
Build mentoring relationships in needed areas.		
Identify stressors and strategies to lesson stress.		
Practice self-selected time-management strategies.		
Schedule appointments with college advisors and develop a schedule for ongoing appointments.		
Identify counselors or therapists on or near college campus (if needed).		
Develop knowledge about the use of drugs, alcohol, prescriptions, and ADHD.		
Develop a schedule for independent administration of prescriptions.		
Determine situations when help is usually needed and develop a plan to solicit assistance.		

STUDENTS WHO HAVE CHRONIC DISEASES OR MEDICAL CONDITIONS

Not only do students with chronic diseases or medical conditions face the same challenges as other students with disabilities when they enroll in college, they may face serious financial issues, experience unpredictable relapses, and may be overlooked by disability office staff who do not have a complete understanding of their conditions (Royster & Marshall, 2008). A number of health-related conditions affect the circulatory, respiratory, neurological, or immune systems of college-age students, and each of these conditions may have levels of severity and affect students very differently (AHEAD, 2002). Conditions such as chronic pain, cancer, lupus, diabetes, AIDS or HIV, epilepsy, asthma, cystic fibrosis, and sickle cell anemia are just a few of the conditions with which students are coping.

Impacts of the disease or condition may include a meticulous regimen of treatments, medication, and eating schedules. The amount of personal care, illness, and frequent hospitalizations and related costs only add to the stress of missing classes and work (AHEAD, 2002). To further complicate the student's situation, medication may have side effects that make academic work very difficult. Medical complications often cause students to medically withdraw for a semester or leave college permanently.

DePaul University's program the Chronic Illness Initiative (CII) was developed specifically for students with chronic illness. The CII's dedication to distance education, a learner-centered approach to studies, and college personnel who have experience with students who have complicated situations have given more than two hundred students an opportunity to attend and complete college using a alternate delivery system (Royster & Marshall, 2008). Some college-bound students with chronic diseases or medical conditions have found that participating in a camp geared to building coping skills and independence before their transitions to college is helpful to them and their families. One example, *Life after High School* sponsored by the Joslin Diabetes Center in Boston, gives students the knowledge and skills they will need to manage diabetes when they become independent college students or community members. High school students can investigate camps and programs unique to their specific diseases and conditions by visiting Web sites, talking to physicians, or talking to peers with similar conditions.

Planning for transition to college will entail long-range preparation but must also must be flexible and fluid because of the unpredictable nature of some illnesses and conditions. Students who choose to leave their hometowns may need to find physicians in new cities and transfer insurance benefits to hospitals, clinics, and pharmacies. High school students with chronic illness or medical conditions may find the following checklist helpful as they get ready for college.

Checklist for Students with Chronic Illness or Medical Conditions

Steps	Partners	Done!
Investigate camps or orientations to college life for students with specific illnesses or conditions.		
Choose doctor(s) and health facilities in college community.		
Investigate insurance options and make arrangements to transfer insurance benefits.		
Determine housing options. Some students choose to live in single residence hall rooms or apartments to accommodate treatments or medical routines.		
Notify residence hall or apartment manager about any accommodations you need.		
Check to see that documentation for your illness or condition is current. Discuss accommodations with medical professionals.		
Investigate and evaluate assistive technology that may help in living or academic settings.		
Develop a plan to communicate with your family members during time at college.		
Investigate parking for students with disabilities on campus.		
Manage dietary needs independently.		
Manage and administer medical routines and medicines independently.		
Develop an action plan in case of health emergencies.		
Share information with the college disability support office and student health office.		

STUDENTS WITH EMOTIONAL DISABILITIES OR MENTAL ILLNESSES

Unfortunately, many high schools are without the resources and essential support needed for academic, behavioral, and social success of students with emotional disturbances or mental illnesses (Crundwell & Killu, 2007). According to the National Longitudinal Transition Study-2 (NLTS-2) report, high school students with emotional disabilities experience difficulties with poor grades, even if their levels of performance are closer to grade level than other students with disabilities. Further, this group of students, particularly those with emotional disturbances, may have had the least amount of access to general curriculum classes, and thus, may have limited academic skills needed for postsecondary education (Wagner & Cameto, 2004). The added stress of college responsibilities may add to the symptoms of an emotional disability or mental illness (Gecker, 2007).

During high school, students should learn about their disabilities or illnesses and the unique behaviors or signs that may signal emotional episodes. Among common behaviors are poor hygiene, constant cigarette smoking, drug or alcohol abuse, atypical sleep patterns, inability to concentrate, inappropriate emotional responses, delusions, isolation, lack of interest in school or other activities, or hallucinations. As Colin suggested, students should learn about the individual characteristics of their disabilities and determine what form of help they will seek if these symptoms appear. High school students may depend on family members or school personnel to recognize these signals, but in a postsecondary environment, students must self-recognize symptoms or have a plan in place to enlist the assistance of counselors or advisors. As part of the transition to college, students need to develop plans and practice administering their medications independently and offer feedback to their physicians about the medication's effectiveness. As part of transition planning, students should have candid discussions with their counselors and physicians about how drugs and alcohol interact with their medications and illnesses.

The lack of data about evidence-based practices and accommodations for these students gives added responsibility to the student and his or her IEP team (Crundwell & Killu, 2007). Students must be diligent in documenting accommodations that were effective and enhanced learning, and the history of useful accommodations should be highlighted on the student's SOP. The following checklist has been created to facilitate students' successful transition to colleges and universities.

Checklist for Students with Emotional Disturbances and Mental Illnesses

Steps	Partners	Done!
Collaborate with your IEP team, mental health counselors, and vocational evaluator to choose a career path that represents your preferences and interests.		
Identify colleges that have an accredited counseling center.		
Identify colleges that have a disability support office that offers accommodations to students with emotional disturbances or mental illnesses.		
Identify physicians, therapists, social workers, or mental health personnel in the college community.		
Build a history of accommodations and justification of their uses with the help of your physician or licensed mental health counselor. Include this information on your SOP.		
Develop a plan to self-recognize symptoms that may signal emotional episodes of your disability or illness. Include steps you will take to enlist help of physicians, counselors, or advisors.		
Develop a plan to self-administer your medications and report your usage to your physician or mental health counselor.		
Develop a plan that includes strategies you can use when you are under stress.		
Learn about how alcohol and drugs may affect your disability or illness along with negative medication interactions you could experience.		
Develop a strategy for building a support network of friends and advisors on campus.		
Think of fitness and recreational activities you would like to do while in college.		

STUDENTS WHO ARE DEAF OR HARD OF HEARING

All students with disabilities must develop essential knowledge and skills for succeeding in postsecondary institutions, but for students who are deaf or hard of hearing, gaining a "generalized knowledge of society" (Howlett, 2000) may be a necessary component of precollege preparation. Those who shift from a high school setting with an ASL focus to a college format designed for hearing students are at risk and must take special care with planning and preparing.

Although the numbers of college students who are deaf or hard of hearing has dramatically increased since 1987 (Wagner, Newman, Cameto, & Levine, 2005), many of these students may exit college before they earn a degree (English, 1997). In response to these statistics, students must learn about their disabilities accompanied with metacognitive information, broad academic knowledge, and scholarly skills that will increase the likelihood of success in college (Luckner, 2002). Of the students who complete college, most report that they have successful careers, are economically self-sufficient, and earn similar salaries as their hearing colleagues (Punch, Hyde, & Power, 2007; Schroedel & Geyer, 2000).

Schroedel (1992) found that many high school students who were deaf lacked an expansive knowledge about the array of available careers or jobs, and as a result, had very low career aspirations. This information should lead high school personnel, families, and agency partners to encourage a wide exploration of career possibilities, rather than aspire to those jobs to which he or she may have ready access. To enhance lifetime earnings, Schroedel and Geyer (2000) urged students who were deaf or hard of hearing to obtain the highest degree they are able to attain. Though the numbers of students who are gaining access to college have increased, underemployment and an overrepresentation in blue-collar jobs continues to be an issue for individuals who are deaf or hard of hearing (Luckner, 2002).

Accommodations for students vary according to need and also to the method in which they have been instructed. Among the accommodations students may use in college are interpreters, note takers, captioning services, assisted listening, or alternate tests or exams. The following checklist will help students identify the services and resources they may need for college enrollment.

Checklist for Students Who Are Deaf or Hard of Hearing

Steps	Partners	Done!

- Participate in comprehensive vocational evaluation that includes preferences and potential skills and abilities.
- Investigate colleges dedicated to students who are deaf/hard of hearing and colleges primarily for hearing students. Choose the college that meets your needs.
- Contact the disability support office on campus and communicate with the specialist for students who are deaf/hard of hearing.
- Investigate counseling services and access for students who are deaf/hard of hearing.
- Investigate academic support services and access for students who are deaf/hard of hearing.
- Learn about levels of interpreter certification at your college choices and determine your needs.
- Attend camps for college-bound students who are deaf/hard of hearing.
- Have an assistive technology evaluation to find assistive listening devices or equipment that will enhance learning.
- Investigate Communication Access Real-time Translation (CART), Caption-to-Print (C-Print), or real-time captioning services to determine compatibility with student needs.
- Identify and practice using accommodations that enhance learning (e.g., note taker).
- Make requests for interpreters for class, school activities, and community events.
- Practice using an interpreter in a lecture class format and identify student preferences for seating. Ask questions of the interpreter if you don't understand.
- Learn about levels of certification (national or state certified) among the interpreters at your college choices and determine your needs.
- Identify and practice with signal devices such as lighted alarm clocks, timers, doorbells, message relay systems, closed-captioning, and other equipment for students who are deaf/hard of hearing.
- Communicate equipment needs to college housing office as early as possible after college admission acceptance.
- Visit college campus before enrollment and attend orientation by admission and disability offices.

STUDENTS WHO ARE BLIND OR HAVE LOW VISION

High school students with visual disabilities may receive extensive support services without asking for them, have personnel who advocate for them, and have instructors who automatically adapt instruction (Erin & Wolffe, 1999). Like other disabilities, each visual disability is different. For example, students have different acuity levels, varied abilities to read print, or sensitivity to light (Schneider, 2001). Because students who are blind or have low vision frequently use a combination of equipment or aids, these students and their transition teams are urged to plan early with agency partners and families.

The NTLS-2 indicates that students who are blind or have low vision are entering all levels of postsecondary education at significantly higher rates than they did in the 1987 longitudinal study (Wagner et al., 2005), but like their peers with hearing disabilities, they are less likely to finish college (American Foundation for the Blind, 2005). These data are hardly surprising when one thinks of the complicated issues faced by these students that include access, mobility, accommodations, technology, and personal care along with academic work (Avila, 2002).

Erin and Wolffe (1999) believe that students with visual disabilities may not identify options for solving problems as readily because they may not see the problem solver attempting various solutions to the problem. Likewise, they may be slow to recognize that a person is actively involved in work and not able to interact with them at that moment. Erin and Wolffe advise families, friends, teachers, and all others involved in the student's life to discuss the steps in critical thinking or problem solving and solutions that worked or didn't work. Building critical thinking skills will help the student plan and act proactively, rather than depending on others for assistance.

Whether students use Braille, enlarged print, electronic books, or books on tapes or CDs, they must plan ahead to have these materials for college classes. Of course, disability support personnel can offer some assistance with textbooks and materials, but to gain independence in campus life, students should plan accordingly to avoid delays in receiving books and class materials. High school students can research ready resources and appropriate equipment through partnerships with community, state, or national agencies who serve individuals who are blind or have low vision. Many of these agencies offer mobility and orientation training on the college campus and summer transition programs in some areas. Summer transition camps offer students practice in areas such as living skills, personal management, independent use of transportation, and campus safety (Dahm, 2002; Hanye, 1998; Jaitly, 1998). A checklist for students who are blind or have low vision will help them build skills in independence and assist them with effective transition planning.

Checklist for Students Who Are Blind or Have Low Vision

Steps	Partners	Done!
• Participate in comprehensive vocational evaluation that includes preferences and potential skills and abilities.		
• Investigate summer or second-year senior college preparatory programs for students who are blind or have low vision.		
• Investigate colleges to determine which ones meet your unique needs.		
• Partner with community and state agencies to determine equipment appropriate for your learning. Practice with equipment to become proficient.		
• Prepare for college entrance exams and practice using accommodations.		
• Identify and independently order books from electronic and audio book sources.		
• Participate in a comprehensive vocational evaluation to determine skills and areas of potential talent.		
• Schedule appointments with specialists to assist you with mobility and orientation on campus.		
• Communicate your needs to housing personnel. Inform housing if you have a service dog.		
• Inform disability support office about the accommodations and equipment you need.		
• Learn to do laundry.		
• Learn to groom yourself.		
• Learn to manage money and use an ATM machine.		
• Learn to clean your room.		

STUDENTS WITH AUTISM SPECTRUM DISORDERS

The number of individuals in the United States who have autism spectrum disorders (ASD), including those who have Asperger Syndrome, has increased dramatically to 1.5 million (Autism Society of America, 2008). With growing numbers of students with ASD choosing to enter colleges and universities, schools and transition partners need to ensure that students are ready for all facets of postsecondary education. Despite the large number of students with ASD, high schools have collected little data about effective learning practices and social skill strategies (Newman, 2007). Jurecic (2007) describes the influx of students with ASD on college campuses as a "historic moment" (p. 422), and despite the lack of adequate information and training for high school and college instructors, colleges must be ready partners with these students. The other partner in this relatively new relationship is the student with ASD, and he or she must be equipped to meet the complexities of college life.

The appropriate choice of a college is integral to the success the student with ASD has in college. Community colleges may offer smaller classes that some student prefer, but larger campuses may have more diversity and students with similar interests (Adreon & Durocher, 2007). Once students choose colleges that meet their needs, they must consider critical options such as living at home or in a residence hall, eating in the cafeteria or bringing food from home, and driving or taking public transportation.

Temple Grandin, a successful college professor with ASD, advises students to shift the fixations some students have into motivators. She suggests students use some of their passionate interests to define career paths and find mentors to help guide their direction and growth (Grandin, 2007). Other students with ASD have found paid and unpaid mentors helpful in both social and academic situations (Moreno, 2005). With guidance and coaching, individuals with ASD will approach the transition to college in ways that align with their unique needs. The following checklist may serve as a guide for students and their IEP teams.

FINAL THOUGHTS

In his book, *the First Year Out: Understanding American Teens After High School,* Clydesdale (2007) describes college freshmen as stowaways from their religious, political, racial, and family identities in exchange for

Checklist for Students with ASD

Steps	Partners	Done!
• Investigate the variety of postsecondary institutions (e.g., community college, vocational technical school, four-year college).		
• Create lists of pros and cons for each of these choices.		
• Discuss housing arrangements with your IEP team.		
• Develop an action plan to make sure you are comfortable with cleaning, shopping, washing clothes, and cooking.		
• Discuss eating arrangements at college (e.g., meal plans, lunch from home, cook in room).		
• Create a book of information that includes how to operate appliances and computer, emergency numbers, daily schedule, medical information, insurance, and other important information to you.		
• Identify accommodations that assist you in your studies.		
• Practice using accommodations in high school classes.		
• Practice decision-making skills with real-life problems such as alcohol and drugs, sleep schedules, and peer pressure.		
• Develop a daily schedule of your high school classes, events, and activities.		
• Practice daily routine of getting up with an alarm clock, grooming, getting ready for class, planning exercise, and studying.		
• Visit the disability support service on campus before you officially enroll.		
• Choose a mentor to help you with social support. Visit the campus with your mentor.		
• Visit the counseling center on campus and attend an orientation for that office.		
• Attend an orientation on your campus as early as possible to have time to plan for this transition. If possible, attend an Open House or orientation before your senior year.		

acknowledgment by the mainstream culture on campus. Results from his research indicate that as a group, these youth have difficulty with long-range planning and limited understanding of worldly or political issues. Knowing current trends are helpful when facilitating the transitions of students with disabilities because some of their challenges may be heightened by this generation's inclinations and beliefs.

Students with a wide range of disabilities are accessing postsecondary education in ever-increasing numbers. How they aim for this education, the skills and knowledge they build in high school, their success in college, and their adult outcomes are dependent on the preparation and planning they independently complete in high school. The National Council on Disability (2003a) provided evidence that students who graduate share similar characteristics of resiliency, determination, and resourcefulness in compensating for learning deficits. These characteristics are not usual or innate in any of us, but must be nurtured, facilitated, and maintained—by students and their partners in transition.

Resource A

Summary of Functional Performance Template

This template was developed by the National Transition Documentation Summit © 2005 based on the initial work of Stan Shaw, Carol Kochhar-Bryant, Margo Izzo, Ken Benedict, and David Parker. It reflects the contributions and suggestions of numerous stakeholders in professional organizations, school districts, and universities. The template has been developed with participation of the Council for Exceptional Children (CEC) as well as several of its divisions, including the Division on Career Development and Transition (DCDT), Division on Learning Disabilities (DLD), and Council on Educational Diagnostic Services (CEDS), Learning Disability Association (LDA), the Higher Education Consortium for Special Education (HECSE), and the Council for Learning Disabilities (CLD). *It is available to be freely copied or adapted for educational purposes.*

The authors recommend that any SOP be implemented with maximum participation of the student or that the process be student driven to the extent possible.

PART 1: BACKGROUND INFORMATION

Student Name: _____ Date of Birth: _____

Year of Graduation/Exit: _____

Address: _____

(Street): _____ (TownState): _____ (Zip code) _____

Telephone Number: _____ Primary Language: _____

Current School: _____ City: _____

Student's primary disability (Diagnosis): _____

Student's secondary disability (Diagnosis), if applicable: _____

When was the student's disability (or disabilities) formally diagnosed? _____

If English is not the student's primary language, what services were provided for this student as an English language learner? _____

_____

Date of most recent IEP or most recent 504 plan: _____

Date this Summary was completed: _____

This form was completed by: Name: _____

Title: _____

School: _____ E-mail: _____ Telephone Number: _____

Please check and include the most recent copy of assessment reports that you are attaching that diagnose and clearly identify the student's disability or functional limitations or information that will assist in postsecondary planning:

o Psychological/cognitive	o Response to Intervention (RTI)
o Neuropsychological	o Language proficiency assessments
o Medical/physical	o Reading assessments
o Achievement/academics	o Communication
o Adaptive behavior	o Behavioral analysis
o Social/interpersonal skills	o Classroom observations (or in other settings)
o Community-based assessment	o Self-determination
o Career/vocational or transition	o Assistive technology assessment

o Informal assessment: _____

o Informal assessment: _____

o Other: _____

PART 2: STUDENT'S POSTSECONDARY GOAL(S)

1.

2.

3.

If employment is the primary goal, the top three job interests: _____

_____

_____

_____

_____

PART 3: SUMMARY OF PERFORMANCE (COMPLETE ALL THAT ARE RELEVANT TO THE STUDENT)

Academic Content Area	Present Level of Performance (Grade level, standard scores, strengths, needs)	Essential Accommodations, Modifications, or Assistive Technology Used in High School, and Why Needed
Reading (Basic reading/decoding; reading comprehension; reading speed)		
Math (Calculation skills, algebraic problem solving; quantitative reasoning)		
Language (Written expression, speaking, spelling)		
Learning Skills (Class participation, note taking, keyboarding, organization, homework management, time management, study skills, test-taking skills)		
Cognitive Areas	Present Level of Performance (Grade level, standard scores, strengths, needs)	Essential Accommodations, Modifications and/or Assistive Technology Used in High School, and Why Needed
General Ability and Problem Solving (Reasoning/processing)		
Attention and Executive Functioning (Energy level, sustained attention, memory functions, processing speed, impulse control, activity level)		
Communication (Speech/language, assisted communication)		

Functional Areas	Present Level of Performance (Strengths and needs)	Essential accommodations, modifications and/or assistive technology used in high school, and why needed
Social Skills and Behavior (Interactions with teachers/peers, level of initiation in asking for assistance, responsiveness to services and accommodations, degree of involvement in extra-curricular activities, confidence and persistence as a learner)		
Independent Living Skills (Self-care, leisure skills, personal safety, transportation, banking, budgeting)		
Environmental Access/Mobility (Assistive technology, mobility, transportation)		
Self-Determination/Self-Advocacy Skills (Ability to identify and articulate postsecondary goals, learning strengths and needs)		
Career-Vocational/Transition/Employment (Career interests, career exploration, job training, employment experiences and supports)		
Additional important considerations that can assist in making decisions about disability determination and needed accommodations (e.g., medical problems, family concerns, sleep disturbance)		

PART 4: RECOMMENDATIONS TO ASSIST THE STUDENT IN MEETING POSTSECONDARY GOALS

Suggestions for accommodations, adaptive devices, assistive services, compensatory strategies, or collateral support services to enhance access in the following post–high school environments (only complete those relevant to the student's postsecondary goals).

Higher Education or Career-Technical Education	
Employment	
Independent living	
Community participation	

PART 5: STUDENT INPUT (HIGHLY RECOMMENDED)

Summary of Performance: Student Perspective

A. How does your disability affect your schoolwork and school activities (such as grades, relationships, assignments, projects, communication, time on tests, mobility, extracurricular activities)?

B. In the past, what supports have been tried by teachers or by you to help you succeed in school (aids, adaptive equipment, physical accommodations, other services)?

C. Which of these accommodations and supports have worked best for you?

D. Which of these accommodations and supports have not worked?

E. What strengths and needs should professionals know about you as you enter the postsecondary education or work environment?

I have reviewed and agree with the content of this Summary of Performance.

Student Signature: _____ Date: _____

Next sections:

Assistive Tech/Technology

Metacognitive strategies (these are both under the same general heading)

New small section: Family involvement

New small section: Counselors and other professional involvement

Source: Shaw, S., Kochhar-Bryant, C., Izzo, M., Benedict, K., & Parker, D. (2005). *A model template for the summary of performance.* National Transition Documentation Summit. Stors, CT: University of Connecticut.

POSTSECONDARY EDUCATION EXPLORATION WORKSHEET EXPLORING CHOICES AND SELECTING AND APPLYING FOR POSTSECONDARY EDUCATION

Make and use a copy of these pages for each college you are considering.

Name of College:

Internet Address of College:

CHARACTER AND SETTING	
Services/Program Characteristics	*Comments*
Highly competitive academically	
Moderately competitive	
Not competitive	
Average class rank of current freshman class	
High school grade point average of incoming freshman class	
Average SAT/ACT score	
Size of college	
Size of city/town	
Sororities/fraternities on campus	
Clubs or organizations of interest	
Sports activities (participant or spectator)	
Other	

GETTING THERE/GETTING AROUND	
Miles from home	
Car pools available	
Public transportation available	
Access to buildings	
Effect of weather, construction, and other factors on mobility access	
Cafeteria/food availability	
Access to support services	
Access to fitness facilities	
Access to computer labs	
Other	
ADMISSION REQUIREMENTS	
Minimum ACT score of:	
Minimum SAT score of:	
Acceptance of nonstandard administration of ACT/SAT	
Open admission/no admission requirements	
Waived ACT/SAT scores	
Class ranking based on high school grade point average	
Admissions interview	

Modified admission for students with disabilities	
Foreign language/math/other specific requirement	
Documentation of intelligence and achievement tests	
Recommendations from high school faculty	
MAJOR FIELD OF STUDY	
Availability of major in chosen career	
Full-time years of study for a degree or certificate	
Part-time years of study for a degree or certificate	
Requirements for admission into the program of study	
Requirements to remain in the program of study	
CLASSES	
Orientation classes	
Learning-strategies classes	
Study-skills classes	
Time-management classes	
Developmental-reading classes	
Basic English classes	
Basic mathematics classes	
Foreign language/math/other requirement waived	
Other	

FINANCIAL CONSIDERATIONS	
High tuition fees	
Moderate tuition fees	
Low tuition fees	
Scholarships available	
Financial aid available	
Work-study jobs available	
Books or material rental fees or costs to purchase	
Tutoring fees	
Room-and-board costs	
Costs for special services	
SERVICES FOR STUDENTS WITH DISABILITIES	
Alternative test administration (computers, oral, other)	
Extended time for tests	
Flexible format for completing assignments	
Note takers	
Readers	
Scribes/writers	

Taped textbooks and alternative formats for course materials	
Assistive technology available	
Computers available	
Study groups	
Subject-matter tutoring	
Modified instruction	
Opportunities for counseling with support staff	
Peer support group	
Opportunities to receive diagnostic testing	
Development of educational plan	
Career placement services	
Interpreters	
Other	
COUNSELING SERVICES	
Student advisors	
Career counselors	
Financial advisors	
Personal counselors	
Health care providers	

HOUSING	
Off-campus housing availability and affordability	
Residence halls and dining halls on campus	
Halls with no drinking or smoking	
Single-occupancy rooms	
Coed halls	
Male-/female-only halls	
Limited guest visitation	
Quiet floors for study	
Study rooms available	
Internet access in rooms	
Computers in residence hall	
Cooking facilities available	

Source: Adapted from *Transition to Post-Secondary Education: Strategies for Students With Disabilities,* by K. Weist-Webb, 2000. Reprinted with permission of the author.

GUIDEPOSTS FOR SUCCESS

General Needs	Specific Needs
School-Based Preparatory Experiences	To perform at optimal levels in all education settings, all youth need to participate in educational programs grounded in standards, clear performance expectations, and graduation exit options based upon meaningful, accurate, and relevant indicators of student learning and skills. The following are necessary components of all educational programs: • Academic programs that are based on clear state standards; • Career and technical education programs that are based on professional and industry standards; • Curricular and program options based on universal design of school, work, and community-based learning experiences; • Learning environments that are small and safe, including extra supports such as tutoring, as necessary; • Supports from and by highly qualified staff; • Access to an assessment system that includes multiple measures; and • Graduation standards that include options. In addition, youth with disabilities need to do the following: • Use their individual transition plans to drive their personal instruction, and use strategies to continue the transition process postschooling; • Have access to specific and individual learning accommodations while they are in school; • Develop knowledge of reasonable accommodations that they can request and control in educational settings, including assessment accommodations; and • Be supported by highly qualified transitional support staff that may or may not be school staff.
Career Preparation and Work-Based Learning Experiences	Career preparation and work-based learning experiences are essential for youth to form and develop aspirations and to make informed choices about careers. These experiences can be provided during the school day or through after-school programs, and require collaborations with other organizations. All youth need information on career options, including the following: • Career assessments to help identify students' school and postschool preferences and interests; • Structured exposure to postsecondary education and other lifelong learning opportunities; • Exposure to career opportunities that ultimately lead to a living wage, including information about educational requirements, entry requirements, income and benefits potential, and asset accumulation; and • Training designed to improve job-seeking skills and workplace basic skills (sometimes called "soft skills"). To identify and attain career goals, youth need to be exposed to a range of experiences, including the following: • Opportunities to engage in a range of work-based exploration activities such as site visits and job shadowing;

General Needs	Specific Needs
	• Multiple on-the-job training experiences, including community service (paid or unpaid), that are specifically linked to the content of a program of study and school credit; • Opportunities to learn and practice their work skills (so-called "soft skills"); and • Opportunities to learn first-hand about specific occupational skills related to a career pathway. In addition, youth with disabilities need to do the following: • Understand the relationships between benefits planning and career choices; • Learn to communicate their disability-related work support and accommodation needs; and • Learn to find, request formally, and secure appropriate supports and reasonable accommodations in education, training, and employment settings.
Youth Development and Leadership	Youth development is a process that prepares young people to meet the challenges of adolescence and adulthood through a coordinated, progressive series of activities and experiences that help them gain skills and competencies. Youth leadership is part of that process. To control and direct their own lives based on informed decisions, all youth need the following opportunities: • Mentoring activities designed to establish strong relationships with adults through formal and informal settings; • Peer-to-peer mentoring opportunities; • Exposure to role models in a variety of contexts; • Training in skills such as self-advocacy and conflict resolution; • Exposure to personal leadership and youth development activities, including community service; and • Opportunities that allow youth to exercise leadership and build self-esteem. Youth with disabilities have the following additional needs: • Mentors and role models, including persons with and without disabilities; and • An understanding of disability history, culture, and disability public policy issues, as well as their rights and responsibilities.
Connecting Activities	Young people need to be connected to programs, services, activities, and supports that help them gain access to chosen postschool options. All youth may also need one or more of the following: • Mental and physical health services; • Transportation; • Tutoring; • Financial planning and management; • Postprogram supports thorough structured arrangements in postsecondary institutions and adult service agencies; and • Connection to other services and opportunities (e.g., recreation).

(Continued)

(Continued)

General Needs	Specific Needs
	Youth with disabilities may need one or more of the following: • Acquisition of appropriate assistive technologies; • Community orientation and mobility training (e.g., accessible transportation, bus routes, housing, and health clinics); • Exposure to postprogram supports such as independent living centers and other consumer-driven community-based support service agencies; • Personal assistance services, including attendants, readers, interpreters, or other such services; and • Benefits-planning counseling, including information regarding the myriad benefits available and their interrelationships so that youth may maximize those benefits in transitioning from public assistance to self-sufficiency.
Family Involvement and Supports	Participation and involvement of parents, family members, or caring adults promotes the social, emotional, physical, academic, and occupational growth of youth, leading to better postschool outcomes. All youth need parents, families, and other caring adults who do the following: • Have high expectations that build upon the young person's strengths, interests, and needs and that foster each youth's ability to achieve independence and self-sufficiency; • Remain involved in their lives and assist them toward adulthood; • Have access to information about employment, further education, and community resources; • Take an active role in transition planning with schools and community partners; and • Have access to medical, professional, and peer support networks. In addition, youth with disabilities need parents, families, and other caring adults who have the following: • An understanding of the youth's disability and how it affects his or her education, employment, and daily living options; • Knowledge of rights and responsibilities under various disability-related legislation; • Knowledge of access to programs, services, supports, and accommodations available for young people with disabilities; and • An understanding of how individualized planning tools can assist youth in achieving transition goals and objectives.

Source: National Alliance for Secondary Education and Transition. (2005). *National standards and quality indicators: Transition toolkit for systems improvement*. Minneapolis: University of Minnesota, National Center on Secondary Education and Transition. Used with permission.

References

Abrams, L., & Gibbs, J. (2000). Planning for school change: School–community collaboration in a full-service elementary school. *Urban Education, 35*(1), 79–103.

Achieve, Inc. (2004). *The expectations gap: A 50 state review of high school graduation requirements.* Washington, DC: Author.

Adams, G., Gullotta, T., & Montemayor, R. (1992). *Adolescent identity formation.* Newbury Park, CA: Sage.

Adelman, H., & Taylor, L. (1997). Addressing barriers to learning: Beyond school-linked services and full service schools. *American Journal of Orthopsychiatry, 67*(3), 408–421.

Adreon, D., & Durocher, J. S. (2007). Evaluating the college transition needs of individuals with high-functioning autism spectrum disorders. *Intervention in School and Clinic, 42*(5), 271–280.

Allsopp, D. H., Minskoff, E. H., & Bolt, L. (2005). Individualized course-specific strategy instruction for college students with learning disabilities and ADHD: Lessons learned from a model demonstration project. *Learning Disabilities Research and Practice, 20*(2), 103–118.

Alssid, J. L., Gruber, D., Jenkins, D., Mazzeo, C., Roberts, B., & Stanback-Stroud, R. (2002, October). *Building a career pathways system: Promising practices in community college-centered workforce development.* Retrieved October 28, 2006, from http://199.237.204.112/publications/promising_practices.pdf

American College Testing (ACT). (2008). *Services for students with disabilities.* Retrieved January 6, 2008, from http://www.act.org/aap/disab/index.html

American Foundation for the Blind. (2005). *Educational attainment.* Retrieved March 3, 2008, from http://www.afb.org/Section.asp?SectionID=15&Mode#ed

Americans with Disabilities Act (ADA) of 1990, PL 101–336, 42 U.S.C., § 12101 et seq.

American Youth Policy Forum, & Center for Workforce Development. (2000, June). *Looking forward: School-to-work principles and strategies for sustainability.* Washington, DC: Authors.

Amundson, N., Borgen, W. A., & Tench, E. (1996). Personality and intelligence in career education and vocational guidance counseling. In D. H. Saklofske & M. Zeidner (Eds.), *International handbook of personality and intelligence* (pp. 603–619). New York: Plenum.

Amundson, N., Harris-Bowlsbey, J., & Niles, S. (2005). *Essential elements of career counseling.* Columbus, OH: Merrill Prentice Hall.

Annunziata, D., Hogue, A., Faw, L., & Liddell, H. A. (2006). Family functioning and school success in at-risk inner-city adolescents. *Journal of Youth and Adolescence, 35*(1), 105–113.

Arnold, E. (1994). *Can I make it? A course for college bound students with special learning needs*. Rochester, NY: Arncraft Publisher.

Arnsten, A. F., & Shansky, R. M. (2004). Adolescence: Vulnerable period for stress-induced prefrontal cortical function? *Annals of the New York Academies of Science, 1021*, 143–147.

Association for Career and Technical Education (ACTE). (2006). *Reinventing the American high school for the 21st century* (A position paper). Arlington, VA: Author.

Association on Higher Education and Disability (AHEAD). (2002). *College students who have ADHD*. Huntersville, NC: Author.

Association on Higher Education and Disability (AHEAD). (2004). *AHEAD best practices*. Huntersville, NC: Author.

Autism Society of America. (2008). *What are autism spectrum disorders?* Retrieved March 4, 2008, from http://www.autism-society.org/site/PageServer?pagename=about_whatis

Avila, K. (2002, July). *E.X.P.L.O.R.E. the possibilities! An approach to transition*. Paper presented at the meeting of the Association for Education and Rehabilitation of the Blind and Visually Impaired, Toronto, Canada.

Ayala, C., & Striplen, A. (2002). *A career introduction model for first-generation college freshmen students* (ERIC Document Reproduction Service No. ED469996). Washington, DC: U.S. Department of Education.

Baer, R. M., & Kochhar-Bryant, C. A. (2008). How can school collaboration and system coordination promote progress of high school students? In C. A. Kochhar-Bryant (Ed.), *Collaboration and system coordination for students with special needs: Early childhood to postsecondary*. Columbus, OH: Merrill/Prentice Hall.

Baer, R. M., Flexer, R. W., Beck S., Amstutz N., Hoffman L., Brothers, J., et al. (2003). A collaborative followup study on transition service utilization and post-school outcomes. *Career Development for Exceptional Individuals, 26*, 7–25.

Bassett, D. S., & Kochhar-Bryant, C. A. (2006). Strategies for aligning standards-based education and transition. *Focus on Exceptional Children, 39*(2), 1–19.

Bassett, D. S., & Lehmann, J. (2002). *Student-focused conferencing and planning*. Austin, TX: Pro-Ed.

Baumberger, J. P., & Harper, R. E. (1999). *Assisting students with disabilities: What counselors can and must do*. Thousand Oaks, CA: Corwin Press.

Bee, H., & Mitchell, S. (1980). *The developing person: A life-span approach*. San Francisco: Harper & Row.

Benz, M., Lindstrom, L., & Yovanoff, P. (2000). Improving graduation and employment outcomes of students with disabilities: Predictive factors and student perspectives. *Exceptional Children, 66*, 529.

Benz, M., Yovanoff, P., & Doren, B. (1997). School-to-work components that predict postschool success for students with and without disabilities. *Exceptional Children, 63*(2), 155–165.

Berry, H., & Jones, M. (2000). *Social security disability insurance and supplemental security income for undergraduates with disabilities: An analysis of the National Postsecondary Student Aid Survey* (NPSAS 2000). Honolulu, HI: National Center for the Study of Postsecondary Education Supports.

Blackorby, J., & Wagner, M. (1996). Longitudinal outcomes for youth with disabilities: Findings from the National Longitudinal Transition Study. *Exceptional Children, 62*(5), 399–413.

Blackorby, J., & Wagner, M. (2002). *Special Education Elementary Longitudinal Study*. Menlo Park, CA: SRI International.

Blanck, P. D. (Ed.). (2000). *Employment, disability, and the Americans with Disabilities Act: Issues in law, public policy, and research.* Evanston, IL: Northwestern University Press.

Blos, P. (1962). *On adolescence.* New York: Free Press.

Blos, P. (1979). *The adolescent passage.* New York: International University Press.

Borgen, W. A., Amundson, N. E., & Reuter, J. (2004). Using portfolios to enhance career resilience. *Journal of Employment Counseling, 41,* 50–59.

Bragg, D. D. (1997). A critical response to Grubb. *Journal of Vocational Education Research, 22*(2), 123–132.

Bremer, C., & Madzar, S. (1995). Encouraging employer involvement in youth apprenticeship and other work-based learning experiences for high school youth. *Journal of Vocational and Technical Education, 12*(1), 15–26.

Bremer, C., Kachgal, M., & Schoeller, K. (2003, April). Self-determination: Supporting successful transition. *NCSET Research to Practice Brief: Improving Secondary Education and Transition Services Through Research, 2,* 91.

Brinckerhoff, L. C., & Banerjee, M. (2007). Misconceptions regarding accommodations on high-stakes tests: Recommendations for preparing disability documentation for test takers with learning disabilities. *Learning Disabilities Research and Practice, 22,* 246–255.

Brinckerhoff, L. C., McGuire, J., & Shaw, S. F. (2002). *Postsecondary education and transition for students with learning disabilities.* Austin, TX: Pro-Ed.

Brown, D. S. (2000). *Learning a living: A guide to planning your career and finding a job for people with learning disabilities, attention deficit disorder, and dyslexia.* Bethesda, MD: Woodbine House.

Burgstahler, S. (2002). Bridging the digital divide in postsecondary education: Technology access for youth with disabilities. *National Center for Secondary Education and Transition Information Brief, 9,* 1–4.

Cameto, R. (2005). *Employment of youth with disabilities after high school* (National Longitudinal Transition Study-2 [NLTS-2]). Menlo Park, CA: SRI International.

Cameto, R., Marder, C., Wagner, M., & Cardoso, D. (2003). Youth employment: NLTS2 data brief. *Report from the National Longitudinal Transition Study, 2,* 1–3.

Camp, W. G. (1982). Social efficiency revisited: A cornerstone of our foundation. *The Journal of the American Association of Teacher Educators in Agriculture, 20*(3), 11–18.

Camp, W. G. (1983). Social efficiency and vocational education: An examination of our changing philosophies. *Journal of Vocational Education Research, 8*(3), 10–19.

Camp, W. G., & Hillison, J. H. (1983). Prosser's sixteen theorems: Time for a reconsideration. *Journal of Vocational and Technical Education. 1*(1), 5–12.

Carl D. Perkins Career and Technical Education Improvement Act of 2006. 20 U.S.C. 2301 et seq. as amended by P.L. 109–270.

Carnevale, A. P., & Derochers, D. M. (2003). *Standards for what? The economic root of K-16 reform.* Princeton, NJ: Educational Testing Service.

Carter, E. W., Lane, K. L., Pierson, M. R., Glaeser, B. (2006). Self-determination skills and opportunities of transition-age youth with emotional disturbance and learning disabilities. *Exceptional Children, 72,* 333–346.

Casey, B. J., Giedd, J. N., & Thomas, K. M. (2000). Structural and functional brain development and its relation to cognitive development. *Biological Psychology, 54,* 241–257.

Castellano, M., Stone, J. R., Stringfield, S., Farley, E. N., & Wayman, J. C. (2004, July). *The effect of CTE-enhances whole-school reform on student coursetaking and performance in English and science.* Columbus, OH: National Research Center for Career and Technical Education, University of Minnesota.

Castellano, M., Stringfield, S., Stone, J. R., & Lewis, M. V. (2002). *Career and technical education reforms and comprehensive school reforms in high school: Their impact on education outcomes for at-risk youth* (The Highlight Zone: Research @ Work No. 8). St. Paul: National Research Center for Career and Technical Education, University of Minnesota.

Center for Workforce Development. (1998). *The teaching firm: Where productive work and learning converge.* Newton, MA: Education Development Center.

Chadsey, J., & Sheldon, D. (1998). Moving toward social inclusion in employment and postsecondary school settings. In F. R. Rusch & J. Chadsey (Eds.), *Beyond high school: Transition from school to work* (pp. 406–437). Belmont, CA: Wadsworth Publishing.

Chiba, C., & Low, R. (2007). A course-based model to promote successful transition to college for students with learning disorders. *Journal of Postsecondary Education and Disability, 20*(1), 40–53.

Christie, K. (2005). Changing the nature of parent involvement. *Phi Delta Kappan, 86*(9), 645–646.

Christle, C. A., Jolivette, K., & Nelson, M. (2007). School characteristics related to high school drop out rates. *Remedial and Special Education, 28,* 325–339.

Clark, G. M., & Patton, J. R. (2006). *The transition planning inventory.* Austin, TX: Pro-Ed.

Clark, G. M., & Patton, J. R. (2006). *Transition planning inventory—updated version: Administration and resource guide.* Austin, TX: Pro-Ed.

Clark, G. M., Patton, J. R., & Moulton, L. R. (2000). *Informal assessments for transitions planning.* Austin, TX: Pro-Ed.

Clark, R. W. (2001). *Dual credit: A report of programs and policy that offer high school students college credits.* Seattle, WA: Institute for Educational Inquiry.

Clark, S., & Lillie, T. (2000). Growing up with disabilities: Education law and the transition. *Disability Studies Quarterly, 20*(4), 383–398.

Clydesdale, T. (2007). *The first year out: Understanding American teens after high school.* Chicago: University of Chicago Press.

Cobb, J. (2003). *Learning how to learn: Getting into and surviving college when you have a learning disability.* Washington, DC: Child & Family Press.

Cobb, P. (1994). Where is the mind? A coordination of sociocultural and cognitive constructivist perspectives. In C. T. Fosnot (Ed.), *Constructivism: Theory, perspectives, and practice* (pp. 34–52). New York: Teachers College Press.

College Board. (2008). *Services for students with disabilities.* Retrieved January 6, 2008, from http://www.collegeboard.com/ssd/student/index.html

CORD, & Hull, D. (2005). *Career pathways: Education with a purpose.* Retrieved November 1, 2006, from http://www.cord.org/uploadedfiles/

Council of State Administrators of Vocational Rehabilitation (CSVAR). (2006). *Public vocational rehabilitation: An investment in America.* Bethesda, MD: Author.

Council of State Administrators of Vocational Rehabilitation (CSVAR), Comments on HR 27, Job Training Improvement Act of 2005, House Education and the Workforce, Committee, February 14, 2005. Washington, DC.

Crundwell, R. M., & Killu, K. (2007). Understanding and accommodating students with depression in the classroom. *Teaching Exceptional Children, 40,* 48–54.

Cuban, L., & Usdan, M. (2002). *Powerful reforms with shallow roots: Getting good schools in 6 cities.* New York: Teachers College Press.

Dahm, S. D. (2002). New territory? Rehabilitation teaching at a state school for the blind. *Rehabilitation Education Review* (RE:view), *34*(2), 77–85.

Dalke, C., & Schmitt, S. (1987). Meeting the transition needs of college-bound students with learning disabilities. *Journal of Learning Disabilities, 20,* 176–180.

Dare, D. (2006). The role of career and technical education in facilitating student transitions to postsecondary education. *New Directions for Community Colleges, 135,* 73–80.

DiFino, S. M., & Lombardino, L. J. (2004). Language learning disabilities: The ultimate foreign language challenge. *Foreign Language Annals, 37*(3), 390–400.

Dixon, K. A., Kruse, D., & Van Horn, C. E. (2003). *Restricted access: A survey of employers about people with disabilities and lowering barriers to work.* Retrieved August 15, 2005, from the John J. Heldrich Center for Workforce Development Web site: www.heldrich.rutgers.edu

Dole, J. A., & Sinatra, G. M. (1998). Reconceptualizing change in the cognitive construction of knowledge. *Educational Psychologist, 33*(2/3), 109–128.

Doolittle, P. E., & Camp, W. G. (1999). Constructivism: The career and technical education perspective. *Journal of Vocational and Technical Education, 16.* Retrieved January 26, 2008, from http://scholar.lib.vt.edu/ejournals/JVTE/v16n1/doolittle .html

Duffy, J. T., & Gugerty, J. (2005). The role of disability support services. In E. E. Getzel & P. Wehman (Eds.), *Going to college* (pp. 89–115). Baltimore: Paul H. Brookes.

Durlak, C. M., Rose, E., & Bursuck, W. D. (1994). Preparing high school students with learning disabilities for the transition to postsecondary education: Teaching the skills of self-determination. *Journal of Learning Disabilities, 27,* 51–59.

Eckes, S. E., & Ochoa, T. A. (2005). Students with disabilities: Transitioning from high school to higher education. *American Secondary Education, 33*(3), 6–20.

Educational and Industrial Testing Service (EdITS). (1995). *Career orientation and placement survey.* San Diego, CA: Author.

Education Commission of the States. (2004). *Dual/concurrent enrollment.* Retrieved April 27, 2004, from http://www.ecs.org/html/IssueSection.asp?issueid= 214&s=Quick+Facts

Eisenman, L. T. (2007). Self-determination interventions: Building a foundation for school completion. *Remedial and Special Education, 28,* 2–8.

Eisenman, L. T., & Chamberlin, M. (2001). Implementing self-determination activities: Lessons from schools. *Remedial and Special Education, 22,* 138–147.

Ekpone, P. M., & Bogucki, R. (n.d.) *A postsecondary resource guide for students with psychiatric disabilities. HEATH Resource Center.* Washington, DC: The George Washington University.

English, K. M. (1997). *Self advocacy for students who are deaf or hard of hearing.* Austin, TX: Pro-Ed.

Erikson, E. H. (1968). *Identity youth and crisis.* New York: W. W. Norton.

Erin, J. N., & Wolffe, K. E. (1999). *Transition issues related to students with visual disabilities.* Austin, TX: Pro-Ed.

Fabian, E., Lent, R., & Willis, S. (1998). Predicting work transition outcomes for students with disabilities: Implications for counselors. *Journal of Counseling & Development, 76,* 311–316.

Family Educational Rights and Privacy Act (FERPA) of 1974. 20 U.S.C. § 1232g; 34 CFR Part 99.

Ferri, B. A., & Conner, D. J. (2005). Tools of exclusion: Race, disability, and (re)segregated education. *Teachers College Record, 107*(3), 453–474.

Field, S., & Hoffman, A. (1996). Increasing the ability of educators to promote youth self-determination. In L. E. Powers, G. H. S. Singer, & J. Sowers (Eds.), *Promoting self-competence among children and youth with disabilities: On the road to autonomy* (pp. 171–187). Baltimore: Paul H. Brookes.

Field, S., & Hoffman, A. (2002). Preparing youth to exercise self-determination. *Journal of Disability Policy Studies, 13*(2), 114–119.

Field, S., Hoffman, A., & Spezia, S. (1998). *Self-determination strategies for adolescents in transition.* Austin, TX: Pro-Ed.

Field, S., Martin, J. Miller, R., Ward, M., & Wehmeyer, M. (1998). *A practical guide for teaching self-determination.* Reston, VA: Council for Exceptional Children.

Flowers, C. R., Edwards, D., & Pusch, B. (1996, July–September). Rehabilitation cultural diversity initiative: A regional survey of cultural diversity within CILs. *Journal of Rehabilitation, 62,* 22–27.

Forest, M., & Pearpoint, J. C. (1992). Putting all kids on the map. *Educational Leadership, 50,* 26–31.

Friesen, B., & Poertner, J. (Eds.). (1997). *From case management to service coordination for children with emotional, behavioral, or mental disorders: Building on family strengths.* Baltimore: Paul H. Brookes.

Fuchs, L. S., Fuchs, D., & Capizzi, A. M. (2005). Identifying appropriate test accommodations for students with learning disabilities. *Focus on Exceptional Children, 37*(6), 1–8.

Fuller, W. E., & Wehman, P. (2003). College entrance exams for students with disabilities: Accommodations and testing guidelines. *Journal of Vocational Rehabilitation, 18,* 191–197.

Gaylord, V., Johnson, D. R., Lehr, C. A., Bremer, C. D., & Hasazi, S. (Eds.). (2004). *Impact: Feature Issue on Achieving Secondary Education and Transition Results for Students with Disabilities, 16*(3). Minneapolis: University of Minnesota, Institute on Community Integration.

Gecker, E. (2007). How do I know if my student is dangerous? *Academe, 93*(6), 38–40.

George, P. S., McEwin, C. K., & Jenkins, J. M. (2000). *The exemplary high school.* Fort Worth, TX: Harcourt College Publishers.

Gerber, P. J., & Reiff, H. B. (1994). *Speaking for themselves: Ethnographic interviews with adults with learning disabilities.* Ann Arbor: The University of Michigan Press.

Gerber, P. J., Ginsberg, R., & Reiff, H. B. (1992). Identifying alterable patterns in employment for highly successful adults with learning disabilities. *Journal of Learning Disabilities, 25,* 475–487.

German, S., Martin, J., Marshall, L., & Sale, H. (2000, Spring). Promoting self-determination: Using "Take Action" to teach goal attainment. *Career Development for Exceptional Individuals, 23,* 27–38.

Getzel, E. E. (2005). Preparing for college. In E. E. Getzel & P. Wehman (Eds.), *Going to college* (pp. 69–83). Baltimore: Paul H. Brookes.

Getzel, E. E., & Wehman, P. (2000). *Going to college: Expanding opportunities for people with disabilities.* Baltimore: Paul H. Brookes.

Getzel, E. E., & Wehman, P. (Eds.). (2005). *Going to college.* Baltimore: Paul H. Brookes.

Getzel, L., Stodden, R. A., & Briel, L. (2001). Pursuing postsecondary education opportunities for individuals with disabilities. In P. Wehman (Ed.), *Life beyond the classroom: Transition strategies for young people with disabilities* (3rd ed.). Baltimore: Paul H. Brookes.

Gibran, K. (1923). *The prophet*. New York: Alfred A. Knopf Publisher.

Gil, L. A. (2007). Bridging the transition gap from high school to college: Preparing students with disabilities a successful postsecondary experience. *Teaching Exceptional Children, 40*, 12–15.

Gilmore, D. S., Bose, J., & Hart, D. (2002). Postsecondary education as a critical step toward meaningful employment: Vocational rehabilitation's role. *Job Training & Placement Report, 26*, 1–3.

Ginsberg, E., Ginsberg, S., Axelrod, S., & Herman, H. (1951). *Occupational choice: An approach to a general theory*. New York: Columbia University.

Glomb, N. K., Buckley, L. D., Minskoff, E. D., & Rogers, S. (2006). The learning leaders mentoring program for children with ADHD and learning disabilities. *Preventing School Failure, 50*(4), 31–35.

Gordon, H. (1999). *History and growth of vocational education in America*. Boston: Allyn & Bacon.

Grandin, T. (2007). Autism from the inside. *Educational Leadership, 64*(5), 29–32.

Greenbaum, B., Graham, S., & Scales, W. (1995). Adults with learning disabilities: Educational and social experiences during college. *Exceptional Children, 61*(5), 460–471.

Greene, G., & Kochhar, C. (2003). *Pathways to successful transition for youth with disabilities*. Upper Saddle River, NJ: Merrill/Prentice Hall.

Greene, G., & Nefsky, P. (1999). Transition for culturally and linguistically diverse youth with disabilities: Closing the gaps. *Multiple Voices for Ethnically Diverse Exceptional Learners, 3*, 15–24.

Gregg, N. (2007). Underserved and unprepared: Postsecondary learning disabilities. *Learning Disabilities Research & Practice, 22*(4), 219–228.

Gregg, N., Scott, S., McPeek, D., & Ferri, B. A. (1999). Definitions and eligibility criteria applied to the adolescent and adult populations with learning disabilities across agencies. *Learning Disabilities Quarterly, 22*, 213–123.

Halpern, A. S. (1999). *Transition: Is it time for another rebottling?* Paper presented at the 1999 Annual OSEP Project Directors' Meeting, Washington, DC.

Halpern, A. S., Herr, C. M., Doren, B., & Wolf, N. K. (2000). *Next S.T.E.P.: Student transition and educational planning*. Austin, TX: Pro-Ed.

Hanye, R. (1998). The missing link: Real work experiences for people who are visually impaired. *Journal of Visual Impairment & Blindness, 92*(12), 844–847.

Harris, R., & Robertson, J. (2001). Successful strategies for college-bound students with learning disabilities. *Preventing School Failure, 45*(3), 125–131.

Hart, D., Zafft, C., & Zimbrich, K. (2001). Creating access to postsecondary education for all students. *The Journal for Vocational Special Needs Education, 23*, 19–30.

Hart, D., Zimbrich, K., & Whelley, T. (2002). *Challenges in coordinating and managing services and supports in secondary and postsecondary options* (Issue Brief, 1(6)). Minneapolis: University of Minnesota, National Center on Secondary Education and Transition.

Hasnain, R. (2001). *Entering adulthood with a disability: Individual, family, and cultural challenges*. Unpublished doctoral dissertation, Boston University, Boston, MA.

HEATH Resource Center. (2005). *Frequently asked questions*. Retrieved July 21, 2006, from The George Washington University Web site: http://www.heath.gwu.edu/taxonomy/term/5

Henderson, A. T., Mapp, K., Jordan, C., Orozco, E., Averett, A., & Donnelly, D., et al. (2003). *A new wave of evidence: The impact of school, family, and community connections on student achievement*. Austin, TX: Southwest Educational Development Laboratory.

Hennessey, M. L., Roessler, R., Cook, B., Unger, D., & Rumrill, P. (2006). Employment and career development concerns of postsecondary students with disabilities: Service and policy implications. *Journal of Postsecondary Education and Disability, 19*(1), 39–55.

Hitchings, W. E., Luzzo, D. A., Ristow, R., Horvath, M., Retish, P., & Tanners, A. (2001). The career development needs of college students with learning disabilities: In their own words. *Learning Disabilities Research and Practice, 16*(1), 8–17.

Hitchings, W. E., Retish, P., & Horvath, M. (2005). Academic preparation of adolescents with disabilities for postsecondary education. *Career Development for Exceptional Individuals, 28,* 26–35.

Hock, M. F. (2005). Students with learning disabilities or attention-deficit/hyperactivity disorder. In E. E. Getzel & P. Wehman (Eds.), *Going to college* (pp. 233–252). Baltimore: Paul H. Brookes.

Hodgkinson, B. (2003). *Leaving too many children behind: A demographer's view on the tragic neglect of American's youngest children.* Washington, DC: Institute on Educational Leadership.

Hoffman, A., & Field, S. (2005). *Steps to self-determination: A curriculum to help adolescents learn to achieve their goals* (2nd ed.). Austin, TX: Pro-Ed.

Hogansen, J. M., Powers, K., Geenen, S., Gil-Kashiwabara, E., & Powers, L. (2008). Transition goals and experiences of females with disabilities: Youth, parents, and professionals. *Exceptional Children, 74*(2), 215–234.

Hong, B. S. S., Ivy, W. F., Gonzalez, H. R., & Ehrensberger, W. (2007). Preparing student for postsecondary education. *Teaching Exceptional Children, 40,* 32–38.

Horne, R. (2001, September). *The Workforce Investment Act (WIA): Creating opportunities for youth with disabilities* (Teleconference). Minneapolis, MN: National Center for Secondary Education and Transition.

Horowitz, S. H. (2007, September). Learning styles vs. learning disabilities: The same or different? *LD News.* Retrieved June 9, 2008, from the National Center for Learning Disabilities Web site: http://www.ncld.org/content/view/1285/480

Howlett, L. (2000). *Transitioning to college: From dependence to independence.* Rochester, NY: Northeast Technical Assistance Center (NETAC).

Hughes, K. L., & Karp, M. M. (2004, February). *School-based career development: A synthesis of the literature.* New York: Columbia University, Teachers College, Institute on Education and the Economy.

Hughes, K. L., Bailey, T. R., & Mechur, M. J. (2001). *School-to-work: Making a difference in education: A research report to America.* New York: Columbia University Teachers College, Institute on Education and the Economy.

Imel, S. (2001). *The Workforce Investment Act: Some implications for adult and vocational education* (Trends and Issues Alert No. 11). Columbus: ERIC Clearinghouse on Adult, Career, and Vocational Education, Center on Education and Training for Employment, College of Education, The Ohio State University.

Individuals with Disabilities Education Act Amendments of 2004, P.L. 108-446, 20 USC §1400 et seq. (2004).

Individuals with Disabilities Education Act of 2004. 20 U.S.C. §1400 et seq. (2004).

Individuals with Disabilities Education Act of 2004. 20 U.S.C. §Sec. 300.305(e)(3).

Intagliata, J., & Willer, R. B. (1982). Reinstitutionalization of mentally retarded persons successfully placed into family-care and group homes. *American Journal of Mental Deficiency, 87,* 34–39.

Izzo, M., & Lamb, M. (2002). *Self-determination and career development: Skills for successful transitions to postsecondary education and employment* (White Paper).

Retrieved June 10, 2008, from http://www.ncset.hawaii.edu/publications/pdf/self_determination.pdf

Izzo, M., Hertzfeld, J., Simmons-Reed, E., & Aaron, J. (2001). Promising practices: Improving the quality of higher education for students with disabilities. *Disability Studies Quarterly, 21*.

Jackson, T. (2003). *Secondary transition coordinators at the state level* (Project forum brief). Alexandria, VA: National Association of State Directors of Special Education.

Jaitly, M. (1998). Closing the gap: Schools forge a bridge to community in Colorado: Partnership with community college enables students; successful transitions. *Perspectives in Education and Deafness, 16*(5), 14–16.

Janiga, S. J., & Costenbader, V. (2002). The transition from high school to post-secondary education for students with a learning disability: A survey of college service coordinators. *Journal of Learning Disabilities, 35*(5), 462–468.

Jeynes, W. H. (2005). Effects of parent involvement and family structure on the academic achievement of adolescents. *Marriage & Family Review, 37*, 99–116.

Job Accommodation Network (JAN). (2008). *Employees' practical guide to requesting and negotiating reasonable accommodations under the Americans with Disabilities Act (ADA)*. Retrieved January 20, 2008, from http://www.jan.wvu.edu/EeGuide/

Johnson, D. R., Stodden, R. A., Emanuel, E. J., Luecking, R., & Mack, M. (2002). Current challenges facing secondary education and transition services: What research tells us. *Exceptional Children, 68*, 519–531.

Johnson, D. R., & Thurlow, M. L. (2003). *A national study on graduation requirements and diploma options* (Tech. Rep. No. 36). Minneapolis: University of Minnesota, Institute on Community Integration, National Center on Secondary Education and Transition and National Center on Educational Outcomes. Retrieved May 25, 2005, from http://cehd.umn.edu/nceo/OnlinePubs/Technical36.htm

Joslin Diabetes Center. (2008). *Life after high school: Camp Joslin*. Boston: Harvard Medical School.

Jurecic, A. (2007). Neurodiversity. *College English, 69*(5), 421–442.

Justesen, T. R., & Justesen, T. R. (2000). Helping more students with disabilities prepare for college: A review of research literature and suggested steps GEAR UP grantees can take. Washington, DC: U.S. Department of Education, Office of Postsecondary Education, Gaining Early Awareness and Readiness for Undergraduate Programs (GEAR UP).

Kaminski, P. L., Turnock, P. M., Rosen, L. A., & Laster, S. A. (2006). Predictors of academic success among college students with attention disorders. *Journal of College Counseling, 9*(1), 60–71.

Kant, I. (1946). *Critique of pure reason* (J. M. D. Meiklejohn, Trans.). New York: Dutton.

Kato, M. M., Nulty, B., Olszewski, B. T., Doolittle, J., & Flannery, B. (2006). Postsecondary academies: Helping students with disabilities transition to college. *Teaching Exceptional Children, 37*, 18–37.

Kaye, H. S. (2000). *Computer and Internet use among people with disabilities* (Disability Statistics Report 13). Washington, DC: U.S. Department of Education.

Kinzie, J., Palmer, M., Hayek, J., Hossler, D., Jacob, S. A., & Cummings, H. (2004). Fifty years of college choice: Social, political, and institutional influences on the decision-making process. *New Agenda Series, 5*(3), 1–76.

Kochhar-Bryant, C. A. (2002). Implementing interagency agreements for transition. In G. Greene & C. Kochhar-Bryant (Eds.), *Pathways to successful transition for youth with disabilities* (pp. 314–379). Columbus, OH: Prentice Hall/Merrill.

Kochhar-Bryant, C. A. (2008). *Collaboration and system coordination for students with special needs: From early childhood to the postsecondary years.* Columbus, OH: Merrill/Prentice Hall.

Kochhar-Bryant, C. A., & Bassett, D. S. (Eds.). (2002). *Aligning transition and standards-based education: Issues and strategies.* Arlington, VA: Council for Exceptional Children.

Kochhar-Bryant, C. A., & Greene, G. (2008). *Pathways to successful transition for youth with disabilities: A developmental process.* Columbus, OH: Merrill/Prentice Hall.

Kochhar-Bryant, C. A., & Izzo, M. V. (2006). Access to post-high school services: Transition assessment and the summary of performance. *Career Development for Exceptional Individuals, 29,* 70–89.

Kochhar-Bryant, C. A., Shaw, S., & Izzo, M. (2007). *What every teacher should know: Transition and IDEA 2004.* Boston: Pearson.

Kokaska, C. J., & Brolin, D. E. (1985). *Career education for handicapped individuals* (2nd ed.). Columbus, OH: Merrill.

Konrad, M., Fowler, C. H., Walker, A. R., Test, D. W., & Wood, W. M. (2007). Effects of self-determination interventions on the academic skills of students with learning disabilities. *Learning Disability Quarterly, 20*(2), 89–113.

Kozminsky, L. (2003). Successful adjustment of individuals with learning disabilities. In S. A. Vogel, G. Vogel, V. Sharonie, & O. Dahan (Eds.), *Learning disabilities in higher education and beyond* (pp. 259–277). Baltimore: York Press.

Kreider, H. Caspe, M., Kennedy, S., & Weiss, H. (2007). *Family involvement in middle and high school students' education* (Harvard Family Research Project, No. 3). Cambridge, MA: Harvard University.

Krentz, J., Thurlow, M., Shyyan, V., & Scott, D. (2005). *Alternative routes to the standard diploma* (Synthesis Report 54). Minneapolis: National Center on Educational Outcomes, University of Minnesota.

Krup, J. (1987). Counseling with an increased awareness of the transition process. *Counseling and Human Development, 19,* 2–15.

Kupper, L. (1997). *The Individuals with Disabilities Education Act amendments of 1997.* Washington, DC: National Information Center for Children and Youth with Disabilities.

Lamb, P. (2003). Case study on the role of the rehabilitation counselor in transitioning youth with disabilities to postsecondary education and employment. Paper presented at Capacity Building Institute, Professional Employment for Individuals with Disabilities Issues of Preparation and Transition. Retrieved April 13, 2008, from http://www.ncset.hawaii.edu/institutes/feb2003/papers/pdf

Lamb, P. (2007). Implications of the summary of performance for vocational rehabilitation counselors. *Career Development for Exceptional Individuals, 30*(1), 3–12.

Lane, K. L., Pierson, M. R., & Givner, C. C. (2004). Secondary teachers' views on social competence: Skills essential for success. *Journal of Special Education, 38,* 174–186.

Lapan, R. T., Gysbers, N. C., & Sun, Y. (1997). The impact of more fully implemented guidance programs on the school experiences of high school students: A statewide evaluation study. *Journal of Counseling & Development, 75,* 292–302.

Leake, D., & Black, R. (2005). *Cultural and linguistic diversity: Implications for transition personnel. Essential tools: Improving secondary education and transition for youth with disabilities.* Minneapolis: National Center on Secondary Education and Transition, University of Minnesota.

Leake, D., & Cholymay, M. (2002). Addressing the needs of culturally and linguistically diverse students with disabilities in postsecondary education. *Information Brief, 3*(1). Minneapolis: National Center on Secondary Education and Transition, University of Minnesota.

Leake, D., & Cholymay, M. (2004, February). *Addressing the needs of culturally and linguistically diverse students with disabilities in postsecondary education* (NCSET Issue Brief Vol. 3 (1)). Minneapolis, MN: National Center for Secondary Education and Transition.

Lindstrom, J. H. (2007). Determining appropriate accommodations for postsecondary students with reading and written expression disorders. *Learning Disabilities Research & Practice, 22*(4), 229–236.

Luckner, J. L. (2002). *Facilitating the transition of students who are deaf or hard of hearing.* Austin, TX: Pro-Ed.

Luecking, R., & Certo, N. (2002). Integrating service systems at the point of transition for youth with significant disabilities: A model that works. *Addressing Trends and Developments in Secondary Education and Transition, 1*(4), 1–3.

Luecking, R., & Fabian, E. S. (2000). Paid internships and employment success for youth in transition. *Career Development for Exceptional Individuals, 23,* 205–221.

Lynch, R. L. (1996). In search of vocational and technical teacher education. *Journal of Vocational and Technical Education, 13*(1), 5–16.

MacArthur Research Network on Transitions to Adulthood. (2005). *Adolescence and the transition to adulthood: Rethinking public policy for a new century.* Retrieved March 12, 2008, from http://tinyurl.com/2w64y7

Madaus, J., (2003). What high school students with learning disabilities need to know about college foreign language requirements. *Teaching Exceptional Children, 36,* 62–66.

Madaus, J. (2005). Navigating the college transition maze: A guide for students with learning disability. *Teaching Exceptional Children, 37,* 32–37.

Madaus, J., & Shaw, S. F. (2004). Section 504: Differences in the regulations for secondary and postsecondary education. *Intervention in School and Clinic, 40*(2), 81–87.

Martin, J. E., Hughes, W., Marshall, L. H., Jerman, P., & Maxon, L. (2000). *Choosing educational goals.* Longmont, CO: Sopris West.

Martin, J. E., Marshall, L. H., Maxon, L. M., & Jerman, P. L. (1996). *The self-directed IEP.* Longmont, CO: Sopris West.

Martin, J. E., Van Dycke, J., D'Ottavio, M., & Nickerson, K. (2007). The student-directed summary of performance: Increasing student and family involvement in the transition planning process. *Career Development for Exceptional Individuals, 30*(1), 13–26.

Martin, J. E., Van Dycke, J., Greene, B., Gardner, J. E., Christensen, W. R., Woods, L. L., et al. (2006). Direct observation of teacher-directed meetings: Establishing the need for student IEP meeting instruction. *Exceptional Children, 72,* 187–200.

McCarthy, D. (2007). Teaching self-advocacy to students with disabilities. *Wiley InterScience, 12*(5), 10–16.

McGahee-Kovac, M. (2002). *A student's guide to the IEP* (2nd ed.). Washington, DC: National Information Center for Children and Youth with Disabilities.

McGuire, J. M. (1997). Documenting a need for dialogue about documentation. *Postsecondary Disability Network News,* 1–2, 5.

McGuire, J. M., & Shaw, S. F. (2002). *Postsecondary education and transition for college students with learning disabilities.* Austin, TX: Pro-Ed.

McNabb, J. G. (1997). Key affective behaviors of students as identified by a select group of secondary school teachers using the SCANS categories [Online serial]. *Journal of Industrial Teacher Education, 34*(4).

McNeil, J. M. (2000, June 29–July 3). *Employment, earnings, and disability.* Paper presented at the 75th Annual Conference of the Western Economic Association International, Vancouver, British Columbia, Canada.

Meers, G. (1980). *Introduction to special vocational needs education.* Rockville, MD: Aspen Publications.

Mellard, D. (2005). Strategies for transition to postsecondary educational settings. *Focus on Exceptional Children, 37*(9), 1–19.

Mellard, M. F., & Berry, G. (2001). *Current status report of services to students with disabilities in postsecondary setting.* Lawrence: University of Kansas, Center for Research on Learning, Division of Adult Studies.

Michaels, C. (1994). *Transition strategies for persons with learning disabilities.* San Diego, CA: Singular.

Miller, R. J., Lombard, R. C., & Corbey, S. A. (2006). *Transition assessment: Planning transition and IEP development for youth with mild to moderate disabilities.* Columbus, OH: Allyn & Bacon.

Milsom A., & Hartley, M. T. (2005). Assisting students with learning disabilities transitioning to college: What school counselors should know. *Professional School Counseling, 8,* 436–441.

Mithaug, D. E. (1996). The optimal prospects principle: A theoretical basis for rethinking instructional practices for self-determination. In D. J. Sands & M. L. Weymeyer (Eds.), *Self-determination across the lifespan: Independence and choice for people with disabilities* (pp. 147–168). Baltimore: Paul H. Brookes.

Mooney, C. (2007). Choosing a college: Student voices. *Chronicle of Higher Education, 53*:B24.

Mooney, J., & Cole, D. (2000). *Learning outside the lines: Two ivy league students with learning disabilities and ADHD give you the tools for academic success and educational revolution.* New York: Simon and Schuster.

Mooney, M., & Scholl, L. (2004, Spring). Students with disabilities in Wisconsin youth apprenticeship programs: Supports and accommodations. *Career Development for Exceptional Individuals, 27,* 7–26.

Moore, D. T. (1999). *Toward a theory of work-based learning.* New York: Institute on Education and the Economy, Teachers College, Columbia University.

Moore, R. (2003). *Students with disabilities face financial aid barriers.* Retrieved February 3, 2008, from The National Council on Disability Web site: http://www.ncd.gov/newsroom/advisory/youth/yac_aidbarriers.htm

Moreno, S. (2005, Winter). On the road to a successful college experience: Preparations make the difference. *Autism Spectrum Quarterly,* 16–19.

Morningstar, M. E., Kleinhammer-Trammill, P. J., & Lattin, D. L. (1999). Using successful models of student-centered transition planning and services for adolescents with disabilities. *Focus on Exceptional Children, 31,* 1–19.

Mortimer, J. T., & Larson, R. W. (2002). *The changing adolescent experience: Societal trends and the transition to adulthood.* Cambridge, UK: Cambridge University Press.

Mull, C., & Sitlington, P. L. (2003). The role of technology in the transition to postsecondary education of students with learning disabilities. *Journal of Special Education, 37,* 26–32.

Mull, C., Sitlington, P., & Alper, S. (2001). Postsecondary education for students with learning disabilities: A synthesis of the literature. *Exceptional Children, 68,* 1, 97–116.

Murray State University, First Year Experience. (2005). *The differences: High school vs. college.* Retrieved February 12, 2008, from http://www.murraystate.edu/secsv/fye/hsvscollege.htm

National Academy of Science. (1996). *National science education standards.* Washington, DC: National Academy Press.

National Alliance for Secondary Education and Transition. (2005). *National standards and quality indicators: Transition toolkit for systems improvement.* Minneapolis: University of Minnesota, National Center on Secondary Education and Transition.

National Association of State Directors of Career Technical Education Consortium, States' Career Clusters Initiative. (n.d.). *A career cluster journey.* Retrieved October 28, 2006, from http://www.acteonline.org/convention/upload/CareerClusters101.ppt

National Association of State Directors of Career Technical Education Consortium, States' Career Clusters Initiative. (n.d.). *Career clusters: Architecture and construction cluster/pathway model.* Retrieved October 28, 2006, from http://www.career clusters.org/clusters/

National Association of State Directors of Career Technical Education Consortium, States' Career Clusters Initiative. (n.d.). *Career clusters: A plan of education for a global economy.* Retrieved October 28, 2006, from http://www.careertech .org/uploaded_files/

National Association of State Directors of Career Technical Education Consortium, States' Career Clusters Initiative. (n.d.). *Career clusters brochures.* Retrieved October 28, 2006, from http://www.careerclusters.org/preferred.cfm

National Association of State Directors of Career Technical Education Consortium, States' Career Clusters Initiative. (n.d.). *Career clusters interest inventory.* Retrieved October 28, 2006, from http://www.careerclusters.org/whatsnew.cfm

National Association of State Directors of Career Technical Education Consortium, States' Career Clusters Initiative. (n.d.). *Career clusters tour guide—Module 1: Introduction.* Retrieved October 28, 2006, from http://www.careerclusters .org/whatsnew.cfm

National Association of State Directors of Career Technical Education Consortium, States' Career Clusters Initiative. (n.d.). *Preferred products. .* Retrieved October 28, 2006, from http://www.careerclusters.org/preferred.cfm

National Center for Education Statistics (NCES). (2000). *Vocational education in the United States: Toward the year 2000.* Washington, DC: U.S. Department of Education.

National Center for Education Statistics (NCES). (2005a). *Dual enrollment of high school students at postsecondary institutions: 2003–2003.* Washington, DC: U.S. Department of Education.

National Center for Education Statistics (NCES). (2005b). *Dual credit and exam-based courses in U.S. public high schools: 2002–03.* Washington, DC: U.S. Department of Education.

National Center for Education Statistics (NCES). (2005c). *The condition of education.* Washington, DC: U.S. Department of Education.

National Center for Education Statistics (NCES). (2007). *College navigator.* Retrieved January 6, 2008, from http://nces.ed.gov/collegenavigator

National Center for the Study of Postsecondary Educational Supports (NCSPES). (2000). *Technical report: National survey of educational support provision to students with disabilities in postsecondary education settings.* Honolulu, HI: Author.

National Center on Outcomes Research. (2001). *Practice guidance for delivery outcomes in service coordination.* Towson, MD: Author.

National Center on Secondary Education and Transition (NCSET). (2002). *Integrating services systems at the point of transition for youth with significant disabilities: A model that works* (Information brief, 1(4)). Minneapolis, MN: Author.

National Center on Secondary Education and Transition (NCSET). (2003). *Preparing for postsecondary education.* Minneapolis, MN: Author.

National Center on Secondary Education and Transition (NCWL). (2004a). *Current challenges facing secondary education and transition services for youth with disabilities in the United States.* Retrieved May 26, 2005, from University of Minnesota, National Center on Secondary Education and Transition Web site: http://www.ncset.org/publications/discussionpaper/default.asp

National Center on Secondary Education and Transition. (NCSET). (2004b). *Person-centered planning: A tool for transition.* Retrieved May 26, 2005, from University of Minnesota, National Center on Secondary Education and Transition Web site: http://www.ncset.org/publications/viewdesc .asp?id=1431

National Collaborative on Workforce and Disability for Youth (NCWD). (2004). *Organizational and programmatic components of effective youth programs.* Retrieved December 10, 2007, from http://www.ncwd-youth.info/ resources_&_Publications/jump_Starts//youth_Development/table_com ponents.html

National Collaborative on Workforce and Disability for Youth (NCWD). (2007). *Tunnels & cliffs: A guide for workforce development practitioners and policy makers serving youth with mental health needs.* Washington, DC: Institute for Educational Leadership.

National Commission on the High School Senior Year. (2001). *Raising our sights: No high school senior left behind.* Retrieved May 25, 2005, from the Woodrow Wilson National Fellowship Foundation Web site: http://www.woodrow .org/images/pdf/policy/raising_our_sights.pdf

National Consortium on Health Science and Technology Education. (n.d.). *Critical components: Health science career cluster critical components.* Retrieved November 1, 2006, from http://www.nchste.org/ViewPage.cfm?NavID=62

National Council for Support of Disability Issues. (2005). *Scholarship opportunities.* Retrieved January 6, 2008, from http://ncsd.org/scholar/scholarship.htm

National Council for the Social Studies. (1994). *Expectations of excellence: Curriculum standards for social studies.* Washington, DC: Author.

National Council of Teachers of Mathematics. (1989). *Curriculum and evaluation standards for school mathematics.* Reston, VA: Author.

National Council of Teachers of Mathematics. (1991). *Professional standards for teaching mathematics.* Reston, VA: Author.

National Council on Disability. (2003a). *People with disabilities and postsecondary education* (Position paper). Washington, DC: Author.

National Council on Disability. (2003b, January 24). *Youth advisory committee to the national council on disability* (Record of personal meeting, teleconference). Washington, DC: Author.

National Information Center for Children and Youth with Disabilities. (1999). Child outcomes when child care center classes meet recommended standards for quality. Early Child Care Research Network. *American Journal of Public Health, 89,* 1072–1077.

National Information Center for Children and Youth with Disabilities. (2002). *Technical assistance guide: Helping students develop their IEPs* (2nd ed.). Washington, DC: Author.

National Institute for Literacy. (2007). *What content area teachers should know about adolescent literacy.* Washington, DC: National Institute of Child Health and Human Development.

National Joint Committee on Learning Disabilities (NJCLD). (2007). The documentation disconnect for students with learning disabilities: Improving access to postsecondary disability services. *Learning Disability Quarterly, 30*(4), 265–274.

National Longitudinal Transition Study-2 (NLTS-2). (2005). *Changes over time in postschool outcomes of youth with disabilities.* Retrieved June 5, 2007, from http://nlts2.org/pdfs/str6_completereport.pdf

National Occupational Competency Testing Institute. (2006). *Increasing student achievement: Educators' guide to secondary career and technical education assessment.* Big Rapids, MI: Author.

National Organization on Disability. (2000, October). *Conflicting trends in employment of people with disabilities 1986–2000.* Washington, DC: Louis Harris & Associates.

National Resource Center on AD/HD. (2002). *Education issues: College.* Retrieved February 14, 2007, from http://www.help4adhd.org

National Secondary Transition Technical Assistance Center. (2007, September). *Web-based examples and nonexamples for SPP/APR Indicator 13 Checklist.* Retrieved January 26, 2008, from http://www.nsttac.org/?FileName=examples_i13_checklist

Newcomb, L. H., McCracken, D. G., & Warmbrod, R. J. (1993). Methods of teaching agriculture (2nd ed.). Danville, IL: The Interstate Printers and Publishers.

Newman, L. (2006). *Facts from NLTS2: General education participation and academic performance of students with learning disabilities.* Retrieved February 19, 2008, from http://www.nlts2.org/fact_sheets/nlts2_fact_sheet_2006_07.pdf

Newman, L. (2007). *Facts from NLTS2: Secondary school experiences of students with autism.* Retrieved February 19, 2008, from http://www.nlts2.org/fact_sheets/nlts2_fact_sheet_2007_04.pdf

O'Brien, J., & Lovett, H. (1993). *Finding a way toward everyday lives: The contribution of person-centered planning.* Harrisburg: Pennsylvania Office of Mental Retardation.

Office of Civil Rights. (2007). *Transition of students with disabilities to postsecondary education: A guide for high school educators.* Jessup, MD: Education Publications Center, U.S. Department of Education.

Office of Special Education and Rehabilitative Services. (2008). *Vocational rehabilitation agencies.* Retrieved February 4, 2008, from http://www.jan.wvu.edu/cgi-win/TypeQuery.exe?902

Office of Vocational and Adult Education (OVAE). (2008). *Community college research symposium, June 2008.* Retrieved February 15, 2008, from the U.S. Department of Education Web site: http://www.ed.gov/about/offices/list/ovae/pi/cclo/index.html

Ofiesh, N. S. (2007). Math, science, and foreign language: Evidence-based accommodation decision making at the postsecondary level. *Learning Disabilities Research & Practice, 22*(4), 237–245.

Osborne, E. W. (1999). *Distinguished lecture.* Paper presented at the Southern Agricultural Education Research Conference, Memphis, TN.

Osipow, S. H. (1983). *Theories of career development.* Upper Saddle River, NJ: Prentice Hall.

Osipow, S. H., & Fitzgerald, L. F. (1996). *Theories of career development* (4th ed.). Boston: Allyn & Bacon.

Pannabecker, J. R. (1996). Diderot, Rousseau, and the mechanical arts: Disciplines, systems, and social context. *Journal of Industrial Teacher Education, 33,* 6–22.

Partnership for 21st Century Skills. (2003). *Learning for the 21st century: A report and mile guide for 21st century skills.* Retrieved May 25, 2005, from http://www.21stcenturyskills.org/downloads/P21_Report.pdf

Pearpoint, J., Forest, M., & O'Brien, J. (1998). *PATH (Planning alternative tomorrows with hope): A workbook for planning possible futures* (3rd ed.). Toronto, Canada: Inclusion Press.

Phelan, P., Davidson, A., & Yu, H. (1998). *Adolescents' worlds: Negotiating family, peers, and school* New York: Teachers College Press.

Phelps, L. A., & Hanley-Maxwell, C. (1997). School-to-work transition for youth with disabilities: A review of outcomes and practices. *Review of Educational Research, 67*(2), 197–226.

Phillips, D. C. (1995). The good, the bad, and the ugly: The many faces of constructivism. *Educational Researcher, 24*(7), 5–12.

Piaget, J. (1973). *To understand is to invent.* New York: Viking Press.

Piaget, J. (1977). *The development of thought: Equilibrium of cognitive structures.* New York: Viking Press.

Picciotto, L. P. (1996). *Student-led parent conferences.* New York: Scholastic Professional Books.

Pierangelo, R., & Crane, R. (1997). *Complete guide to special education transition services.* West Nyack, NY: Center for Applied Research in Education.

Pierce, D. R. (2001). *Student pathways through high school to college. Preschool through postsecondary.* Denver, CO: Education Commission of the States. (ERIC Document Reproduction Service No. ED468538)

Pitre, P. E. (2006). College choice: A study of African American and white student aspirations and perception related to college attendance. *College Student Journal, 40*(3), 562–574.

Plank, S. (2001). *Career and technical education in the balance: An analysis of high school persistence, academic achievement, and postsecondary destinations.* St. Paul: National Research Center for Career and Technical Education, University of Minnesota.

Postsecondary Innovative Transition Technology (Post-ITT). (2007). *Know, disclose, and document your disability.* Retrieved November 20, 2007, from http://www.postitt.org/studentcourse/student9.htm

Powers, L. E., Ellison, R., Matuszewski. J., Turner, A. (1999). *Take charge for the future.* Portland: Oregon Health Sciences University.

President's Commission on Excellence in Special Education. (2002). *A new era: Revitalizing special education for children and their families.* Jessup, MD: Educational Publications.

Price, L. (2002). The connections among psychosocial issues, adult development, and self-determination. In L. C. Brinckerhoff, J. M. McGuire, & S. F. Shaw, *Postsecondary education and transition for students with learning disabilities* (pp. 131–155). Austin, TX: Pro-Ed.

Punch, R., Hyde, M., & Power, D. (2007). Career and workplace experiences of Australian university graduates who are deaf or hard of hearing. *Journal of Deaf Studies and Deaf Education, 12*(4), 504–517.

Queen, J. A. (1999). *Curriculum practice in elementary and middle school.* Upper Saddle River, NJ: Merrill.

Quinn, P. O. (2001). What is attention deficit disorder? In P. O. Quinn (Ed.), *ADD and the college student.* Washington, DC: Magination Press.

Raskind, M. H., Goldberg, R. J., Higgins, E. L., & Herman, K. L. (1999). Patterns of change and predictors of success in individuals with learning disabilities: Results from a twenty-year longitudinal study. *Learning Disabilities Research & Practice, 14*, 35–49.

Reiff, H. B. (2007). *Self-advocacy skills for students with learning disabilities: Making it happen in college and beyond—A resource for students, parents, and guidance counselors.* New York: Dude Publishing.

Reis, S. M., Neu, T. W., & McGuire, J. M. (1997). Case studies of high-ability students with learning disabilities who have achieved. *Exceptional Children, 63*(4), 463–479.

Repetto, J. B., Webb, K. W., Neubert, D. A., & Curran, C. (2006). *The middle school experience: Successful teaching transition planning for diverse learners.* Austin, TX: Pro-Ed.

Research and Training Center on Service Coordination. (2001). *Data report: Service coordination policies and models.* Farmington, CT: University of Connecticut Health Center, Research and Training Center on Service Coordination, Division of Child and Family Studies.

Roessler, R. T., & Rumrill, P. D. (1998). Self-advocacy training: Preparing students with disabilities to request classroom accommodations. *Journal of Postsecondary Education and Disability, 13*, 20–31.

Royster, L., & Marshall, O. (2008). The chronic illness initiative: Supporting college students with chronic illness needs at DePaul University. *Journal of Postsecondary Education and Disability, 20*(2), 120–125.

Ryan, R. M., & Deci, E. L. (2000). Self-determination theory and the facilitation of intrinsic motivation, social development, and well-being. *American Psychologist, 55*, 68–78.

Salend, S. J., & Rohena, E. (2003). Students with attention deficit disorder: An overview. *Intervention in School and Clinic, 38*(5), 259–266.

Salvia, S. J., & Ysseldyke, J. (2004). *Assessment in special and inclusive education.* Boston: Houghton Mifflin.

Sander, W. (1992). The effects of ethnicity and religion on educational attainment. *Economics of Education Review, 11*, 119–135.

Sands, D. J., & Wehmeyer, M. L. (1996). *Self-determination across the lifespan.* Baltimore: Paul H. Brookes.

Schargel, F., & Smink, J. (2001). *Strategies to help solve our school dropout problem.* Larchmont, NV: Eye on Education.

Schiller, E., Burnaska, K., Cohen, G., Douglas, Z., Joseph, C., Johnston, P., et al. (2003). *Study of state and local implementation and impact of the Individuals with Disabilities Education Act—Final report on selected findings.* Bethesda, MD: Abt Associates Inc.

Schneider, K. (2001). *Students who are blind or visually impaired in postsecondary education.* Washington, DC: The George Washington University HEATH Resource Center.

Scholl, L., & Mooney, M. (Spring, 2005). Students with learning disabilities in work-based learning programs: Factors that influence success. *The Journal for Vocational Special Needs Education, 26*, 4–6.

Schroedel, J. G. (1992). Helping adolescents and young adults who are deaf make career decisions. *Volta Review, 94*(1), 37–46.

Schroedel, J. G., & Geyer, P. D. (2000). Long-term career attainments of deaf and hard of hearing college graduates: Results from a 15-year follow-up survey. *American Annals of the Deaf, 145*(4), 303–314.

Settersten, R., Furstenberg, F., & Rumbaut, R. (Eds.). (2004). *On the frontier of adulthood: Theory, research and public policy.* Chicago: University of Chicago Press.

Sharpe, M. N., & Johnson, D. R. (2001). A 20/20 analysis of postsecondary support characteristics. *Journal of Vocational Rehabilitation, 16*, 169–177.

Sharpe, M. N., Bruininks, B. D., Blacklock, B. A., Benson, & Johnson, D. M. (September, 2004). *The emergence of psychiatric disabilities in postsecondary education.* Retrieved May 27, 2008, from the National Center on Secondary Education and Transition Web site: http://www.ncset.org/publications/viewdesc.asp?id=1688

Sharpe, M. N., Johnson, D. R., Izzo, M., & Murray, A. (2003). An analysis of instructional accommodations and assistive technologies used by postsecondary graduates with disabilities. *Journal of Vocational Rehabilitation, 22,* 3–11.

Shaw, S. F. (2005). IDEA will change the face of postsecondary disability documentation. *Disability Compliance for Higher Education, 11,* 7.

Shaw, S. F. (2006). Legal and policy perspectives on transition assessment and documentation [Special issue]. *Journal of the Division on Career Development and Transition, 29,* 108–113.

Shaw, S. F., & Dukes, L. L. (2001). Program standards for disability services in higher education. *Journal of Postsecondary Education and Disability, 14,* 81–90.

Shaw, S. F., Kochhar-Bryant, C., Izzo, M., Benedict, K., & Parker D. (2005). *Summary of Performance under IDEA 2004. National Documentation Summit.* Storrs: University of Connecticut.

Silverberg, M., Warner, E., Fong, M., & Goodwin, D. (2004, June). *National assessment of vocational education: Final report to Congress: Executive summary.* Washington, DC: U.S. Department of Education, Office of the Under Secretary, Policy and Program Studies Service.

Sitlington, P. L. (2003). Postsecondary education: The other transition. *Exceptionality, 11,* 103, 113.

Sitlington, P. L., Clark, G. M., & Kolstoe, O. P. (2000). *Transition education & services for adolescents with disabilities* (3rd ed.). Needham Heights, MA: Allyn & Bacon.

Skinner, M. E. (2004). College students with learning disabilities speak out: What it takes to be successful in postsecondary education. *Journal on Postsecondary Education and Disability, 17,* 91–104.

Skinner, M. E., & Lindstrom, B. D. (2003). Bridging the gap between high school and college: Strategies for the successful transition of students with learning disabilities. *Preventing School Failure,* 132–137.

Smink, J., & Schargel, F. P. (2004). *Helping students graduate: A strategic approach to dropout prevention.* Larchmont, NV: Eye on Education.

Smith, T., Price, B., & Marsh, G. (1986). *Mildly handicapped children and adults.* St. Paul, MN: West.

Southern Methodist University, Altshuler Learning Enhancement Center. (2007). *How is college different from high school?* Retrieved February 12, 2008, from http://www.smu.edu/alec/whyhighschool.html

Spinks, S. (2002). *Adolescent brains are works in progress: Here's why.* Retrieved August 2, 2005, from http://www.pbs.org/wgbh/pages/frontline/shows/teen brain/work/adolescsent.html

Spivey, N. N. (1997). *The constructivist metaphor.* Boston: Academic Press.

Stewart, M. A., & Post, P. (1990). Minority students' perception of variables affecting their selection of a large university. *Journal of Multicultural Counseling and Development, 18* 154–162.

Stodden, R. A., Jones, M. A., & Chang, K. (2002). Services, supports and accommodations for individuals with disabilities: An analysis across secondary education, postsecondary education and employment. Retrieved February 15, 2005, from the University of Hawaii at Manoa, Center on Disability Studies Web site: http://www.rrtc.hawaii.edu/capacity/papers/StoddenJones_formatted.htm

Stodden, R. A., Galloway, L. M., & Stodden, N. J. (2003). Secondary school curricula issues: Impact on postsecondary students with disabilities. *Exceptional Children, 70,* 9–25.

Stodden, R. A., Whelley, T., Chang, C., & Harding, T. (2001). Current status of educational support provision to students with disabilities in postsecondary education. *Journal of Vocational Rehabilitation, 16,* 189–198.

Stone, J. R., III, & Aliaga, O. A. (2003). *Career and technical education, career pathways, and work-based learning: Changes in participation 1997–1999.* Retrieved October 28, 2006, from the National Dissemination Center for Career and Technical Education Web site: http://www.nccte.org/publications/

Study of Personnel Needs in Special Education (SPeNSE). (2002). *General education teacher's role in special education.* Retrieved April 7, 2005, from the University of Florida Web site: http://ferdig.coe.ufl.edu/spense/gened11-29.pdf

Study of State and Local Implementation and Impact of the Individuals with Disabilities Education Act (SLIIDEA). (2003). *Highlights from the 1999–2000 School Year—Year 1 data collection.* Bethesda, MD: Abt Associates.

Super, D. E. (1963). *Career development: Essays in vocational development.* New York: College Entrance Examination Board.

Syracuse University, Office of Supportive Services. (2004). *Differences between high school and college.* Retrieved February 12, 2008, from http://www.oss.syr.edu/differences.html

Taymans, J. M., West, L. L., & Sullivan, M. (Eds.). (2000). *Unlocking potential: College and other choices for people with LD and AD/HD.* Bethesda, MD: Woodbine House.

Thoma, C. A., & Wehmeyer, M. L. (2005). Self-determination and the transition to postsecondary education. In E. E. Getzel & P. Wehman (Eds.), *Going to college* (pp. 49–68). Baltimore: Paul H. Brookes.

Thoma, C. A., Williams, J. M., & Davis, N. J. (2005). Teaching self-determination to students with disabilities: Will the literature help? *Career Development for Exceptional Individuals, 28,* 104–115.

Thompson, S. J., Morse, A. B., Sharpe, M., & Hall, S. (2005). *The accommodations manual: How to select, administer, and evaluate use of accommodation for instruction and assessment of students with disabilities.* Retrieved December 19, 2005, from http://www.ccsso.org/content/pdfs/AccommodationsManual.pdf

Thuli, K. J., & Hong, E. (1998). *Employer toolkit.* Washington, DC: National Transition Alliance for Youth with Disabilities, Academy for Educational Development.

Thurlow, M. (2005). *The implications of standards, assessments, and accountability for graduation requirements and diploma options.* Minneapolis: University of Minnesota, National Center on Educational Outcomes.

Thurlow, M., House, A., Boys, C., Scott, D., & Ysseldyke, J. (2000). *State participation and accommodation policies for students with disabilities: 1999 update* (Synthesis Report No. 33). Retrieved January 16, 2004, from the University of Minnesota, National Center on Educational Outcomes Web site: http://www.education.umn.edu/NCEO/OnlinePubs/Synthesis33.html

Timmons, J. (2007). *Models of collaboration and cost sharing in transition programming* (Information brief). Retrieved January 23, 2008, from the National Center on Secondary Education and Transition Institute on Community Integration Web site: http://www.ncset.org/publications/viewdesc.asp?id=3447

Timmons, J., Podmostko, M., Bremer, C., Lavin, D., & Wills, J. (2005). *Career planning begins with assessment: A guide for professionals serving youth with educational & career development challenges.* Retrieved January 23, 2008, from the National Collaborative on Workforce and Disability for Youth, Institute for Educational

Leadership Web site: www.ncwd-youth.info/resources_&_Publications/manuals.php

Trainor, A. A. (2005). Self-determination perceptions and behaviors of diverse students with LD during the transition planning process. *Journal of Learning Disabilities, 38,* 233–249.

Trainor, A. A. (2007). Perceptions of adolescent girls with LD regarding self-determination and postsecondary transition planning. *Learning Disability Quarterly, 30*(1), 31–45.

Unger, K. (1998). *Handbook on supported education: Providing services to students with psychiatric disabilities.* Baltimore: Paul H. Brookes.

University of Hawaii at Manoa. (2000, June). National survey of education support provision to students with disabilities in postsecondary education settings (Tech. Rep.). Retrieved May 27, 2008, from the University of Hawaii at Manoa Rehabilitation, Research and Training Center Web site: http://www.rrtc.hawaii.edu/documents/products/phase1/037-H01.pdf

U.S. Department of Education. (2001, Fall). *Career education for special populations—welfare to work: Considerations for adult and vocational educational programs.* Washington, DC: U.S. Government Printing Office.

U.S. Department of Education. (2001). *Challenges to providing secondary education and transition services for youth with disabilities. Twenty-third annual report to Congress on the implementation of the Individuals with Disabilities Education Act* (pp. I-19–I-31). Washington, DC: U.S. Government Printing Office.

U.S. Department of Education. (2005, February). *FERPA: General guidance for students.* Retrieved January 8, 2008, from http://www.ed.gov/print/policy/gen/guid/fpco/ferpa/students.html

U.S. Department of Education. (2007). *Special demonstration programs, model demonstration projects: Improving the postsecondary and employment outcomes of youth with disabilities* (Federal Register Vol. 72, No. 31, 7427-7430). Washington, DC: Government Printing Office.

U.S. Department of Education. (2008). *Community college research symposium, June 2008.* Retrieved February 15, 2008, from http://www.ed.gov/about/offices/list/ovae/pi/cclo/index.html

U.S. Department of Health and Human Services. (2003). *President's new freedom commission on mental health final report. Achieving the promise: Transforming mental health care in America* (DHHS Publication No. SMA-03-3832). Washington, DC: Author.

U.S. Department of Health and Human Services, Office of Civil Rights. (2007). *Part 84—nondiscrimination Nondiscrimination on basis of handicap in programs and activities receiving or benefiting from federal financial assistance* (45 CFR Part 84). Washington, DC: Author.

U.S. Department of Labor. (2007). *Occupational outlook handbook (OOH), 2008–09 edition.* Washington, DC: U.S. Bureau of Labor Statistics.

U.S. Department of Labor, Employment & Training Administration. (1991, June). *The Secretary's commission on achieving necessary skills. A SCANS report for America 2000: What work requires of schools.* Retrieved October 28, 2006, from http://wdr.doleta.gov/SCANS/

U.S. Department of Labor, Office of Disability Employment Policy. (2004). *Working while disabled: A guide to plans for achieving self-support* (SSA Publication No. 05-11017). Washington, DC: Author.

U.S. Department of Labor, Office of Disability Employment Policy. (2005). *Opening doors to job accommodations.* Retrieved July 22, 2005, from http://www.dol.gov/odep/archives/ek98/jan.htm

U.S. Government Accountability Office. (2003a). *College completion: Additional efforts could help education with its completion goals* (GAO-03-568). Washington, DC: U.S. Government Printing Office.

U.S. Government Accountability Office. (2003b). *Federal actions can assist state in improving postsecondary outcomes for youth* (GAO-03-773). Washington, DC: U.S. Government Printing Office.

U.S. Government Accountability Office. (2004). *Foster youth: HHS actions could improve coordination of services and monitoring of states' independent living programs* (GAO- 05-25).Washington, DC: U.S. Government Printing Office.

Van Reusen, A. K., Bos, C. S., Schumaker, J. B., & Deshler, D. D. (1994). *The self-advocacy strategy.* Lawrence, KS: Edge Enterprises.

Virginia Department of Education, Office of Career and Technical Education Services. (n.d.). Path to industry certification: High school industry credentialing. Richmond, VA: Author.

Vreeburg-Izzo, M., Hertzfeld, J., Simmons-Reed, E., & Aaron, J. (2001, Winter). Promising practices: Improving the quality of higher education for students with disabilities. *Disability Studies Quarterly, 21.*

Wagner, M., & Cameto, R. (2004, August). *The characteristics, experiences, and outcomes of youth with emotional disturbance* (A NLTS2 data brief, vol. 3 (2) of findings from the National Longitudinal Transition Study [NLTS] and the National Longitudinal Transition Study-2 [NLTS2]). Retrieved February 20, 2008, from the National Center on Secondary Education and Transition Web site: http://www.ncset.org/publications/viewdesc.asp?id=1687

Wagner, M., Cadwallader, T. W., Newman, L., Marder, C., Levine, P., Garza, N., et al. (2003). *Life outside the classroom for youth with disabilities. A report from the National Longitudinal Transition Study-2 (NLTS2).* Menlo Park, CA: SRI International.

Wagner, M., Newman, L., Cameto, R., Garza, N., & Levine, P. (2005). *After high school: A first look at the postschool experiences of students with disabilities. A report from the National Longitudinal Transition Study-2 (NLTS2).* Retrieved September 20, 2007, from www.nlts2.org/pdfs/afterhighschool_execsum.pdf

Wagner, M., Newman, L., Cameto, R., & Levine, P. (2005, June). *Changes over time in the early postschool outcomes of youth with disabilities. A report of findings from the National Longitudinal Transition Study (NLTS) and the National Longitudinal Transition Study-2 (NLTS2).* Retrieved February 19, 2008, from http://www.nlts2.org/reports/2005_06/nlts2_report_2005_06_complete.pdf

Wagner, M., Newman, L., Cameto, R., & Levine, P. (2006). *The academic achievement and functional performance of youth with disabilities* (NCSER 2006-3000). Menlo Park, CA: SRI International.

Wagner, M., Newman, L., Cameto, R., Levine, P., & Marder, C . (2007). *Perceptions and expectations of youth with disabilities. A special topic report of findings from the National Longitudinal Transition Study-2 (NLTS2).* Retrieved February 19, 2008, from http://www.nlts2.org/reports/2007_08/nlts2_report_2007_08_completepdf

Walter, R. (1993). Development of vocational education. In C. S. Anderson & L. C. Ramp (Eds.), *Vocational education in the 1990s. Sourcebook for strategies, methods, and materials* (pp. 1–20). Ann Arbor, MI: Pakken Publications.

Ward, M. J., & Berry, H. G. (Summer, 2005). *Students with disabilities and postsecondary education: A tale of two data sets.* Washington, DC: HEATH Center.

Webb, K. W. (1995). *A descriptive analysis of variables influencing college selection and career choice among college students with learning disabilities.* Unpublished doctoral dissertation, University of New Mexico, Albuquerque.

Webb, K. W. (2000). *Transition to postsecondary education: Strategies for students with*

Webb, K. W., & Peller, J. (2004). *Dare to dream for adults.* Tallahassee, FL: Bureau of Exceptional Education and Student Services, Florida Department of Education.

Webb, K. W., Peller, J., & Phillips, M. (2004). *Dare to dream for adults.* Tallahassee, FL: Bureau of Exceptional Education and Student Services, Florida Department of Education.

Webster, D. D. (2004). Giving voice to students with disabilities who have successfully transitioned to college. *Career Development for Exceptional Individuals, 27,* 151–174.

Webster, D. D., Clary, G., & Griffith, P. L. (2001). Postsecondary education and career paths. In R. W. Flexer, T. J. Simmons, P. Luft, & R. M. Baer (Eds.), *Transition planning for secondary students with disabilities* (pp. 439–473). Upper Saddle River, NJ: Prentice Hall.

Wehman, P. (1996). *Life beyond the classroom: Transition strategies for young people with disabilities.* Menlo Park, CA: SRI International.

Wehman, P. (2006). *Life beyond the classroom: Transition strategies for young people with disabilities.* Baltimore: Paul H. Brookes.

Wehmeyer, M. (1992). Self-determination and the education of students with mental retardation. *Education and Training of the Mentally Retarded, 27,* 302–314.

Wehmeyer, M. L., Agran, M., & Hughes, C. (1998). *Teaching self-determination to youth with disabilities: Basic skills for successful transition.* Baltimore: Paul H. Brookes.

Wehmeyer, M. L., Agran, M., & Hughes, C. (2000). A national survey of teachers' promotion of self-determination and student-directed learning. *The Journal of Special Education, 4,* 58–68.

Wehmeyer, M. L., & Palmer, S. B. (2003). Adult outcomes for students with cognitive disabilities three years after high school: The impact of self-determination. *Education and Training in Developmental Disabilities, 38,* 131–144.

Wehmeyer, M. L., & Schalock, R. L. (2001). Self-determination and quality of life: Implications for special education services and supports. *Focus on Exceptional Children, 33,* 1–16.

Wehmeyer, M. L., & Schwartz, M. (1997). Self-determination and positive adult outcomes: A follow-up study of youth with mental retardation or learning disabilities. *Exceptional Children, 63,* 245–255.

Wehmeyer, M. L., Palmer, S. B., Agran, M., Mithaug, D. E., & Martin, J. E. (2000). Promoting causal agency: The self-determined learning model of instruction. *Exceptional Children, 66,* 439–453.

West, L. L., Corbey, S., Boyer-Stephens, A., Jones, B., Miller, R. J., & Sarkees-Wircenski, M. (1999). *Integrating transition planning into the IEP process* (2nd ed.). Arlington, VA: Council for Exceptional Children.

West, L., & Taymans, J. (2001). *Selecting a college for students with learning disabilities or attention deficit hyperactivity disorder.* Washington, DC: The George Washington University HEATH Resource Center.

Wills, J. L. (1998). *Employers talk about building school-to-work systems: Voices from the field.* Washington, DC: American Youth Policy Forum & Center for Workforce Development, Institute for Educational Leadership.

Wilson, L., & Horch, H. (2004, September). Implications of brain research for teaching young adolescents. *Middle School Journal,* 57–61.

Wisconsin Department of Public Instruction (2007, September). *Opening doors to postsecondary education and training.* Retrieved April 24, 2008, from http://dpi.state.wi.us/sped/pdf/tranopndrs.pdf

Wolanin, T., & Steele, P. (2004). *Higher education opportunities for students with disabilities.* Washington, DC: The Institute for Higher Education Policy.

Yuen, J. W. L., & Shaughnessy, B. (2001). Cultural empowerment: Tools to engage and retain postsecondary students with disabilities. *Journal of Vocational Rehabilitation, 16,* 199–207.

Index

**CORWIN
PRESS**

The Corwin Press logo—a raven striding across an open book—represents the union of courage and learning. Corwin Press is committed to improving education for all learners by publishing books and other professional development resources for those serving the field of PreK–12 education. By providing practical, hands-on materials, Corwin Press continues to carry out the promise of its motto: **"Helping Educators Do Their Work Better."**

Mission Statement

The mission of DCDT is to promote national and international efforts to improve the quality of and access to, career/vocational and transition services, increase the participation of education in career development and transition goals and to influence policies affecting career development and transition services for persons with disabilities.

Made in the USA
Las Vegas, NV
13 January 2022

41320924R00138